THE NEW CAMBRIDGE SHAKESPEARE

GENERAL EDITOR
Brian Gibbons

ASSOCIATE GENERAL EDITOR
A. R. Braunmuller, *University of California, Los Angeles*

From the publication of the first volumes in 1984 the General Editor of the New Cambridge Shakespeare was Philip Brockbank and the Associate General Editors were Brian Gibbons and Robin Hood. From 1990 to 1994 the General Editor was Brian Gibbons and the Associate General Editors were A. R. Braunmuller and Robin Hood.

THE MERCHANT OF VENICE

The Merchant of Venice has been performed more often than any other comedy by Shakespeare. Molly Mahood pays special attention to the expectations of the play's first audience, and to our modern experience of seeing and hearing the play.

In a substantial new addition to the Introduction, Charles Edelman focuses on the play's sexual politics and recent scholarship devoted to the position of Jews in Shakespeare's time. He surveys the international scope and diversity of theatrical interpretations of *The Merchant* in the 1980s and 1990s and their different ways of tackling the troubling figure of Shylock.

THE NEW CAMBRIDGE SHAKESPEARE

All's Well That Ends Well, edited by Russell Fraser
Antony and Cleopatra, edited by David Bevington
As You Like It, edited by Michael Hattaway
The Comedy of Errors, edited by T. S. Dorsch
Coriolanus, edited by Lee Bliss
Cymbeline, edited by Martin Butler
Hamlet, edited by Philip Edwards
Julius Caesar, edited by Marvin Spevack
King Edward III, edited by Giorgio Melchiori
The First Part of King Henry IV, edited by Herbert Weil and Judith Weil
The Second Part of King Henry IV, edited by Giorgio Melchiori
King Henry V, edited by Andrew Gurr
The First Part of King Henry VI, edited by Michael Hattaway
The Second Part of King Henry VI, edited by Michael Hattaway
The Third Part of King Henry VI, edited by Michael Hattaway
King Henry VIII, edited by John Margeson
King John, edited by L. A. Beaurline
The Tragedy of King Lear, edited by Jay L. Halio
King Richard II, edited by Andrew Gurr
King Richard III, edited by Janis Lull
Love's Labour's Lost, edited by William C. Carroll
Macbeth, edited by A. R. Braunmuller
Measure for Measure, edited by Brian Gibbons
The Merchant of Venice, edited by M. M. Mahood
The Merry Wives of Windsor, edited by David Crane
A Midsummer Night's Dream, edited by R. A. Foakes
Much Ado About Nothing, edited by F. H. Mares
Othello, edited by Norman Sanders
Pericles, edited by Doreen DelVecchio and Antony Hammond
The Poems, edited by John Roe
Romeo and Juliet, edited by G. Blakemore Evans
The Sonnets, edited by G. Blakemore Evans
The Taming of the Shrew, edited by Ann Thompson
The Tempest, edited by David Lindley
Timon of Athens, edited by Karl Klein
Titus Andronicus, edited by Alan Hughes
Troilus and Cressida, edited by Anthony B. Dawson
Twelfth Night, edited by Elizabeth Story Donno
The Two Gentlemen of Verona, edited by Kurt Schlueter
The Two Noble Kinsmen, edited by Robert Kean Turner and Patricia Tatspaugh
The Winter's Tale, edited by Susan Snyder and Deborah T. Curren-Aquino

THE EARLY QUARTOS
The First Quarto of Hamlet, edited by Kathleen O. Irace
The First Quarto of King Henry V, edited by Andrew Gurr
The First Quarto of King Lear, edited by Jay L. Halio
The First Quarto of King Richard III, edited by Peter Davison
The First Quarto of Othello, edited by Scott McMillin
The First Quarto of Romeo and Juliet, edited by Lukas Erne
The Taming of a Shrew: The 1594 Quarto, edited by Stephen Roy Miller

THE MERCHANT OF VENICE

Edited by
M. M. MAHOOD
Emeritus Professor of English Literature
University of Kent

CAMBRIDGE
UNIVERSITY PRESS

University Printing House, Cambridge CB2 8BS, United Kingdom

Cambridge University Press is part of the University of Cambridge.

It furthers the University's mission by disseminating knowledge in the pursuit of education, learning and research at the highest international levels of excellence.

www.cambridge.org
Information on this title: www.cambridge.org/9780521532518

First published 1987
Reprinted 1989, 1992, 1993, 1996, 1998, 2000, 2001
Updated edition 2003
13th printing 2014

Printed in the United Kingdom by Clays, St Ives plc.

A catalogue record for this publication is available from the British Library

Library of Congress Cataloguing in Publication data
Shakespeare, William, 1564–1616.
The merchant of Venice
(The New Cambridge Shakespeare).
I. Mahood, M.M. (Molly Maureen). II. Title.
III. Series: Shakespeare, William, 1564–1616. Works.
1984. Cambridge University Press.
PR2825.A2M34 1987 822.3′3 86-28413

ISBN 978-0-521-82544-3 Hardback
ISNB 978-0-521-53251-8 Paperback

CONTENTS

ILLUSTRATIONS

Illustrations 5, 8, 11, 12 and 13 are reproduced by courtesy of the Shakespeare Centre Library, Stratford-upon-Avon.

PREFACE

The Merchant of Venice is a play which calls for unobtrusive editing. Though the reader, or the actor studying his lines, is nowhere brought to a halt by a major textual or linguistic problem, there are many places where he or she may be glad of a reassuring clarification of sixteenth-century usage or ideas. One of the pleasures of preparing this edition has been that of receiving this kind of help from several of the play's early editors, who had the advantage of being closer to Elizabethan speech and Elizabethan ways of thinking than, for all our research into the period, we can be today. Among the play's recent editors, my main debt has been to John Russell Brown, whose Arden edition was the first to take full cognisance of the probability that the printers of the play's first quarto were working from Shakespeare's manuscript.

In preparing the Introduction and Appendix I have sought the advice on particular points of many correspondents, friends, and colleagues, all of whom have responded generously; among them, Daniel Cohn-Sherbok, Bernice Hamilton, Peter Laven, and Brian Simpson have cast an expert eye over portions of the typescript. The General Editor of the series has offered encouragement just at the times when it was most needed. Throughout my preparation of the edition I have had invaluable help from the Associate General Editor, Robin Hood, whose painstaking attention to textual minutiae has never obscured his enthusiastic awareness of the play as theatre. At a later stage, the sharp-eyed accuracy of Paul Chipchase as press reader has preserved me from many errors and inconsistencies.

Mary White and Sylvia Morris of the Shakespeare Centre Library have not only borne with my demands for volume after volume but helped me as well with the choice of illustrations. Moira Mosley, Giorgio Melchiori, Marilla Battilana, and Gianfranco Donella all aided me in my quest for a sixteenth-century Gobbo on the Rialto (illustration 2). I owe the photographs on pp. 46 and 174 to the speedy and efficient work of Sussex University's Photographic Unit.

M. M. M.

University of Kent

ABBREVIATIONS AND CONVENTIONS

Shakespeare's plays, when cited in this edition, are abbreviated in a style modified slightly from that used in the *Harvard Concordance to Shakespeare*. Other editions of Shakespeare are abbreviated under the editor's surname (Furness, Hudson), or, in certain cases, under the series title (Cam., Clarendon). When more than one edition by the same editor is cited, later editions are discriminated with a raised figure (Delius³). All quotations from Shakespeare, except those from *The Merchant of Venice*, use the text and lineation of *The Riverside Shakespeare*, under the general editorship of G. Blakemore Evans.

1. Shakespeare's plays

Ado	*Much Ado about Nothing*
Ant.	*Antony and Cleopatra*
AWW	*All's Well That Ends Well*
AYLI	*As You Like It*
Cor.	*Coriolanus*
Cym.	*Cymbeline*
Err.	*The Comedy of Errors*
Ham.	*Hamlet*
1H4	*The First Part of King Henry the Fourth*
2H4	*The Second Part of King Henry the Fourth*
H5	*King Henry the Fifth*
1H6	*The First Part of King Henry the Sixth*
2H6	*The Second Part of King Henry the Sixth*
3H6	*The Third Part of King Henry the Sixth*
H8	*King Henry the Eighth*
JC	*Julius Caesar*
John	*King John*
LLL	*Love's Labour's Lost*
Lear	*King Lear*
Mac.	*Macbeth*
MM	*Measure for Measure*
MND	*A Midsummer Night's Dream*
MV	*The Merchant of Venice*
Oth.	*Othello*
Per.	*Pericles*
R2	*King Richard the Second*
R3	*King Richard the Third*
Rom.	*Romeo and Juliet*
Shr.	*The Taming of the Shrew*
STM	*Sir Thomas More*
Temp.	*The Tempest*
TGV	*The Two Gentlemen of Verona*
Tim.	*Timon of Athens*
Tit.	*Titus Andronicus*
TN	*Twelfth Night*

TNK	*The Two Noble Kinsmen*
Tro.	*Troilus and Cressida*
Wiv.	*The Merry Wives of Windsor*
WT	*The Winter's Tale*

2. Other works cited and general references

Abbott	E. A. Abbott, *A Shakespearian Grammar*, 1869 (references are to numbered paragraphs)
Alexander	*William Shakespeare, The Complete Works*, ed. Peter Alexander, 1951
AV	The Authorised Version of the Bible, 1611 (also known as the King James Bible)
BB	The 'Bishops' Bible', 1568 (a revision of the Great Bible of 1539)
Boswell	*The Plays and Poems of William Shakspeare*, [ed. James Boswell,] 21 vols., 1821, V
Brown	*The Merchant of Venice*, ed. John Russell Brown, 1955; reprinted with corrections and additions, 1961 (Arden)
Bulloch	John Bulloch, *Studies on the Text of Shakespeare*, 1878
Bullough	*Narrative and Dramatic Sources of Shakespeare*, ed. Geoffrey Bullough, I, 1957
Cam.	*The Works of William Shakespeare*, ed. William George Clark, John Glover and William Aldis Wright, 9 vols., 1863–6, II
Capell	*Mr William Shakespeare his Comedies, Histories, and Tragedies*, [ed. Edward Capell,] 10 vols., 1767–8, III
conj. Capell	Edward Capell, *Notes and Various Readings to Shakespeare*, I, 1783
Chew	S. C. Chew, *The Crescent and the Rose*, 1937
Clarendon	*The Merchant of Venice*, ed. William George Clark and William Aldis Wright, 1869 (Clarendon Shakespeare)
Collier	*The Works of William Shakespeare*, ed. J. Payne Collier, 8 vols., 1842–4, II
Collier[2]	*The Plays of Shakespeare. The text regulated by the old copies, and by the recently discovered Folio of 1632*, ed. J. Payne Collier, 1853
Collier[3]	*Shakespeare's Comedies, Histories, Tragedies, and Poems*, ed. J. Payne Collier, 6 vols., 1858, II
conj.	conjecture
Cowden Clarke	*The Plays of Shakespeare*, edited and annotated by Charles and Mary Cowden Clarke, 3 vols., 1864–8, I
Delius	*Complete Works of William Shakespeare*, [ed. Nicolaus Delius,] 1854
Delius[2]	*Shakspere's Werke*, herausgegeben von Nicolaus Delius, 7 vols., 1854–65, V
Delius[3]	*Shakspere's Werke*, herausgegeben von Nicolaus Delius, 2 vols., 1876, I
Dyce	*The Works of William Shakespeare*, ed. Alexander Dyce, 6 vols., 1857, II
Dyce[2]	*The Works of William Shakespeare*, ed. Alexander Dyce, 9 vols., 1864–7, II
Eccles	*The Merchant of Venice*, [ed. I. A. Eccles,] 1805
ELH	*ELH: A Journal of English Literary History*
ELN	*English Language Notes*

ETJ	*Educational Theatre Journal*
F	*Mr. William Shakespeares Comedies, Histories, & Tragedies*, 1623
F2	*Mr. William Shakespeares Comedies, Histories, and Tragedies*, 1632
F3	*Mr. William Shakespear's Comedies, Histories, and Tragedies*, 1664
F4	*Mr. William Shakespear's Comedies, Histories, and Tragedies*, 1685
Fletcher	*The Merchant of Venice*, ed. R. F. W. Fletcher, 1938 (New Clarendon)
Furness	*The Merchant of Venice*, ed. H. H. Furness, 1888 (Variorum)
GB	The Geneva translation of the Bible, 1560
Golding	*Shakespeare's Ovid: being Arthur Golding's Translation of the Metamorphoses*, ed. W. H. D. Rouse, 1961
Hanmer	*The Works of Mr. William Shakespear*, [ed. Thomas Hanmer,] 6 vols, 1743–4, II
Hanmer[2]	*The Works of Mr. William Shakespear*, [ed. Thomas Hanmer,] 6 vols., 1770–1, II
conj. Hawkins	*see* Reed
Hudson	*The Complete Works of William Shakespeare*, ed. H. N. Hudson, 20 vols., 1881, III
Johnson	*The Plays of William Shakespeare*, ed. Samuel Johnson, 8 vols., 1765, I
Keightley	*The Plays of William Shakespeare*, ed. Thomas Keightley, 6 vols., 1864, I
Kellner	Leon Kellner, *Restoring Shakespeare*, 1925
Knight	*The Pictorial Edition of the Works of Shakspere*, ed. Charles Knight, 8 vols., 1838–43, *Comedies*, I
conj. Lawrence	*see* NS
conj. Lettsom	*see* Cam.
Ludowyk	*The Merchant of Venice*, ed. E. F. C. Ludowyk, 1964
Malone	*The Plays and Poems of William Shakespeare*, ed. Edmond Malone, 10 vols., 1790, III
Merchant	*The Merchant of Venice*, ed. W. Moelwyn Merchant, 1967 (Penguin)
MLQ	*Modern Language Quarterly*
MLR	*Modern Language Review*
Myrick	*The Merchant of Venice*, ed. Kenneth Myrick, 1965 (Signet)
n.d.	no date
Neilson and Hill	*The Complete Plays and Poems of William Shakespeare*, ed. William Allan Neilson and Charles Jarvis Hill, 1942
Noble	Richmond Noble, *Shakespeare's Biblical Knowledge*, 1935
NQ	*Notes and Queries*
NS	*The Merchant of Venice*, ed. Arthur Quiller-Couch and John Dover Wilson, 1926, revised 1953 (New Shakespeare)
ns	new series
OED	*The Oxford English Dictionary*, ed. Sir A. A. H. Murray, W. A. Craigie and C. T. Onions, 13 vols., 1933
Onions	C. T. Onions, *A Shakespeare Glossary*, 2nd edn, 1919
Plutarch's *Lives*	*The Lives of the Nobel Grecians and Romans, compared together by... Plutarke...translated...into French by Sir James Amyot, and...into English by Sir Thomas North* (1579). 8 vols., 1928
PMLA	*Publications of the Modern Language Association of America*
Pooler	*The Merchant of Venice*, ed. Charles Knox Pooler, 1905 (Arden)
Pope	*The Works of Mr William Shakespear*, ed. Alexander Pope, 6 vols., 1723–5, II

PQ	*Philological Quarterly*
Q1	*The most excellent Historie of the Merchant of Venice*...by William Shakespeare...Printed by I.R. for Thomas Heyes, 1600
Q2	*The excellent History of the Merchant of Venice*...by W. Shakespeare. Printed by J. Roberts, 1600 [for 1619]
Q3	*The most excellent History of the Merchant of Venice*...by William Shakespeare...Printed by M.P. for Laurence Hayes, 1637
Rann	*The Dramatic Works of Shakespeare*, ed. Joseph Rann, 6 vols., 1786–94, II
Reed	*The Plays of William Shakspeare*, [ed. Isaac Reed,] 10 vols., 1785, III
Reed²	*The Plays of William Shakspeare*, ed. Isaac Reed, 21 vols., 1803, VII
RES	*Review of English Studies*
Ritson	Joseph Ritson, *Remarks, Critical and Illustrative, on the Text and Notes of the Last Edition of Shakespeare*, 1783
Riverside	*The Riverside Shakespeare*, ed. G. Blakemore Evans, 1974
Rosser	*The Merchant of Venice*, ed. G. C. Rosser, 1964
Rowe	*The Works of Mr. William Shakespear*, ed. Nicholas Rowe, 6 vols., 1709, II
Rowe²	*The Works of Mr. William Shakespear*, ed. Nicholas Rowe, 8 vols., 1714, II
SAB	*Shakespeare Association Bulletin*
SB	*Studies in Bibliography*
SD	Stage direction
SEL	*Studies in English Literature*
SH	Speech heading
Sisson	*William Shakespeare: The Complete Works*, ed. Charles Jasper Sisson, 1954
SQ	*Shakespeare Quarterly*
S.St.	*Shakespeare Studies*
S.Sur	*Shakespeare Survey*
Staunton	*The Plays of Shakespeare*, ed. Howard Staunton, 3 vols., 1858–60, I
Steevens	*The Plays of William Shakespeare*...notes by Samuel Johnson and George Steevens, 10 vols., 1773, III
Steevens²	*The Plays of William Shakspeare*, 10 vols., 1778, III
Steevens³	*The Plays of William Shakspeare*, 15 vols., 1793, V
subst.	substantively
Theobald	*The Works of Shakespeare*, ed. Lewis Theobald, 7 vols., 1733, II
Theobald²	*The Works of Shakespeare*, 8 vols., 1740, II
conj. Thirlby	Christopher Spencer and John Velz, 'Styan Thirlby: a forgotten "editor" of Shakespeare', *S.St.* 6 (1970), 327–33
Tilley	Morris Palmer Tilley, *A Dictionary of the Proverbs in England in the Sixteenth and Seventeenth Centuries*, 1950 (references are to numbered proverbs)
Tilley / Dent	R. W. Dent, *Shakespeare's Proverbial Language: An Index*, 1981 (references are to numbered proverbs)
TLS	*Times Literary Supplement*
Warburton	*The Works of Shakespear*, ed. William Warburton, 8 vols., 1747, II
White	*Mr. William Shakespeare's Comedies, Histories, Tragedies, and Poems*, ed. Richard Grant White, 3 vols., 1883, I

INTRODUCTION

Date and source

The magnificent sailing ships of the sixteenth century are an unseen presence throughout *The Merchant of Venice*. 'Argosies with portly sail' dominate the opening dialogue, and in the last scene our sense of an ending is satisfied by the news that three of Antonio's ships 'are richly come to harbour'. So it is highly fitting that the clearest indication within the play of the date at which it was written should be an allusion to a real ship of the period.

In June 1596 an English expedition under the Earl of Essex made a surprise attack on Cadiz harbour. The first objective was four richly appointed and provisioned Spanish galleons; worsted in the fight, these cut adrift and ran aground. Two of them, the San Matias and the San Andrés, were captured before they could be fired, and were triumphantly taken into the English fleet as prize vessels.[1] It is generally agreed that the San Andrés, renamed the Andrew, is the ship alluded to as a byword for maritime wealth at line 27 of the play's first scene:

> I should not see the sandy hourglass run
> But I should think of shallows and of flats,
> And see my wealthy Andrew docked in sand,
> Vailing her high top lower than her ribs
> To kiss her burial. (1.1.25–9)

The phrase 'my wealthy Andrew' is small but significant evidence that *The Merchant of Venice* was written not earlier than the late summer of 1596.[2]

The latest possible date for the play is only two years after this. As the first step towards publication, its title was entered in the Stationers' Register on 22 July 1598. Some six weeks later, on 7 September, Francis Meres's *Palladis Tamia* was entered in the same Register; a compact account of the state of English literature, it lists six comedies by Shakespeare, of which *The Merchant of Venice* is the last. Between them, these entries make clear both that the play was in the repertory of Shakespeare's company, and that a manuscript of it had been sold for publication, by the late summer of 1598.

So the play could have been a new one in either the 1596–7 or the 1597–8 acting season. The 'wealthy Andrew' allusion does not clearly favour one date rather than the other, since, as John Russell Brown has shown, the Andrew was several times in the news and several times in danger of 'shallows and of flats' between July 1596 and October 1597.[3] The fact that she was 'docked in sand' at Cadiz and that she nearly

[1] Sir William Slingsby, 'A Relation of the Voyage to Cadiz', *The Naval Miscellany I*, ed. J. K. Laughton, 1902, pp. 25–92.

[2] The allusion was identified by Ernest Kuhl in a letter to the *TLS* 27 December 1928, p. 1025.

[3] Brown, pp. xxvi–vii.

ran aground subsequently in the Thames estuary would make an allusion apposite enough in 1596. She was, however, rather more likely to have become a household name in the next year, when, after weathering the terrible storms of August which disabled her sister galleon, she served as a troop carrier in the Islands voyage. On her return in the storm-ridden month of October, Essex was unwilling to let her sail past the Goodwin Sands where, Shakespeare's play reminds us, 'the carcases of many a tall ship lie buried' (3.1.4–5; compare 2.8.28–31). Essex had good cause to be apprehensive; the weather was such that it scattered and damaged a whole Spanish armada. Men's minds were a good deal occupied with 'peril of waters, winds, and rocks' in the autumn of 1597. And as the shareholders in the Islands voyage began to realise what a fiasco it had been, a play about failed maritime ventures would have taken on a sombre contemporaneity.

The strongest indication that the play originated in the theatrical season of 1597–8 comes, however, not from any internal allusion but from a proviso in the Stationers' Register that it should not be printed without the consent of the Lord Chamberlain – by which we may understand the agreement of Shakespeare's company, the Lord Chamberlain's Men. The most reasonable explanation of this safeguard is that the actors did not want the play to appear in print while it was still enjoying the success of a theatrical novelty.[1] Even if we had no objective evidence such as this of the play's date, 1597 would strike most readers of *The Merchant of Venice* as about right. The play's skilful blending of several plots, its enterprising and emancipated heroine and its supple, pellucid style all serve to link it to the group of mature comedies, *Much Ado about Nothing* (1598), *As You Like It* (1599), and *Twelfth Night* (1601–2). It has a strong affinity also, despite the difference in genre, with the *King Henry IV* plays (1597 and 1598): we recognise in the first words of Shylock and Falstaff the same new-found and boldly grasped power to individualise a character dramatically through the sounds, rhythms, idioms and images of prose speech.

The same confidence shows itself in Shakespeare's handling of his main source. Like several other of his romantic comedies, the mood and atmosphere of which it presages, *The Merchant of Venice* is based on an Italian *novella* or short story; in this case the tale of Giannetto of Venice and the Lady of Belmont, which forms part of the collection called *Il Pecorone* ('the big sheep', or simpleton – the English equivalent would be 'the dumb ox') written in the late fourteenth century by Ser Giovanni of Florence and published at Milan in 1558. No Elizabethan translation is known, but as several modern ones are available only a brief synopsis is attempted here.[2]

A rich merchant of Venice called Ansaldo adopts his orphaned godson Giannetto. When the young man wants to join in a trading expedition, Ansaldo provides him with a splendid ship and rich cargo. On the voyage out, Giannetto is diverted to the port of Belmont, whose Lady has let it be known that she will marry none but the man who is able to spend a successful night with her; those who fail this test must be prepared to lose all they possess. She for her part makes sure of her suitors' failure by giving them drugged wine. Giannetto falls for the trick and duly loses his ship to

[1] See Textual Analysis, p. 180 below.

[2] Translations are given in Brown, pp. 140–53; Bullough, pp. 463–76; T. J. B. Spencer, *Elizabethan Love Stories*, 1968, pp. 177–96.

the Lady. He returns to Venice where he hides in shame; but Ansaldo seeks him out and, on being told the ship has been lost at sea, equips his godson for a second voyage. Everything, not surprisingly, happens exactly as it did the first time. To finance a third voyage, Ansaldo now has to borrow beyond his means, so he pledges a pound of his flesh to a Jew in return for a loan of ten thousand ducats. This time, a 'damsel' warns Giannetto not to drink the proffered wine, and he is able to win the Lady. He lives happily as the Lord of Belmont, and does not think about the bond until the day of reckoning comes round. Then he tells the Lady of Ansaldo's plight and she sends him off to Venice with a hundred thousand ducats. The Jew, however, is not to be deflected from his murderous intentions. The Lady herself now arrives in Venice, disguised as a lawyer, and having failed to persuade the Jew to accept ten times the sum lent, takes the case to the open court. There she tells the Jew that he is entitled to his forfeiture, but that if he takes more or less than the exact pound, or sheds a single drop of blood, his head will be struck off. Unable to recoup even the original loan, the Jew in rage tears up the bond. The grateful Giannetto offers payment to the lawyer, who asks instead for his ring, which he yields after much protestation of his love and loyalty for the Lady who gave it him. In company with Ansaldo, Giannetto now returns to Belmont, where he gets a very cool reception. Only when the Lady has reduced him to tears by her reproaches does she tell him who the lawyer was. Finally Giannetto bestows the obliging 'damsel' on Ansaldo in marriage.

This synopsis highlights the differences as well as the similarities between Ser Giovanni's story and Shakespeare's play. Clearly the flesh-bond plot is virtually the same in both. So is the affair of the ring, though Shakespeare handles this with a lighter touch, omitting the sentimental reflections with which Giannetto relinquishes the keepsake, and doubling the entertainment of the ending by involving Gratiano and Nerissa in its contretemps. That Shakespeare read Ser Giovanni's story, either in the original or in a very faithful translation, is put beyond doubt in any close comparison of the two works. Shakespeare seizes upon all the vivid details of the Lady's intervention to save Ansaldo – her taking the bond and reading it, her conceding its validity so firmly that the Jew approaches the merchant with his razor bared, her dramatic last-minute halt to the proceedings. Generations of actors who have never read *Il Pecorone* have instinctively felt it right for the thwarted Shylock to tear up his bond. One puzzling feature of the play, the discrepancy between Bassanio's long sea voyage to Belmont and Portia's headlong coach ride to the Venetian ferry, is cleared up in the Italian source: 'Take a horse at once, and go by land, for it is quicker than by sea.'[1]

Even more important than these details is the emotional cast of the tale. Much is made of Ansaldo's generosity and long-suffering, and of his readiness to risk his life for his godson, whose shiftiness forebodes the difficulties that faced Shakespeare when he sought to make Bassanio an attractive hero. Ansaldo's behaviour after Giannetto's first two mishaps is described in language which recalls the Prodigal Son's father, and these resonances may have given rise to Gratiano's image of the 'scarfèd bark' (all Giannetto's ships are gay with banners) setting forth 'like a younger or a prodigal'

[1] Bullough, p. 471.

but returning 'lean, rent, and beggared by the strumpet wind' (2.6.15–20). The Jew in the Italian tale is a less realised character than the merchant, but as in the play his obduracy has a clear religious and commercial motivation: 'he wished to commit this homicide in order to be able to say that he had put to death the greatest of the Christian merchants'.[1] Finally, there are enough close verbal parallels to prove conclusively that Shakespeare knew and made use of Ser Giovanni's story.[2]

Not everything in the tale of Giannetto was to Shakespeare's purpose. He forestalled the absurd match of the merchant and the damsel by having Nerissa marry Gratiano in Act 3. More importantly, the ribald story of the bed test, which makes nonsense of all the talk of the Lady's generosity, is replaced by the highly moral tale of the three caskets, which has survived in a number of versions from the ninth century onwards.[3] The medieval collection known as the *Gesta Romanorum* includes the story of a choice between vessels of gold, silver and lead which is made a test of marriage-worthiness – though of a woman, not a man. In translation, this forms part of a selection from the *Gesta Romanorum* published in London in 1577 and, with revisions, in 1595. We can be reasonably sure this last was the edition used by Shakespeare, because in its translation of the casket story there occurs the unusual word 'insculpt' which is also used by Morocco when he is making his choice of casket (2.7.57).[4] Shakespeare handles the tale very freely, making the caskets the test for a whole series of suitors; this was a common romance pattern, which needed no specific model.

So far we have been assuming that Shakespeare was the first to substitute the story of the caskets for Ser Giovanni's tale of the drugged wine. This assumption grows into a near certainty when, on subjecting the play to close scrutiny, we discover residual traces of the story that Shakespeare cut out. Among the loose ends is Bassanio's impecunious state at the beginning of the play, which leads the audience to suspect him of wooing Portia in an attempt to mend his fortunes; in the *novella* it is the Lady herself who is responsible for Giannetto being penniless, as she has already seized the ships and cargoes from his first two ventures. Indeed Bassanio's argument that the best way to find a lost arrow is to send another after it, which is almost too much for Antonio's patience, would be nearly valid in the context of Giannetto's triple attempt. In Antonio's expression 'secret pilgrimage' (1.1.119) there is a vestige of the secrecy with which Giannetto hid his quest from his trading companions; and Bassanio's costly gifts are likewise a reminder of the high price Giannetto paid for his first two voyages. Perhaps too it was the recollection of the risk run by the Lady's suitors that caused Shakespeare to invent such hard conditions for those who woo Portia, and, in his adaptation of the *Gesta Romanorum* tale, to change the inscription on the leaden casket from 'Whoso chooseth me shall find that God hath disposed' to 'Who chooseth me, must give and hazard all he hath' (2.7.16).[5]

[1] *Ibid.*, p. 472.

[2] Bernard Grebanier, *The Truth about Shylock*, 1962, pp. 136–45, gives a full list. Some particularly interesting ones are noted in the Commentary.

[3] Bullough gives examples, p. 458.

[4] Brown gives the 1595 translation, pp. 172–4. Bullough prints an extract from an earlier version of the complete *Gesta Romanorum*.

[5] See also Milton A. Levy, 'Did Shakespeare join the... plots in *The Merchant of Venice*?', *SQ* 11 (1960), 388–91.

These traces of the story in its original form imply that Shakespeare made his own adaptation of the story direct from the *novella* and did not, as was long supposed, re-work a play in which the flesh-bond plot and the casket plot had already been welded together. Lost source plays are, however, persistent ghosts in Shakespearean scholarship, and the one that haunts discussions of *The Merchant of Venice* has proved particularly hard to lay. It even has a name. The sometime actor Stephen Gosson, in his attack on the immorality of the stage which was published in 1579, exempted from his censure two plays which had been acted at the Red Bull. One of these, *The Jew*, he describes as representing 'the greediness of worldly choosers, and bloody minds of usurers'.[1] This has been taken as proof that a play combining the casket story with that of the pound of flesh already existed in the 1570s, so that Shakespeare had only to re-write it for a new generation of playgoers twenty years later. But it is difficult to see how a play containing the casket story could be said never, in Gosson's phrase, to wound the eye with amorous gesture. Moreover the art of interweaving two or more stories in the manner of Italian intrigue comedy was still unknown to the English stage of the 1570s. Nor is there any need for Gosson's words to refer to a double plot: they can simply mean 'the greediness of those who choose the worldly way of life, such as bloody-minded usurers'; Morocco and Arragon, whatever their short-comings as suitors, hardly deserve to be called 'worldly'.[2] In short, while a play about a Jewish moneylender existed some twenty years before Shakespeare wrote *The Merchant of Venice*, we have no proof whatever of the two plays being connected, whereas the text of Shakespeare's comedy offers ample evidence that he himself inserted the casket tale into the story of Giannetto.

The flesh-bond story has a long ancestry as a folk tale,[3] and Shakespeare is likely to have known other versions beside Ser Giovanni's. The ballad of *Gernutus*, a very basic version which involves only the Jew, his merchant victim from whom he obtains the bond as 'a merry jest', and a judge who, at the moment the Jew is ready 'with whetted blade in hand' to claim his due, intervenes to tell him the pound of flesh must be exact and bloodless, is undated; the phrases quoted are just as likely to have derived from Shakespeare's play as to have contributed to it.[4] Another version could have been read by Shakespeare shortly before he wrote *The Merchant of Venice*: this is the English translation of Alexandre Silvayn's *The Orator* (1596), in which a brief n[illegible]ative 'Of a Jew, who would for his debt have a pound of the flesh of a Christian', [illegible]ollowed by the Jew's appeal against the 'just pound' judgement, and the Ch[illegible]an's speech in reply. One of the Jew's arguments is that there are worse cru[illegible] than exacting a pound of flesh – for example, keeping one's victim in '[illegible]lerable slavery'. Shakespeare perhaps picked up the idea and put it to be[illegible]e in Shylock's 'You have among you many a purchased slave...' (4.1.90–8). C[illegible]ly the tone of Shylock's

[1] Stephen Gosson, *The School of Abuse* (1579), ed. E. Arber [illegible] 40.

[2] The case against *The Jew* as a source has been forcefull[illegible] E. A. J. Honigmann, 'Shakespeare's "lost source-plays"', *MLR* 49 (1954), 293–307.

[3] L. Toulmin Smith, 'On the bond-story in *The* [illegible]*f Venice* and a version of it in *Cursor Mundi*', *New Shakespeare Society* (1875), 18[illegible]7–86; M. J. Landa, *The Shylock Myth*, 1942, [illegible]ez Cardozo, 'The background of Shakespeare's *Merchant of Venice*', *English Studies* [illegible] pp. 18–31; Grebanier, *Truth*, pp. 97–14[illegible]

[illegible]Brown gives *Gernutus*, pp. 153–6.

retorts at the trial is sometimes very close to that of Silvayn's Jew. 'A man may ask why I would not rather take silver of this man, than his flesh...' could well have prompted 'You'll ask me why I rather choose to have / A weight of carrion flesh than to receive / Three thousand ducats...' (4.1.40–2).[1]

The ballad of Gernutus and Silvayn's orations are more in the nature of passing influences than sources. A work which could have been of wider use to Shakespeare, in that it may have given him a lead-in to his elaboration of the flesh-bond plot by means of the duplication of lovers and the added story of Jessica's elopement, is a tale inset into the third book of Antony Munday's romance *Zelauto, or the Fountain of Fame* (1580). The dramatic liveliness of this tale has led to the suggestion that a play by Munday himself, based on an Italian original, lies behind it;[2] not necessarily a complete play, since the reason Munday was described by Meres as 'our best plotter' could be that he wrote play outlines, or *scenari*, which would have been sold to acting companies and worked up into full-dress dramas by their regular playwrights.[3] The basic situation in the story is that Strabino loves Cornelia, the sister of his friend Rudolfo, who for his part falls in love with Brisana, the daughter of the rich old usurer whom Cornelia is in danger of being forced to marry. The two friends pledge their right eyes as a means of getting a large loan from the usurer, and buy a rich jewel by which they win the consent of Cornelia's father to her marrying Strabino. When the usurer, who has meanwhile agreed to Brisana marrying Rudolfo, discovers that he has been outbid as a suitor by his own money, he summons the young men before a judge and claims the forfeiture. Using the same religious argument as Portia, the judge urges him to show mercy. But he is deaf to entreaty: 'I crave justice to be uprightly used, and I crave no more, wherefore I will have it.'[4] The friends call on their attorneys to speak for them, and Brisana and Cornelia, dressed in scholars' gowns, step forward. Brisana's arguments, which have to do with the failure to repay by a certain date, might be heard in any court; it is Cornelia who clinches the matter by stipulating that the usurer, in taking his due, must spill no blood. Realising that he is not going to get his money back, the usurer capitulates, accepts Rudolfo as a son-in-law, and declares him his heir.

Any influence Munday's tale may have had is secondary to Shakespeare's use of Ser Gio[...]nni's story; Portia's plea is here, but no merchant and no Jew. What is interesting [...] Munday's story, apart from its tone (to which we shall return), is its reduplication [...]overs, by which the usurer is given a son-in-law to inherit his wealth and the heroine [...]mpanion to help bring the trial to a happy end. If Shakespeare did, as is probable, [...]unter Munday's romance, these two characters underwent a second binary fission [...]s imagination, Rudolfo differentiating into Lorenzo and

1 The relevant extract is in B[...] found traces of *The Orator* in [...] 168–72, and Bullough, pp. 482–6. Winifred Nowottny has and *The Orator*', *Bulletin de la F*[...] by Shakespeare, especially in trial scenes; see 'Shakespeare [...] *Lettres de Strasbourg* 43 (1965), 813–33.

2 Janet Spens, *An Essay on Shakespear*[...] and Italian comedy: a study in sources[...] *to Tradition*, 1916, pp. 23–4; Geoffrey Creigh, '*Zelauto* [...] (1968), 161–7. *Zelauto* has been edited by Jack Stillinger, 1963; Brown gives an abridgeme[...] [...]68.

3 I. A. Shapiro, 'Shakespeare and Mundy', [...]61), 30–3.

4 *Zelauto*, ed. Stillinger, p. 176.

Gratiano, and Brisana into Jessica and Nerissa. In this way, the love interest was trebled. Furthermore, the addition to Shakespeare's play of the moneylender's daughter increased a strong theatrical influence to which we must now turn, that of Marlowe's *Jew of Malta*.

Until the allusion to the Andrew was identified, *The Merchant of Venice* was usually dated 1594. It was known that anti-Jewish feeling was rife in that year because of the trial and execution of Ruy Lopez, a Portuguese Jew by birth and physician to Queen Elizabeth, who was convicted of attempting to poison both the Queen and an eminent Spanish refugee called Antonio Pérez.[1] Marlowe's *Jew of Malta* enjoyed a revival during Lopez's trial, and it has been suggested that Shakespeare wrote his play about a Jew to emulate the success of Marlowe's piece. The fact that *The Merchant of Venice* is now generally dated two or three years later does not of itself dissociate the play from the Lopez affair. But Shylock, unlike Marlowe's Jew, bears very little resemblance to Lopez. He is neither a poisoner nor, before his final exit, a convert, and though the choice of the name Antonio could be a faint reverberation of the trial, it was a common Italian name which Shakespeare used for several more characters.[2]

But if Ruy Lopez did not linger in Shakespeare's memory, Marlowe's Barabas certainly did. Shylock has learnt from Barabas how to respond to Christian contempt: Barabas finds it politic to 'Heave up my shoulders when they call me dog' (*Jew of Malta* 2,3.24)[3] and Shylock submits with a 'patient shrug' to being called 'misbeliever, cut-throat dog' (1.3.101, 103). In both, this obsequiousness masks a fierce racial pride: Shylock recalls (1.3.81) the prosperity of Jacob with as much satisfaction as Barabas does the 'blessings promised to the Jews' (*Jew of Malta* 1.1.103). Like Barabas, he believes that without the divine seal of material prosperity, life is not worth living. To those who take away his wealth Barabas cries:

> Why, I esteem the injury far less,
> To take the lives of miserable men,
> Than be the causers of their misery;
> You have my wealth, the labor of my life,
> The comfort of mine age, my children's hope;
> And therefore ne'er distinguish of the wrong (*Jew of Malta* 1.2.146–51)

– a passion heard again from Shylock:

> Nay, take my life and all, pardon not that:
> You take my house when you do take the prop
> That doth sustain my house; you take my life
> When you do take the means whereby I live. (4.1.370–3)

Despite such echoes of *The Jew of Malta*, *The Merchant of Venice* is a different kind

[1] The possible connection between Lopez and Shylock was suggested by Frederick Hawkins, 'Shylock and other stage Jews', *The Theatre* 1 November 1879, and discussed by Sidney Lee, 'The original of Shylock', *Gentleman's Magazine* 246 (1880), 185–220. Lee mistook Antonio Pérez for Dom Antonio, pretender to the Portuguese throne. For Pérez see Gustav Ungerer, *Anglo-Spanish Relations in Tudor England*, 1956, pp. 81–174. Ungerer corrects Lopez's first name, usually given as Roderigo, to Ruy.

[2] See also R. P. Corballis, 'The name Antonio in English Renaissance drama', *Cahiers Élizabéthains* 25 (1984), 61–72.

[3] Quotations are from Richard Van Fossen's edition, 1965.

of play and the product of a different kind of imagination. Marlowe's powerful and grotesque tragedy was so vivid in the memories of Shakespeare's audience that it must have presented itself to him as a challenge rather than a source. When he seems most dependent on it, closer examination often reveals that he is holding it at bay: that is, in the manner of painters – Francis Bacon, for example, 'quoting' Velázquez – he recalls the older work in order to show how far from it his own concerns lie. Marlowe's opening scene exuberantly celebrates the Jew's wealth of gold and silks and spices, in preparation for the portrayal of a world of materialist relationships. In Shakespeare's first scene, argosies with their cargoes of silk and spices are powerfully evoked, but they are made to appear an irrelevance to the world of feeling revealed in Antonio's sadness and his affection for Bassanio; they are the means by which Antonio may serve Bassanio's ends, whereas Barabas's wealth is an end in itself. This fruitful and creative resistance to Marlowe's play is most evident in the contrast between Jessica and Barabas's daughter Abigail. The scene in which the runaway Jessica throws down a casket of her father's jewels to her waiting lover deliberately recalls the night scene in *The Jew of Malta* in which the loyal Abigail extracts the sequestered treasure from her father's house and throws it down to him. Profound differences of character, tone, and circumstance in the two episodes are to make Shylock's 'My daughter! O my ducats! O my daughter!' (2.8.15) as ironic an echo of Barabas's triumphant 'O girl, O gold, O beauty, O my bliss!' (*Jew of Malta* 2.1.54) as is Marlowe's own use of the happy Ovidian lover's *Lente, lente, currite noctis equi* at the dire climax of *Doctor Faustus*. *The Jew of Malta* is not, in the conventional sense, a source of *The Merchant of Venice*. It is a persistent presence, which Shakespeare manipulates with confident skill.[1]

Some attitudes and assumptions behind the play

The Kenyan writer Karen Blixen once told the story of *The Merchant of Venice* to her Somali butler, Farah Aden, who was deeply disappointed by Shylock's defeat. He was sure the Jew could have succeeded, if only he had used a red-hot knife. As an African listener, he had expected a tale about a clever trickster in the Brer Rabbit tradition; Shylock let him down.[2] We can be as far off-course as Farah in our reading of the play if we do not pay some heed to the attitudes of its first audience: their range of expectations about comedy as a genre, and the assumptions they brought to a play set in Venice, to its portrayal of the law, of Jews, and of usury, and to its handling of the theme of love and friendship. Yet in our attempts to understand these background matters we need also to hold fast to the fact that Shakespeare's eminence makes him stand out from his background. The play is not made up of average Elizabethan preconceptions. It is made out of the life experience of a highly individual artist, and our sense of that individuality as we gather it from Shakespeare's work as a whole is an important part of our response.

[1] In 'Marlowe and Shakespeare', *SQ* (1964), 41–53, Irving Ribner argues strongly against *The Jew of Malta* being treated as a source. His characterisation, though, of the two plays as 'a tragedy of defeat and negation' and 'a comedy of affirmation' oversimplifies both plays.

[2] B. E. Obumselu, 'The background of modern African literature', *Ibadan* 22 (1966), 46.

KINDS OF COMEDY

First and foremost *The Merchant of Venice* is a romantic play. The triumph of love and friendship over malice and cruelty is the theme of most medieval romances, of countless short stories of the Italian Renaissance, and, from the 1570s onward, of many English plays.[1] In comedies such as those of Robert Greene, love is an ennobling experience, far removed from the absurdities of courtship displayed in *Love's Labour's Lost* and *A Midsummer Night's Dream*. Unlike these earlier Shakespearean works which have the flavour of Lyly's court comedies, *The Merchant of Venice* has the feel of a popularly romantic play intended primarily for the public stage. Only occasionally witty, it abounds in proverbial wisdom – 'good sentences, and well pronounced' (1.2.9). And whereas court entertainments were made up of 'happenings' that the dramatist could invent at will, plays in the popular romance tradition had a well-defined story line, and existed rather as narrations than presentations. Disguise, a very important element in such stories, is used to bring home to the audience the heroine's devotion and worth. Far-fetched as such devices may seem, popular stage romance was not experienced as fantasy, and to call *The Merchant of Venice* a fairy tale is to induce a dangerous condescension in the reader and a dangerous whimsy in the director. Romantic comedies could be set in real places, even (like Greene's *James IV*) portray historical figures. Although the Belmont of Ser Giovanni is the conventional court of medieval romance, complete with jousting and damsels, his Jew lives on the mainland at Mestre as most Venetian Jews did in the fourteenth century. Two hundred years later, a public theatre audience took Antonio's perils seriously as befitted members of a rival trading nation. Argosies did not only belong in story books: they sailed into Southampton Water.

Another kind of reality, that provided by the miracle play and the morality, gave further substance to much Elizabethan romantic comedy. Portia intervenes to save Antonio as providentially as the Virgin Mary, in continental miracle plays of the sixteenth century, came to the help of hero or heroine. The notion, traceable to the *Golden Legend*, that souls could be saved even when they were being weighed in the balance and found wanting persisted in several forms: didactically, in the fourteenth-century *Processus Belial*, in which the devil claims that in justice man is forfeit to him and confidently produces scales in which to weigh human sins, but is routed when the Virgin appears as an advocate calling on God to exercise his other great attribute of mercy;[2] visually, in many wall paintings, like the one in illustration 1, of the Weighing of Souls; dramatically, as when Mercy and Peace, in *The Castle of Perseverance*, plead successfully for man's soul before the judgement seat.[3] This strain of underlying seriousness which *The Merchant of Venice* may owe to the miracle tradition was deepened when Shakespeare substituted the caskets for the bed test.

[1] See Leo Salingar, *Shakespeare and the Traditions of Comedy*, 1974, pp. 28–59.

[2] J. D. Rea, 'Shylock and the *Processus Belial*', *PQ* 8 (1929), 311–15.

[3] A. Caiger Smith, *English Medieval Mural Paintings*, 1963, pp. 58–63; Hope Traver, *The Four Daughters of God*, 1907. The part of an actor playing God in a morality about the debate of Justice and Mercy has survived in an Elizabethan MS. See *Malone Society Collections* 2, ed. W. W. Greg, 1931, pp. 239–50.

1 The Weighing of Souls. Wall painting in the church of St James, South Leigh, Oxfordshire. Drawn from the original by Caroline Sassoon

Despite talk of Jason and Hercules, Bassanio's venture has more in common with the Grail story than with the pursuit of the Golden Fleece: it is a test of moral worth, not of prowess or cunning. Moreover we are given a secure feeling, characteristic of romance, that the outcome is under the direction of benign powers; Portia's dead father acts much as the divinely directed Fortune of romance, exercising a protective role over his daughter such as she in her turn is to exercise over Antonio.

Elsewhere, the play relies on a very different set of theatrical expectations, those brought to Italian comedy as it had been naturalised by Gascoigne, Munday, Shakespeare himself in *The Taming of the Shrew*, and possibly several of the writers of comedy named by Meres. Munday's *Zelauto* has the spirit of this Italian comedy; even if it does not have a theatrical source, it represents another aspect of Renaissance fiction which is close in temper to the imbroglios of comedy, the 'merry tale'. Like such stories, Italian Renaissance comedies and their derivatives in France and England tend to be brisk and unsentimental. The setting is urban, often a city at Carnival time.

Its heroines are resourceful and adventurous. Double and treble plots give the young ample opportunity to triumph over the old by means of trickery and disguise. And the trickster is fully in control of his fate and not presented to us as the protégé of Fortune.[1] The inset episode of Jessica's elopement in Shakespeare's second act could well form part of such a comedy of intrigue, though in point of fact no dramatic source for it has been identified. To match its mood we have to turn to the fourteenth story in the *Novellino* of Masuccio of Salerno, which is about a miser's daughter who runs away with her lover after extracting from her father's store 'a much greater sum than anyone could have reckoned sufficient for her dowry'.[2] No sympathy is shown for the miser, who weeps at home day after day and is ready to hang himself in grief for the double loss of his money and his daughter.

The Merchant of Venice thus rouses and satisfies two very different kinds of expectation in its audience, who appear to have had no difficulty, here or elsewhere in Shakespeare's comedies, in shifting their perspective from scene to scene.[3] Those critics who stress the affinity between festivity and comedy point to a comparable coexistence, in the festive season of the year, of affection and charity on the one hand and a zest for brutal practical jokes on the other.[4] Ser Giovanni's story had provided this mixture in some degree by making a trickster of the Lady. When Shakespeare instead made her the prize in a moral contest, he had to turn elsewhere – to his recollection of Munday's tale or some similar work – for a cheerfully amoral love intrigue such as Jessica's flight affords. He also introduced a little levity into the more serious parts of his plot by drawing at moments on his own prior mastery of the comedy of wit. Like Angelina in Greene's *Orlando Furioso*, Portia is courted by the princes of the earth. But whereas Greene starts his play with high-flown declarations of love from all the princes, Shakespeare first gives us Portia's mocking review of her suitors, saving the pomp and rhetoric till 2.1 when they can be undercut by our knowledge of her private thoughts. Later on, when the tension of the trial scene is most strained, Portia is no less sharp-tongued in her reaction to Bassanio's romantic declaration that he would give his wife to save Antonio; here, by exploiting for a moment the use of disguise for a skirmish in the sex war, Shakespeare awakens responses proper to the courtly comedy of love and wit to keep in check other responses that have more to do with melodrama.

This flexibility of response on the part of the audience is one means by which Shakespeare can give his characters substance. A personality is defined in life by an intricate net of relationships, but in a play the audience's extraneous, single-angled relationship to a character makes this multifaceted nature of personality one of the most elusive of dramatic goals. A possible path to its attainment is the use of the audience's prior experience of varied dramatic and literary traditions. Portia may at

1 See also Salingar, *Traditions*, pp. 175–242.
2 Bullough, p. 503. I do not include *Il Novellino* among the sources of the play, as the resemblances are very slight.
3 *Twelfth Night*, for example, in which the romantic main story and the heartless plot against Malvolio both originate in a single collection of stories.
4 See C. L. Barber, *Shakespeare's Festive Comedy*, 1959.

times in the courtroom be the *advocatus dei* of medieval drama, but elsewhere she is the heroine of a quest romance, as good as she is rich as she is beautiful, and elsewhere again a clever schemer from intrigue comedy, with a scathing wit. Shylock too meets several different expectations. At one moment he is the ogre of medieval romance, at another the devil of the morality play, at another the usurer of citizen comedy; from time to time also the proud, even awesome, remnant of the House of Jacob from the Book of Genesis. He may even appear to us fleetingly as the Pantaloon of the *commedia dell' arte*, who was an avaricious Venetian householder with a large knife at his side, plagued by a greedy servant and an errant daughter.[1] But this last image would arise from a closer and more immediate knowledge of Italian culture with its distinctive dramatic modes than we can safely attribute to Shakespeare and his audience.

THE MYTH OF VENICE

The Merchant of Venice was a title that ensured its audience came to the theatre with well-defined expectations about the setting of the play. Shakespeare met these expectations with a fair amount of what would now be called local colour. The Verona, Messina, or Florence of his other plays might be anywhere, but his Venice is particularised by gondolas and *traghetti* and double ducats, the Rialto and the synagogues, *magnifichi* and figures from the famous civil law school at nearby Padua. Speculations have arisen that Shakespeare visited Venice when plague closed the London theatres in 1592–4. But if he did make the journey, it is scarcely conceivable that the ghetto, the first in Europe, could have escaped his notice.[2] Shylock however appears to live in a Christian quarter and employs a non-Jewish servant, much as a Christianised Jew would have done in Elizabethan London.

Shakespeare did not have to travel to Venice to learn about its more picturesque aspects. He could have gathered all he needed from travellers and the guidebooks and histories they brought home with them; and the Italian community in London, though small, included people he was likely to meet.[3] The Queen's Musick included no fewer than eight members of a Venetian family called Bassani: the name as it appears in court records, 'Bassanye', could have given rise to the form 'Bassanio' in the play.[4] Although the community of Venetian merchants in London had dwindled, their factor was sufficiently involved in London life to be one of Essex's spies; his contact in Venice was his merchant brother Antonio.[5] The name 'Gobbo', heard rather than read since Shakespeare appears at first uncertain how to spell it,[6] could

[1] John Robert Moore, 'Pantaloon as Shylock', *Boston Public Library Quarterly* 1 (1949), 33–42.

[2] The ghetto, founded in 1516, is described by Fynes Moryson, who saw it in 1594, and Thomas Coryate who travelled to Venice in 1608. Jews were allowed at that time to employ Christian servants, provided they did not eat, drink, or sleep in the ghetto.

[3] S. Schoenbaum, *William Shakespeare, a Documentary Life*, 1975, p. 127; G. K. Hunter, 'Elizabethans and foreigners', *S.Sur.* 17 (1964), 37–52.

[4] *The New Grove Dictionary of Music and Musicians*, 1980, sv Bassani; Walter L. Woodfill, *Musicians in English Society from Elizabeth to Charles I*, 1953, Appendix E.

[5] Gustav Ungerer, *A Spaniard in Elizabethan England: The Correspondence of Antonio Pérez's Exile*, 1976, II, 174–8. J. W. Draper believes Antonio to be a portrait of the Genoese-born financier, Orazio Palavicino ('Shakespeare's Antonio and the Queen's finance', *Neophilogus* 51 (1967), 178–85).

[6] See collation and Commentary for 2.2.3, 4, 6.

have been picked up from talk with those who knew Venice well. It means 'hunchback', but there is nothing to suggest Lancelot or his father is deformed. Shakespeare could have been told about *il gobbo di Rialto*, the crouching stone figure (illustration 2) supporting the platform from which laws were promulgated, which was credited with innumerable jokes and satires much as was the statue of Pasquino at Rome.[1] Though we cannot be sure that this is the origin of the name, Shakespeare could have hit on no better one for his Venetian clown. Another memorable detail, and one Shakespeare could have found pictured in books about Venice, was the drawing of lots, in the process of election to state offices, by taking gold and silver balls out of three large receptacles.[2] The custom may well have set Shakespeare's thoughts moving in the direction of a 'lottery' involving metals and so brought him to the *Gesta Romanorum* story of the caskets.

Of much greater importance to the play as a whole than any touch of local colour is the underlying set of ideas which Shakespeare and his audience shared about 'the most serene city'. The myth of Venice, as historians now call it, can be watched in steady growth through half a century of publications, from the grudging admiration of William Thomas, an Englishman on the run (1549), to Sir Lewis Lewkenor's ecstatic praise prefixed to his translation of Contarini's *La repubblica e i magistrati di Venezia* in 1599.[3] The sonnets by Spenser and others published with Lewkenor's essay show how strongly established the myth was by the 1590s. At the time *The Merchant of Venice* was written, the Republic was a legend for her independence, wealth, art, and political stability, her respect for law, and her toleration of foreigners.

After the battle of Lepanto (1571), Venice suffered a marked decline in her fortunes as a trading nation. But the traveller could still be dazzled by Venetian opulence, because this maritime decline was masked by the switch of capital to mainland agriculture and industry.[4] Shakespeare, when he lists Antonio's ventures, pays no heed to the loss of the spice trade (1.1.33) nor to the exclusion of Venetian shipping from the new oceanic trade. Antonio's argosies not only ply between Levantine Tripoli, the ports of 'Barbary', Lisbon, and England, but they venture also to India and to Mexico – from both of which they would in real life have been debarred by Iberian interests.[5] Antonio's social standing, too, reflects the heyday of mercantile power, when the city's nobility were also its trading magnates; by the 1590s, there were few who could still be called 'royal merchants'.

[1] Giulio Lorenzetti, *Venice and its Lagoon*, trans. Guthrie, 1975, p. 471. The association was first made by Carl Elze (*Essays*, 1874, p. 281). Lancelot's part, translated literally into Italian, has struck a recent translator, according to Giorgio Melchiori, as 'genuinely Venetian in sentence structure and in the very spirit of the jokes in it'.

[2] Described by Contarini (see next note) and also by Thomas Coryate, *Crudities* (1611), p. 282.

[3] Donato Giannotti, *Libro della repubblica dei veneziani* (1540); Gasparo Contarini, *La repubblica e i magistrati di Venezia* (1543); William Thomas, *History of Italy* (1549); Francesco Sansovino, *Venetia, città nobilissima* (1581); Girolamo Bardi, *Delle cose notabili della città di Venetia* (1592). Shakespeare could have read Giannotti and Contarini together in one edition of 1591. Christopher Whitfield thinks he also had a preview of Lewkenor's translation ('Sir Lewis Lewkenor and *The Merchant of Venice*: a suggested connection', *NQ* ns 11 (1964), 123–33).

[4] J. H. Elliott, *Europe Divided*, 1968, pp. 58–9.

[5] 3.2.267–8. A casual Venetian presence before 1530 in Brazil is indicated by Pierre Chaunu, *Conquête et exploitations des nouveaux mondes*, 1969, p. 221.

2 'Il Gobbo di Rialto', Venice. Sculpture by Pietro Grazioli da Salò, mid sixteenth century

For Spenser, Venice's highest claim to fame was her 'policy of right'. Two particular aspects of Venetian law were highly praised by authors of the time. One was its inviolability, stressed when Portia is urged to wrest the law to her authority and replies that 'no power in Venice / Can alter a decree establishèd' (4.1.214–15). The tyrannical acts of the Council of Ten and its habit of judicial murder were still unknown in England. The other was the law's availability to all; 'equality' is the term repeatedly used. *Othello* shows that Shakespeare believed that in Venice 'a private suit would obtain a fair hearing in the middle of an emergency council of war',[1] and the plot of *The Merchant of Venice* rests on the two facts, widely reported at the period, that Venice recognised bonds to foreigners entered into by its own citizens, and that it gave foreigners full access to its courts.[2] This 'freedom of the state', as it is called at 3.2.277, an intellectual as well as commercial traffic between the men of many countries who comprised the communities known as 'nations', was a source of pride to the Venetians and of admiration to all strangers.

A further feature of the myth of Venice was the belief that the Republic's colony of Jews was a privileged community. Not only had they the same rights of redress in the courts as had other foreigners, but they were allowed openly to practise their religion, and were entitled to lend money at interest – 'by means whereof', says William Thomas, 'the Jews are out of measure wealthy in those parts'.[3] This belief, gained from glimpses of pictureque Levantine figures on the Rialto and reinforced by claims such as that of Sansovino that the Jews enjoyed life in Venice as much as if it had been their Promised Land,[4] was one of the more unreliable aspects of the Venetian myth. Jews were tolerated in Venice, not out of humanitarian feelings, but because their moneylending was an essential service to the poor and saved the authorities the trouble of setting up the state loan banks which, by the end of the century, had largely taken over the function of the Jewish moneylenders on the mainland.[5] In William Thomas's day they had had some chance to grow rich through usury, despite harsh discriminatory taxation, but by the end of the century they were allowed interest of only five per cent.[6] Even this much toleration had its price in an enforced *apartheid* which walled Jews up in the ghetto and set them apart by a yellow badge or by distinctively coloured headgear. The right of choice that Shylock exercises when he first refuses to dine with Bassanio but later goes to his feast could not have been enjoyed by a real Jew of the period.

In these and other respects the myth of Venice can be shown to have been sometimes a long way from the reality. But this disparity would be important to our understanding of *The Merchant of Venice* only if Shakespeare, with or without some portion of his audience, could be seen to be questioning the myth. In fact he and his audience appear to be in perfect accord in admiration for Venice's mercantile power and what Lewkenor called its pure and uncorrupted justice. Only when he encountered the complacency of such Venetians as Sansovino on the subject of the Jews did Shakespeare, perhaps with Marlowe's attacks on Christian hypocrisy fresh in his mind, react with an irony to which we shall return.

[1] J. R. Hale, *England and the Italian Renaissance*, 1954, p. 30.

[2] The French jurist Jean Bodin, in stating that in Venice 'it is lawful to bind a citizen to a stranger', draws a contrast with English custom (*The Six Books of a Commonweal*, trans. Richard Knolles, ed. K. D. McRae, 1962, p. 66).

[3] Thomas, *History*, p. 77.

[4] Sansovino, *Venetia*, p. 137.

[5] Brian Pullen, *Rich and Poor in Renaissance Venice*, 1971, pp. 429–578. See especially the summary, pp. 576–8.

[6] Coryate, in 1608, noted the apparent wealth of many Jews, but not all of it would have been acquired by usury. The only authorised moneylenders among them, the transalpine Jews, were also permitted to trade in second-hand goods, which included costly furniture and hangings.

THE LAW

Audience expectations of 1597 or so, based on the prevailing romantic mode of comedy and on the myth of Venice, were well served by the trial scene. The Duke's curiously ineffectual role is in accord with Venetian custom: the Doge could not act as sole judge in any court, though he could add his voice to those of the appointed judges.[1] Appeals were also addressed to him and this enabled Shakespeare to combine supposedly Venetian procedures with the traditional design of romantic comedy in which a king or governor, exercising clemency, brought everything to a satisfactory conclusion. The fact that Venice was known to have many unique laws may have helped the more informed spectators to swallow the improbability of Shylock being entitled only to an exact and bloodless pound of flesh. But most of the audience would simply have revelled in what is a version of the Wise Judge story: a tale in which the tables are turned on the accuser, just as happens to the Elders in the biblical tale of Susanna so unsuspectingly recalled by Shylock in 'A Daniel come to judgement!'

A pleasure in things as they might have happened long ago and might still happen far away can, however, by no means explain the effect of the trial scene. Primarily, Shakespeare was satisfying his audience's fervent interest in the law as it was practised in sixteenth-century London. His 'gentle' hearers had for the most part studied, or were still studying, at the Inns of Court, and many of the citizens in the theatre would, like Shakespeare's own family, have had frequent recourse to the courts. All were connoisseurs of trial scenes which in one form or another occur in one third of all Elizabethan plays.[2] So however romantic and exotic the events leading to the trial, it had to be conducted in a way that would guarantee the spectators' imaginative involvement. That Shakespeare succeeded in doing this and knew himself to have succeeded is suggested by some lines towards the end of the scene. Judgement has been given and both plaintiff and defendant have declared themselves content. Gratiano throws a last contemptuous remark at Shylock:

> In christening shalt thou have two godfathers:
> Had I been judge, thou shouldst have had ten more,
> To bring thee to the gallows, not the font. (4.1.394–6)

The English-sounding joke about trial by jury deliberately snaps the theatrical illusion as Gratiano, who likes to 'play the Fool' (1.1.79), makes use of a Fool's liberty to step out of a play and ally himself with its audience. For a dramatist thus to switch off one of his most brilliant illusions is an act of bravado, a way of celebrating the success with which he has compelled the audience to suspend all disbelief in what it has witnessed. Gratiano's remark indicates that the trial is both totally impossible – and totally plausible. Nothing of the kind could have taken place in the Court of the Queen's Bench – and yet legal minds of the present have readily engaged with the play's

[1] Comments on the Doge's position range from Thomas's 'an honourable slave' (p. 77), quoted from the Venetians, to Lewkenor's 'strange and unusual form of a most excellent monarchy' (A2v).

[2] This estimate from an unpublished thesis by D. Smith is quoted by O. Hood Phillips, *Shakespeare and the Lawyers*, 1972, p. 84.

handling of fundamental questions of law, much as Shakespeare's legally well-informed audience must have done.

In recent years, legal historians have tended to see the trial as a reflection of the sixteenth-century concern with equity and its relation to common law. They stress that in Shakespeare's day there were in effect two legal systems: a civil case could be settled either in one of the common law courts by a judgement based on statute or precedent, or in Chancery by a decree based upon equity and conscience – in effect, that is, upon the Lord Chancellor's sense of natural justice. Among the pleaders who sought the redress of grievances in Chancery were Shakespeare's parents, who tried in 1597 to recover an estate they had lost in the Queen's Bench ten years previously.[1] In the play, some aspects of the trial, notably Antonio's proposal that he put Shylock's property to 'use', or as we would now say, that he hold it in trust, recall Chancery proceedings; and it has even been claimed that from the moment Portia says 'Tarry a little' (4.1.301), the principles, procedures, and maxims of a court of Chancery are exclusively used.[2] This historical reading of the trial scene has been made much use of by critics who view the play in thematic terms as a confrontation of the principles of mercy and justice. But the equation of common law with strict legalism and Chancery with mercy is an oversimplification of Elizabethan legal thinking.

The concept of equity, so powerfully developed by sixteenth-century writers such as Bodin and Hooker,[3] does indeed lie at the heart of the scene, but it is improbable that Shakespeare's audience, in the midst of so much dramatic excitement, thought of the trial as a vindication of Chancery – the decrees of which were in any case not notably humane. Equity, like its criminal law equivalent, mercy, could be displayed in other legal contexts. It could even be viewed as the basis of justice in Venice; pondering the Venetian custom of arriving at a verdict by means of a judges' ballot, William Thomas concluded (without enthusiasm: he had been imprisoned in Venice) that 'all matters are decided by the judges' consciences and not by the civil nor yet by their own laws'.[4] Nearer home, the Staple Court, set up early in Tudor times to 'give courage' (that is, encouragement) 'to merchant strangers', had as its object the equitable settlement of trade disputes. It was also empowered to turn itself into a criminal court to try anyone accused of committing a felony in its precincts – which is what Portia does when she finds Shylock guilty of an attack on Antonio's life.[5] Above all, a judge had ample scope to uphold the principle of equity within the framework of common law, and equity in this context constitutes the legal interest of *The Merchant of Venice*.

[1] The fullest account of this is in W. Nicholas Knight, 'Equity, *The Merchant of Venice* and William Lambarde', *S.Sur.* 27 (1974), 93–104. The Shakespeares were to get no more joy out of Chancery than did the characters in *Bleak House*.

[2] Besides Knight, Maxime MacKay ('*The Merchant of Venice*: a reflection of the early conflict between courts of law and courts of equity', *SQ* 15 (1964), 371–6), Mark Edwin Andrews (*Law versus Equity in 'The Merchant of Venice'*, 1965) and W. Gordon Zeefeld (*The Temper of Shakespeare's Thought*, 1974, pp. 141–84) all argue that Shakespeare is concerned with Chancery in Act 4.

[3] Philip Brockbank discusses equity as a theme in the work of Hooker and Bodin in 'Shakespeare and the fashion of these times', *S.Sur.* 16 (1963), 30–41.

[4] Thomas, *History*, p. 81.

[5] Henry Saunders, 'Staple Courts in *The Merchant of Venice*', *NQ* ns 31 (1984), 190–1.

If Shakespeare had been concerned with the supposed incompatibility between equity and statutory law, he could very reasonably have had Portia rule that, in equity, a bond whose forfeiture resulted in mutilation was inadmissible. But what he was pursuing was not legal theory but dramatic effect. A judgement that combined a meticulous attention to the letter of the law with a no less meticulous concern for the principle of equity would unite all parts of the house in a common satisfaction. Those spectators who read chapbooks rather than works of jurisprudence would rejoice at Portia's conditions: the magical inviolability of legal words was being upheld, as was right and proper,[1] but for once this mysterious literalism was being handled in a way which ensured the wicked did not prosper. And the 'judicious' spectators, who had been taught at the Inns of Court to apply the principle of equity to the interpretation of statutes, would have been no less delighted. Portia's restriction of the forfeiture to a just pound without blood, while in no way undermining the statutory protection of aliens in Venetian law, is 'an equitable diminishment of the letter of the law according to the reason and intent of true justice'.[2]

The flesh-bond story ends here in many of its versions. But this will not do in the theatre, where we have just witnessed the 'manifest proceeding' of Shylock preparing to kill Antonio in cold blood. Whatever our relief and satisfaction at the legal expertise that has saved Antonio, we are still painfully aware that Shylock has attempted murder, and it would be a deep affront to our sense of justice if he now said, 'I'll stay no longer question' (4.1.342), gave a characteristic shrug and walked out of the courtroom. So Portia declares that the law has another hold on him:

There is a law in Venice, she urges, in virtue of which anyone attempting the life of a citizen forfeits both life and property. There was also a similar law in England, as the audience very well knew. Shylock had attempted 'grievous bodily harm' on Antonio.[3]

Our normal human reaction here is again satisfaction. Shylock has got what was coming to him. Yet there swiftly follows a no less spontaneous misgiving. Like Angelo in *Measure for Measure*, Shylock has willed more evil than he has performed. Because our sense of right decrees that he ought not to die, the equivalent of equity, the mercy of the Duke, in the end overrules statutory law.

But there are conditions to the Duke's pardon, and here a modern audience's responses are likely to differ widely from those of an Elizabethan one. Shylock must cease to be a Jew and a usurer. Those in the original audience, if they reflected on the matter, may have felt that these conditions completed the Duke's god-like act of mercy because they made it possible that Shylock 'should see salvation'. But for us the conditions imply that Shylock is being judged not so much on what he has done as on what he is: his very being as a Jew, and his social role as usurer of which we have seen nothing in the play. The assumptions of the Elizabethans about law and equity are ones that we basically share; their preconceptions about Jews and usury are a good deal more likely to elude us.

[1] Lawrence Danson, *The Harmonies of 'The Merchant of Venice'*, 1978, pp. 86–9.

[2] E. P. J. Tucker, 'The letter of the law in *The Merchant of Venice*', *S.Sur.* 29 (1976), 93–101 – the most persuasive refutation of the idea that Shakespeare is concerned with Chancery in Act 4.

[3] George W. Keeton, *Shakespeare's Legal and Political Background*, 1967, p. 145.

JEWS AND USURERS

Though practising Jews had been excluded from England for three centuries, Elizabethan London had its colony of nominally Christianised Jews from Spain and Portugal. There are indications that attitudes to these Marranos varied between different sections of society. The London populace was xenophobic, and the English apprentices of Marranos seem to have been prepared to spy on their employers and report on the rituals of Jewish family life which they kept up within doors.[1] At Court, however, the Queen not only had a Marrano doctor but even, for a time, a Jewish lady-in-waiting.[2] But these divergences of attitude between classes are likely to have been superficial; as much virulence against the 'vile Jew' Lopez was displayed by the prosecutor at his trial as by the mob at his execution. And it is a hanger-on of the Court, Thomas Coryate, who defines for us the colloquial use of 'Jew': 'sometimes a weather beaten warp-faced fellow, sometimes a frenetic and lunatic person, sometimes one discontented'.[3]

Coryate, who had first-hand acquaintance with Venetian Jews, goes on to declare these preconceptions untrue. The sight in a synagogue of many 'goodly and proper men' and beautiful women moved him to reflect that 'it is a most lamentable case for a Christian to consider the damnable estate of these miserable Jews'.[4] Though Coryate's subsequent attempt to convert a Rabbi now strikes us as appallingly arrogant, his attitude is one we must take into account in our reading of *The Merchant of Venice*. A twentieth-century audience sometimes catches its breath at Shylock's shotgun conversion. It is as if the Jew was to be allowed to win back life and sustenance only at the price of his soul. Sixteenth-century spectators, however, would have regarded his soul as already forfeit in so far as he, like his forebears, refused to acknowledge the Christian Messiah. Baptism alone, it was believed, could put a Jew in the way of salvation.

The genuine concern of many that the 'lost sheep of the house of Israel' should be brought into the fold had its ugly obverse. Jews who resisted proselytisation were thought of as under God's curse for their part in killing his Son. The older members of Shakespeare's audience could in their childhood have watched plays about the Crucifixion in which the mocking Jews were played with horrifying realism. Shakespeare even exploits the association: Shylock's 'My deeds upon my head!' (4.1.202) is clearly an echo of the cry with which the Jerusalem crowd elected to free Barabbas rather than Jesus: 'His blood be on us and on our children!' (Matt. 27.25). Friars in Venice and clergymen in London fulminated from their pulpits against the Jews as deicides; outrageous as this idea now seems, it was until very recently the official doctrine of the Roman Catholic and some reformed Churches. A deicide was

[1] C. J. Sisson, 'A colony of Jews in Shakespeare's London', *Essays and Studies* 23 (1937), 38–51.

[2] Sidney L. Lee, 'Elizabethan England and the Jews', *New Shakespeare Society* (1888), 143–66.

[3] *Crudities*, p. 232. As Coryate was writing early in the new century, a memory of Shylock could have contributed to his definition. But the popular notion that Jews easily became impassioned could have contributed to the occasional 'frenetic' behaviour of Barabas and Shylock.

[4] *Crudities*, p. 233.

by definition capable of every iniquity, so the Jews became established as the arch-villains of medieval literature. It is significant that the villain of the flesh-bond story, not a Jew in the earliest versions, became one only when the story was linked to the medieval legend about the finding of the Cross.[1] The old stories about sacrilege, well-poisoning, and ritual murder were familiar in Shakespeare's day in the form of ballads for the illiterate and, for those who could read, romances such as Chaucer's Prioress's Tale. Such horror stories were also given striking dramatic currency in *The Jew of Malta*.

Charges of heresy and deicide may also be seen as the rationalisation of a simple and primitive emotion, envy of the skill and speed with which Jews were able to amass wealth. From early medieval times, Jews had been usurers; not, as was generally believed, because their Law allowed them to take interest from strangers – in fact both the Talmud and the Midrash condemn usury – but because moneylending was one of the few ways they were permitted to earn a living. Temporal rulers, for their part, were content for it to be a good living, since from time to time they mulcted the Jews of their capital under the pretext that their gains were ill-gotten. Nothing reveals more sharply the economic basis for the ill-tempered toleration of orthodox Jews in Venice than the fact that any Jew who became a Christian had to hand all his possessions over to the Church. The result, Coryate noted, was that 'there are fewer Jews converted to Christianity in Italy, than in any country of Christendom'.[2] Unconverted Jews were of much greater use than converts in the Venetian economy.

Though there were in theory no unconverted Jews in England, economic resentment such as was widely expressed against settlers from the Low Countries may have been behind the cry raised against the prosperous Marrano, Lopez: 'Hang him for he is a Jew!' A folk memory of Jews as moneylenders could have lingered through centuries, to be reinforced by medieval ballads and romances and, later, by Italian stories and plays. Moreover, by Shakespeare's day, English usurers were in their own right a familiar element in the London social scene.

Usury, the Elizabethans were repeatedly told, was contrary to the law of nations, the law of nature, and the law of God. The guidance of the Gospels was clear: the command 'Lend, looking for nothing again' (Luke 6.35) was glossed 'not only not hoping for profit, but to lose the stock and principle'.[3] In addition, popular assent was still given to Aristotle's idea that to make money breed was against the course of nature; while the medieval distinction between making a well-secured loan and courageously casting one's bread upon the waters had been heard as recently as 1594 from a preacher who insisted that usurers do not, unlike 'the merchants that cross the sea, adventure'.[4] With all this obloquy as well as *The Merchant of Venice* behind him, Shakespeare presumably did not ask for interest when a fellow townsman sought to borrow thirty pounds from him in 1598. We do not know if he lent the money, though

[1] In the *Cursor Mundi*, about 1290, a Jew who has tried to take a pound of his debtor's flesh and has consequently been condemned to death is reprieved when he offers to reveal the place where the Cross is buried.

[2] *Crudities*, p. 234.

[3] The gloss is in the Geneva Bible, the version most used by Elizabethans for their private reading.

[4] Quoted by Walter Cohen, '*The Merchant of Venice* and the possibilities of historical criticism', *ELH* 49 (1982), 765–89.

the association progressed in the manner of comedy, Shakespeare's daughter in due course marrying the son of the would-be borrower.

There is something Canute-like about the many sermons preached against usury in the 1590s. The tide had turned towards capitalism with the 1571 Act which, though it did not openly countenance usury, relaxed the prohibition against it.[1] The Elizabethans could no more live without usury than could the Venetians; their multitudinous enterprises had to be floated on borrowed capital, and the more the usurer was needed the more he was hated for his profits. His services were most in demand among the aristocracy,[2] and since the players were under lordly patronage the drama was a ready medium for making the usurer a scapegoat for the economic ills of the age. By the time the theatres closed in 1642, some sixty usurers had been hissed from their stages.[3]

The Jew then was the scapegoat of Christendom and the usurer the scapegoat of a nascent capitalism. But while there is no doubt that the Elizabethans would have brought a whole heap of prejudices to a play about a 'stubborn' Jew who is also a moneylender,[4] the scapegoating of Shylock is (to make use of René Girard's distinction) both structure and theme in *The Merchant of Venice*. Because the realisation that Shakespeare is less concerned with creating a scapegoat than in suggesting how scapegoats are created comes, as Girard says, in intermittent flashes of complicity with the playwright,[5] discussion of it must be left till we take a closer look at the play in action (p. 24 below). Two general points about Shakespeare's manipulation of the wicked Jewish moneylender stereotype can be made here. The first is that the playwright seems to have gone to the Book of Genesis for what we would now call background information about Judaism,[6] and like every other reader he found his imagination stirred by the way the patriarchs are there presented as a chosen people. Shylock is rare among villains in that he claims a holy ancestry. It does not make him any better in our eyes – Lucifer too can recall a God-directed past – but it enables his mean and cringing figure to cast a nobler shadow. The second point is that Shakespeare's play can be seen as the culmination of a series of extant plays about grasping Jews which are all in one way or another critical towards the assumed moral superiority of Christians.

Three such plays preceded *The Merchant of Venice*. *The Croxton Play of the Sacrament* is a miracle drama dealing with the misdeeds of two wicked merchants, one Jewish and the other Christian.[7] Both in the end repent, confess, and are forgiven;

[1] See the full discussion by R. H. Tawney in the introduction to his edition of Thomas Wilson's *Discourse upon Usury* (1572), 1925.

[2] Lawrence Stone, *The Crisis of the Aristocracy 1558–1641*, 1965, pp. 543–4.

[3] Arthur Bivins Stonex, 'The usurer in Elizabethan drama', *PMLA* 31 (1916), 190–210.

[4] He also perhaps has some traits of the puritan. Thomas Wilson associates puritans and usurers, and the puritans' predilection for the Old Testament led in the popular mind to a conflation of Jews and puritans as parsimonious killjoys. See Paul N. Siegel, 'Shylock and the puritan usurers', *Studies in Shakespeare*, ed. A. D. Matthews and Clark M. Emery, 1953, pp. 129–38.

[5] René Girard, '"To entrap the wisest": a reading of *The Merchant of Venice*', in *Literature and Society, Selected Papers from the English Institute* ed. E. Said, 1980, pp. 100–19.

[6] See Appendix, 'Shakespeare's use of the Bible in *The Merchant of Venice*', p. 196 below.

[7] *The Non-Cycle Mystery Plays*, ed. O. Waterhouse, 1909.

but on the Christian, who should have known better, is imposed the penance of never trading again. A sharper contrast is drawn in a morality play of the 1580s, Robert Wilson's *Three Ladies of London.*[1] When Mercadore, the merchant suitor to Lady Lucre, is brought before a Turkish court at the suit of his Jewish creditor Gerontus, he seeks to extricate himself by turning up in Turkish dress and announcing he has reneged his faith. He knows, and this is an oblique comment on the treatment of Jewish converts to Christianity, that converts to Islam are freed from their debts. But Gerontus is horrified at the thought that he has caused a man to repudiate the faith to which he was born. He withdraws his claim, causing the judge to remark 'Jews seek to excel in Christianity and Christians in Jewishness.' In passing it should be noted that Gerontus has no truck with Lady Lucre's servant, Usury – who hails from Venice. The third play, and the one closest to Shakespeare's in time and in the villainy of its Jew, is Marlowe's tragedy. When Shakespeare made use of his audience's memories of the monstrous Barabas and his convertite daughter he was also inviting them to recall the way Barabas likens his guile and hypocrisy to the same traits in the Maltese Christians:

> This is the life we Jews are used to lead,
> And reason too, for Christians do the like. (*Jew of Malta* 5.2.115–16)

It is easy to fit *The Merchant of Venice* into this sequence: 'The villainy you teach me I will execute, and it shall go hard but I will better the instruction' (3.1.56–7). Shakespeare had good precedent for his modification of the simple equation, 'Jewishness plus usury equals villainy.' His chosen genre of romantic comedy demanded, however, that the modification should be more oblique than Wilson's moralisings or Marlowe's satire. And in one respect, his portrayal of the merchant, Shakespeare would seem to have some difficulty in sustaining his objectivity about the Christians of Venice.

'GOD-LIKE AMITY'

The Merchant of Venice, according to the Stationers' Register, was 'otherwise called *The Jew of Venice*'. The alternative suggests where the play's interest lay for the majority; for every spectator who could identify with the merchant's exalted love of his friend, there would have been many whose chief pleasure was in seeing the tables turned upon the usurer. Idealised friendship was a favourite theme of Renaissance literature, but it was a cult only of the educated minority: those who, even if they had not read Plato's *Phaedrus*, would have been familiar with the celebration of Platonic love in a more recent dialogue, in the fourth book of Castiglione's *The Courtier*. These readers were accustomed to the impassioned language of friendship which took for its model the love of David and Jonathan – 'passing the love of women'. They did not assume either a sexual origin or an actively sexual outcome for such emotion, and they believed it could coexist harmoniously with love between the sexes. The conquest of the 'lower' love by the 'higher' friendship, a cerebral and unconvincing theme in the

[1] Ed. J. S. Farmer, 1911 (Tudor Facsimile Reprints).

early *Two Gentlemen of Verona*, is replaced here by an unbroken concord. Portia accepts Bassanio's absence because she has 'a noble and a true conceit / Of god-like amity' (3.4.2–3), while Antonio is no less self-effacing in his concern that his own risks should not enter Bassanio's 'mind of love' (2.8.43).

This reconciliation of love and friendship is matched in the first seventeen of Shakespeare's *Sonnets*, in which he urges his friend to marry. But though marriage is there no impediment to the friends' 'marriage of true minds', other inimical forces are at work. One divisive force is social difference: Shakespeare's friend, a younger man than the poet, is apparently of much higher rank. An even greater danger lies in the friend's character. His past unkindnesses are ungrudgingly forgiven, but there always remains in the poet's mind the dread that one day his friend will repudiate him. These thoughts, and the characteristic group of images which express them, have parallels in the plays of Shakespeare's middle period which, taken together with external evidence, have led some scholars to date the *Sonnets* as late as 1597 or 1598.[1] If they are right, the experiences that underlie the *Sonnets* could have been painfully fresh in Shakespeare's memory when he came to write *The Merchant of Venice*. There would have been an immediate relevance in Ser Giovanni's tale[2] about an older man prepared to give and forgive with unstinted affection and a younger man prone to forget his friend's generosity. The story also provided satisfactions lacking in real life. Ansaldo and Giannetto were social equals, and Ansaldo was the material benefactor of Giannetto, whereas in the *Sonnets* the poet can bestow only devotion and praise on his friend. Best of all, the *Il Pecorone* story offered a happy ending, in which the older man, after the marriage which he had successfully furthered, was taken into his friend's brilliant social circle.

Despite this happy ending, the anxiety which appears to have hampered the real-life relationship is present as an undertone in the play. It is heard in Bassanio's reflections on appearance and reality before his choice of the right casket; these have very close verbal parallels in Sonnet 68, one of a group of particularly ambiguous sonnets which praise the friend for an integrity the poet wants him to have but knows he lacks.[3] It is heard too in Antonio's melancholy, which was to E. K. Chambers 'an echo of those disturbed relations in Shakespeare's private life of which the fuller but enigmatic record is to be found in the *Sonnets*'.[4] As in the *Sonnets*, this melancholy takes the form of a deep self-deprecation. When Antonio sees himself as 'a tainted wether of the flock' (4.1.114), he is close to the poet who writes in Sonnet 88:

> With mine own weakness being best acquainted,
> Upon thy part I can set down a story
> Of faults concealed, wherein I am attainted,
> That thou in losing me shall win much glory.

This rationalisation of the fear of rejection persists in the play even though Bassanio

[1] For example, H. C. Beeching's edition of the *Sonnets*, 1904, pp. xxiv–xxvii, and J. Dover Wilson's edition (NS), 1966, pp. lxxiv–lxxxii.

[2] See the summary and discussion, pp. 2–4 above.

[3] See Commentary on 3.2.95.

[4] *Shakespeare: A Survey*, 1925, p. 117.

is presented in a favourable light. Indeed, the very strength and authenticity of Antonio's feelings may be at the root of the uneasiness that many critics express about Bassanio.

The story of Giannetto, then, could have appealed to Shakespeare first and foremost as the portrayal of a friendship and only secondarily as the story of Ansaldo's escape from the Jew. Here perhaps lies the source of our dissatisfaction with the relationship between Shylock and Antonio. When Antonio, accused by Shylock of having abused him, spat at him, and kicked him, replies that he is likely to do all these things again, we feel that even when allowances have been made for Elizabethan prejudices, something has gone badly wrong. Shakespeare's emotional involvement with one relationship of the character has left him insensitive to the character's other relationships – a point which could arguably be made about Hamlet also.

There is a structural difficulty here as well. In the bond scene, Shakespeare needed to give Shylock strong motives for his hatred if he was to get the story moving. The difficulty was already there in the old tale. One of its first tellers even makes the moneylender, a former serf, hate the knight to whom he lends money because the knight once, 'in a fit of wrath', cut off the moneylender's foot.[1] Though Shakespeare's inventions are less unhappy, they have the effect of transforming Antonio, to whom most people take a liking in the play's first scene, into a self-righteous figure storming defiance at his business rival. The actor of Antonio has his work cut out to give coherence to a role that Shakespeare has left in some confusion. If Shakespeare can be accused of anti-semitism this can be found not so much in his depiction of Shylock as in an involvement with Antonio that results in his letting the merchant's contempt for the Jew go unchallenged, whereas other Christian failings in the play do not go unchallenged. In Shakespeare's imaginative prospect, Antonio perhaps stands too close to his creator to be in perfect focus.

Experiencing the play

The prior involvement of Shakespeare and his audience with the literary genre, setting, and topics of *The Merchant of Venice* has shown itself to be a complex subject, far removed from easy assumptions about 'what the Elizabethans thought'. It follows that the play itself offers its audience a complicated experience. This complexity comes as something of a surprise to the many readers who first saw or read *The Merchant of Venice* when they were very young, and have kept the impression of a straightforward comedy with an energetic clarity of plot and language. We can go on enjoying for the rest of our lives the play's momentum towards its climactic scenes; but with increasing self-awareness, we discover that the reason we enter so wholeheartedly into its most improbable situations is that, like real-life events, they arouse multiple and shifting responses. In Norman Rabkin's vivid description, to watch the play is

[1] Grebanier, *Truth*, p. 103.

a constantly turbulent experience which demands an incessant giving and taking back of allegiance, a counterpoint of ever-shifting response to phrase, speech, character, scene, action, a welter of emotions and ideas and perceptions and surprises and intuitions of underlying unity and coherence rivalled only by our experience in the real world so perplexingly suggested by the artifact to which we yield ourselves.[1]

The commentary on the play's action which follows here is an attempt to preserve this complexity of the theatrical experience. It stops short of attempting to define the 'underlying unity and coherence' in the belief that these, being intuitive, remain the individual possession of each member of an audience.

BELMONT AND VENICE

In the Elizabethan public playhouse, *The Merchant of Venice* would have been performed without a break. It does however divide naturally into five movements, though these do not quite correspond to the act divisions which were introduced in the Folio. A feature of these five natural movements is that each culminates in a spectacular exeunt or the expectation of it; and though only one of these is a wedding procession, the idea of marriage is each time to the fore.

The first movement (Act 1 and Act 2, Scene 1) shuttles us back and forth between Venice and Belmont and so establishes our awareness of the action proceeding in two places. But directors who labour a contrast between them, opposing a gauzily romantic Belmont to a mundanely commercial Venice in which Salarino and Solanio wear the sober black gowns that were the Venetian equivalent of formal city suits, are imposing a pattern which is not discoverable in these four scenes. The costumes of the two gentlemen of Venice should surely correspond to the fantasy of their speeches which so strangely trivialise and fictionalise the hazards of sea trade. Antonio's argosies are seen as comfortable burghers or the water pageants of the tranquil Lagoon (illustration 3), tempests are represented by a storm in a soup bowl (1.1.22–4), disasters at sea are reduced to picturesque conceits such as 'enrobe the roaring waters with my silks' (1.1.34). Salarino's shipwrecks come from the world of Greek romance, in which the venturer always swims ashore to win an heiress, rather than from Shylock's world of calculated risks where 'ships are but boards, sailors but men' (1.3.18).

Antonio for his part is scarcely the conventional business tycoon. As the scene proceeds, we begin to understand that his real venture has been to sink all his emotional capital in a single friendship. When Bassanio appears, Antonio readily lets Salarino and Solanio go with the Elizabethan equivalent of 'Don't let me keep you' (1.1.63–4) and masks himself against Gratiano's curiosity with 'every man must play a part, / And mine a sad one' (78–9). Alone with Bassanio, his speech rhythms quicken with feeling. Spendthrift affection speaks through superlatives – 'my extremest means' (137), 'my uttermost' (155) – or through such an image as 'all unlocked to your occasions' (138), while anxiety is heard in conditional phrases: 'if it stand as you yourself still do / Within the eye of honour' (135–6); 'you do me now more wrong...Than if you had made waste of all I have' (154–6). The possibility that

[1] *Shakespeare and the Problem of Meaning*, 1981, p. 30.

3 Venetian water pageantry. From Giacomo Franco, *Habiti d'huomini et donne venetiane* (*c*. 1609)

Bassanio could make waste of his older friend's store of affection can cause us to react sharply to his deviousness in asking for a loan. Yet this is only one flicker of our 'ever-shifting response'; at the same time and on another level, we are enjoying Bassanio's circumlocutions and hesitations as a familiar comedy routine, the engaging embarrassment of a young man trying to borrow from a rich relation and evoking a fatherly 'Come on, out with it.' Something similar happens with Bassanio's listing of Portia's assets as wealth, beauty, and virtue; the second after he has, we feel, given himself away badly by 'In Belmont is a lady richly left' (160), we recognise 'And she is fair, and – fairer than that word – / Of wondrous virtues' as the climactic 'climbing figure' of Elizabethan rhetoric which shows he has got his priorities right – perhaps. All these varying attitudes to Bassanio are neatly clinched when he speaks of Portia's 'worth' (166); like the equally ambiguous 'thrift' (174) and 'fortunate' (175) in this scene, or 'good', 'interest', and 'dear' later on, such words serve to knit together the many individual threads in an audience's response.

Within two minutes of Portia being presented to us in Bassanio's highly romantic verse as that symbol of almost unattainable 'worth', the Golden Fleece, she is before us as a lively girl anxious about a future husband, and speaking prose which brings back, in its mixture of homely proverbs and elegant antitheses, the atmosphere of Lyly's court comedies. In Portia's mocking review of her suitors, Shakespeare in fact has rewritten a scene from his first attempt at courtly comedy, *Two Gentlemen of Verona*. The effect is to make Portia's Belmont seem rather more down-to-earth than Antonio's Venice. Yet there is no deliberate contrast: melancholy, wealth, and tender feelings for Bassanio serve to link Portia and Antonio in our minds far in advance of their encounter in Act 4.

In contrast to Portia's tones of warm feeling controlled and channelled by an inventive wit, there now comes 'rasping into the play like a file' a voice that varies 'from the strident to the rough, from the scratchy to the growled'.[1] Shylock's speech habits, his idiolect, tell us more about him than just the lack of music in his soul. He repeats words as if they were coins he was counting; his curt phrases are a sort of syntactical book-keeping; and his rare images have to be spelt out with heavy literalism: 'I mean pirates' (1.3.20), 'I mean my casements' (2.5.33). Small wonder that Antonio, coming upon Bassanio and Shylock together, draws his friend aside to question and protest. But with the opportunity that this gives Shylock to soliloquise in tones of prophetic denunciation, our responses to him become, as they are to remain, complex. He is alone among Shakespeare's villains in his conviction that God is on his side, and the story of Jacob and Laban invests him with a patriarchal dignity. Yet just as Elizabethan commentators on the biblical passage hesitated between admiration for Jacob's faith and distaste for his trickery, we sense the deceitfulness in Shylock's eloquence: all this talk of animals is a skilful lead-in to his proposal of a flesh bond.

Our response to Antonio is no less shifting and complex. The air of financial security he imparted in the play's first scene serves to undermine the distinction he now draws in 1.3 between usury and ventures, a distinction less impressive to the Elizabethans,

[1] The phrases are Mark van Doren's, *Shakespeare*, 1941, p. 101.

4 The arrival of the Prince of Morocco. A possible staging of Act 2, Scene 1, by C. Walter Hodges

accustomed to hear all kinds of legal fictions about risk-taking in cases concerning usury, than it is to modern critics. And at Antonio's declaration that friendship would never take a breed of barren metal, there may flash through our minds the thought that friendship does none the less seek a return for its outlay. The gap between merchant and Jew appears to be narrowing: Antonio's self-righteousness, pilloried so effectively in Shylock's sketch of his past behaviour, almost justifies H. B. Charlton's protest: 'It is as if, dashing during closed hours into the bar of a public house, one preached to a landlord a complacent sermon on teetotalism, prior to demanding brandy from him for a fainting friend.'[1] The very weakness of Antonio's case gives Shylock his opening. Antonio, having praised risk-taking, then becomes perhaps a little aware of his own possible hypocrisy, and finally is alerted to his unseemly vehemence by Shylock ('Why look you how you storm!' (1.3.130)). He is now easily trapped into taking a huge and deadly risk – the more easily in that it enables him to demonstrate 'to the uttermost' his love for Bassanio. The odds against him are in any case very long; it is plausible for Shylock to treat the bond as a merry sport, and fleetingly we believe him. Perhaps after all there is much kindness in the Jew. In such ways, our reception of the bond scene is made as fluctuating and open-ended as our immediate response to any real-life situation.

The play's first movement culminates in spectacle as the dark-skinned Moors in white burnouses salute the ladies of Belmont in their colourful silks (illustration 4). Morocco's love quest is in some ways worlds apart from Shylock's bargains on the Rialto, but once again there is as much parallelism as contrast between successive

[1] *Shakespearean Comedy*, 1938, p. 140.

scenes in Venice and Belmont. We are again watching an outsider venturing into an alien society, an outsider too who is grotesque one moment and dignified the next. So Portia counters the absurd flourishes both of Morocco's rhetoric and his scimitar with a demure irony, but meets with a courteous gravity his readiness to risk his future happiness in the quest. The stakes, then, are high in Belmont as well as in Venice; we realise Bassanio will have to venture more than Antonio's ducats, and he goes up in our estimation; we even begin to feel a little uneasiness on his behalf. All our experience as readers of romance tells us that he must succeed, but this trustfulness is skilfully undermined by the ceremonial exeunt to this scene. It is very close to being a wedding procession as Portia and Morocco leave hand-in-hand for the vow-taking in the 'temple'. The after-image is to stay with us teasingly through six scenes in Venice.

THE ELOPEMENT

Nicholas Rowe, the first editor to divide the play into scenes, kept the next five (Act 2, Scenes 2–6) together as an unbroken episode. Even amid the scenic resources of the Victorian stage, Charles Kean preserved this unity, presenting the scenes as continuous action in the grandiose reconstruction of a Venetian street shown in illustration 11. Both Rowe and Kean were responding to something distinctive about this part of the play. Not only do its events, a 'merry tale' of how a young man, helped by a comic servant as go-between, runs away with the daughter and much of the wealth of a rich old miser, constitute a single and self-contained action, but they are set off as a kind of interlude or inset by virtue of their prevailing tone and mood, which recall those of Italian *commedia erudita*. In such comedy, love justifies any behaviour; the old are mocked, deceived, and cheated by the young in the kind of holiday from normal morality that was associated with Carnival.[1] But because Jessica's elopement is only one episode in *The Merchant of Venice*, the proximity of scenes with a totally different atmosphere ensures complex responses even to this most straightforward of stories. Moreover, notes of regret and misgiving can be heard at times through the shrill discord of Carnival's wry-necked fife.

Thus at the very start of the episode, when we should be entering a world free from moral anxieties, we meet (like Jaques in the greenwood of *As You Like It*) a moralising fool. Lancelot, who is not the scheming retainer of Italian comedy but a native product developed from the Vice of morality plays, is debating with a great show of casuistry whether or not a servant may run away from a bad master. Inevitably the question re-forms itself on Jessica's first appearance (2.3): may a daughter run away from a bad father? Jessica herself fears she is lacking in filial piety, and that theme too has been put in our minds by Lancelot's reunion with his father. Critics tend to pass over in some embarrassment this teasing of a blind old man, but there is more to the scene than a crude practical joke. Actually, as a joke, it misfires. Old Gobbo's distress on being told his son is dead overwhelms Lancelot, who struggles to assure his father he

[1] In *Il Vecchio amoroso* of Giannotti, the heroine is abducted amid realistic scenes of Carnival in Pisa. See Marvin T. Herrick, *Italian Comedy in the Renaissance*, 1960, pp. 101–3.

is very much alive. In the end the laugh is not on the father but on the son, whose trick goes out of control not because Old Gobbo cannot see him, but because, being shrewd and only gravel-blind, he does not take long to see what his son is up to and so refuse to play his game. Similarly, when the two Gobbos waylay Bassanio, the plain good sense of Old Gobbo's words is drowned and lost in Lancelot's 'confusions', even though he emerges from the interview convinced that he did very well for himself: 'I cannot get a service, no, I have ne'er a tongue in my head!' (2.2.131–2). Yet for all his big-headedness and his daft impulsiveness (he nearly wrecks Lorenzo's plan by telling Shylock about the masque), 'the patch is kind enough'; it is fitting that the last time we hear from him in the play he is chortling with pleasure at Bassanio's return. He may patronise his aged parent but he is also the prop of his old age; and this most natural of relationships helps to undermine the impression of youth's antagonism to age in this part of the play. His muddled clamour for a blessing – 'I am Lancelot your boy that was, your son that is, your child that shall be' (2.2.70–1) – is still with us when we listen to the neat and chill finality of Jessica's

> Farewell, and if my fortune be not crossed,
> I have a father, you a daughter, lost. (2.5.54–5)

By the time of Shylock's departure for Bassanio's feast, our changing views of Jessica have begun to overlay the one the other in rapid succession. No sooner have we seen her in kindly talk with Lancelot and in inward 'strife' about deserting her father than we learn that the plan to run away with Shylock's gold and jewels is of her devising. This suggests a hardbitten character at home in the world of intrigue. But now, in her only scene with her father, his harsh impersonality makes us eager to see her rescued from a house that is 'hell' (2.3.2); Jessica is starved of affection; hence, in the scene of her escape (2.6), her touching anxiety that Lorenzo will protect her.

The escape scene starts with the entry of 'the masquers, Gratiano and Salarino': perhaps only the two of them, perhaps a colourful crowd. Gratiano in his 'boldest suit of mirth' (2.2.173) appears to be a character born into the amoral world of intrigue comedy. Yet, from the shadow of the 'penthouse', Gratiano suddenly lifts us clear of intrigue and its excitements in the play's most haunting lines:

> All things that are
> Are with more spirit chasèd than enjoyed.
> How like a younger or a prodigal
> The scarfèd bark puts from her native bay,
> Hugged and embracèd by the strumpet wind!
> How like the prodigal doth she return
> With overweathered ribs and ragged sails,
> Lean, rent, and beggared by the strumpet wind! (2.6.13–20)

Many effects are achieved in this double image of the prodigal son and a maritime venture: it acts as a reminder that prodigality is as much of an aberration as avarice; it rouses a shiver of apprehension over Antonio's cargoes; it casts a doubt on the future happiness of impetuous lovers; it recalls a different love, the long-suffering of the prodigal's father, and so of Antonio. Inevitably it complicates our responses to the rest of the scene, slightly souring our amusement at such of Lorenzo's flippancies as 'play the thieves for wives' (2.6.24) and 'here dwells my father Jew' (26), and raising doubts about his characterisation of Jessica as 'wise, fair, and true' (57) at the moment she dashes down to the counting-house to 'gild' herself with more of her father's ducats.

To list such faintly discordant elements is to give them a prominence they cannot have in the theatre, where the audience loves a lover whatever his actions, and rejoices that some of Shylock's gold has fallen into the hands of those who can enjoy it. But their subliminal effect on the elopement episode is that we never quite board the merry-go-round of festive comedy; and if Shakespeare intended to write a masquerading scene with Shylock as its butt, he came to think better of it. So this second movement does not culminate in Lorenzo and Jessica leading out the masquers at the end of a crowded scene of festivity. Instead, the lovers slip off into the night to be married, as their companions are halted by the news that the wind has changed: fair winds, auspicious gales, for Bassanio; but for Antonio, a strumpet wind.

DEBIT AND CREDIT

The play now returns (Act 2, Scene 7 to Act 3, Scene 2) to an alternation of scenes between Belmont and Venice. We watch with mounting satisfaction as first Morocco and then Arragon makes the wrong choice of casket; all is progressing according to the folk-tale pattern in which the third contender always wins. By contrast, the scenes in Venice build up our concern for Antonio; we expect Bassanio to gain Portia and her fortune, but can he do so in time to save his friend? Finally these rising hopes and fears converge with vivid dramatic effect in the beautifully orchestrated scene of Bassanio's success.

We move to Belmont for a solemn occasion. Instead of the central curtains on the stage parting, as we earlier expected them to do, on a noisy embarkation party, they are drawn back at Portia's command to reveal the caskets; instead of a daughter in flight from her father, throwing the casket containing his gold out of the window and in effect flinging herself after it, we are confronted with a daughter who is the passive model of filial duty as she waits for the opening of the casket containing her image. Either we are impressed by the decorum which prevails in Belmont – or we are still so immersed in the world of the Venetian masquers and its post-medieval attitude to women, that we resent Portia's acquiescence in the will of a living daughter being curbed by the will of a dead father. Nor is our response to Morocco single-minded in this scene. The splendour of the verse, reminiscent of Marlowe, in which he praises Portia makes him a convincing lover; and he commands our sympathy when at the last he stands, a Tamburlaine-like figure of frustrated ambition, holding the death's head that 'many men desire'. But there has been absurdity too in his pompous self-satisfaction, though not perhaps enough of it to prevent Portia's brisk dismissal jarring our sensibilities. Again, though, a quick shift occurs: it is a relief to see the first competitor eliminated, the more so if the role has not been played for easy comic effect but in a way that showed the competition was serious.

5 Frontispiece to *The Merchant of Venice* in Thomas Hanmer's edition of Shakespeare, 1743. Drawing by Francis Hayman, engraved by H. F. B. Gravelot

So the loser departs and we are returned to Venice to learn of other losses, sustained by Antonio and Shylock. Antonio grieves for his friend's absence, not for his argosy – 'I think he only loves the world for him' (2.8.51). Shylock on the other hand grieves for his money rather than his daughter. But our uneasiness that Salarino and Solanio should treat the one human relationship with awe and the other with derision serves to blur once more the contrast between the protagonists. The pair of friends go off in quest of some delight to alleviate Antonio's heaviness. Shakespeare alleviates ours with the Prince of Arragon, a role that can be played with some levity; to Portia he is a 'deliberate fool' (2.9.79). We had some time for Morocco, but we have none for this suitor who thinks Portia is no more than he deserves and whose hurt pride explodes in complaints that compare poorly with Morocco's dignified silence. Yet it has been a dynastic pride, as his talk of degrees has suggested, so that in the middle of our relief and laughter we feel the blow with him: the more if he is played as a very young man.[1]

At Arragon's exit, Bassanio is near at hand and, like the audience of a Western, we are waiting for the sound of his horse's hooves. But the scene moves back to Venice where 'meanwhile', as the sub-titles would have it, the villain is ready for the kill. Shylock here both is and is not the grotesque figure described by Solanio in 2.8. The picture drawn there was a kind of anticipatory irony:[2] it prepared us for the ludicrous in Shylock's behaviour but not for the palpable distress in his voice and bearing, which consequently are disturbingly convincing. 'Caught in compulsive, reflexive responses', in C. L. Barber's phrase,[3] he dances like an absurd puppet to Tubal's jerkings; but we see how the jerkings hurt – 'Thou torturest me' (3.1.95). The 'Hath not a Jew eyes?' speech, delivered by generations of actors as a noble appeal for racial equality, may on close inspection turn out to be merely a sophistical justification of revenge; in the actual performance, the cruel goadings of Salarino and Solanio make it a cry from the heart: 'If you prick us, do we not bleed?' (50–1). Much of Shylock's language is as comically repetitive as the 'sans dot' of Molière's miser; yet the declaration 'I would my daughter were dead at my foot, and the jewels in her ear: would she were hearsed at my foot, and the ducats in her coffin' (69–71) echoes with a kind of psalmodic passion the very different repetitiousness of Hebrew poetry. The same voice of lamentation, obscuring the solipsistic nature of what is said, is heard in 'no sighs but o'my breathing, no tears but o'my shedding' (75–6). Leah and her ring disturb us still further, though not enough to obscure the menace of 'I will have the heart of him' (100); an admission of conjugal fidelity, as M. C. Bradbrook remarks, can scarcely be held to outweigh a taste for murder.[4]

Because our responses to the Tubal scene are already so complex, it seems no place to embark on a fresh development in Shylock's character by having him suddenly

[1] Arragon was very young both in Tyrone Guthrie's production (1954) and in Michael Langham's (1960).

[2] By this I mean the kind of effect Shakespeare achieves by having Falstaff and Prince Hal, in the first part of *King Henry IV*, enact in Act 2 the meeting between Hal and the King in Act 3.

[3] *Shakespeare's Festive Comedy*, p. 183.

[4] *Shakespeare and Elizabethan Poetry*, 1951, p. 171.

seize upon the possibility for revenge in a bond which he had proposed as a joke. Such an interpretation flies in the face of contradictory evidence which stretches from Shylock's own 'If I can catch him once upon the hip...' (1.3.38) to Jessica's statement that her father has long sworn to have Antonio's flesh (3.2.283–7). And if Tubal is made to instigate the plan of revenge in Shylock's mind, the play really does become anti-semitic. Shylock is confirming a long-cherished hope when he goes to the synagogue to swear an oath of vengeance. Oaths were traditionally taken in a religious building, and a similar ritual is imposed on Portia's suitors, with the important difference that their vows are prompted by love. Shylock's 'oath in heaven' (4.1.224) is prompted by hate, and Shakespeare was well aware how much his vow was at variance with the teaching of the Jewish scriptures that vengeance belongs to the Lord.

The stage is now thronged with Portia and Bassanio 'and all their trains'. Despite the crowd of extras, this is a love scene, the finest since *Romeo and Juliet*. Portia, whose speeches have hitherto been for the most part either cautiously polite or scornfully dismissive, now reveals a turmoil of emotion in the ebb and flow and eddy of her speech rhythms as she begs Bassanio to delay his choice. But as she tries to 'peize the time' (3.2.22) we remember how inexorably time is moving on in Venice, where we have just heard Shylock ask Tubal to bespeak a catchpole 'a fortnight before' the expiry of the bond. Bassanio (we hear with relief) will not wait; he is on the rack till his choice is made. The image is tossed back and forth in the manner of Elizabethan love talk, but it is not to be dismissed as a 'Petrarchan conceit'; the thought of torture is there to remind us of Shylock's intention to take a long time in killing Antonio.

Here are pointers to the nature of the complexity of this scene. It lies less in the kind of critical undertone we have already detected than in our awareness, as we listen to the happy and triumphant lovers, of other worlds of feeling: especially of Shylock's dangerous hatred, to which Antonio is exposed as the result of his own reckless love. When Portia poetically transforms Bassanio's choice of casket into Hercules' rescue of Hesione from a sea-monster, few if any of the audience recall that Hercules was hoping for a good reward from Hesione's father, let alone see in this an oblique criticism of Bassanio. The lines are much more likely to put us in mind, in the light of the scene we have just watched in Venice, of Shylock's monstrous thirst for vengeance, the sea-change of Antonio's wealth, and Antonio's dependence now for his life on Bassanio's success. The melancholy song about Fancy is another shadow across the scene. But it does not impugn Bassanio's constancy. Rather it is just because his love is not a passing fancy that he is able to generalise from his feelings as a lover in reflections upon the specious and the real; reflections which bring him inevitably to the right choice of casket.

We are not, it is true, allowed to forget that Portia is worth a fortune; she even reminds us of this herself by making her declaration of love, in part, in counting-house terms. But Shakespeare, far from critically distancing us from the lovers by this language, uses it to involve us more closely with them. At this moment of the play we are all fortune-hunters who can scarcely wait for Bassanio to get his hands on Portia's money in order that he may save Antonio. A major irony of the play is of

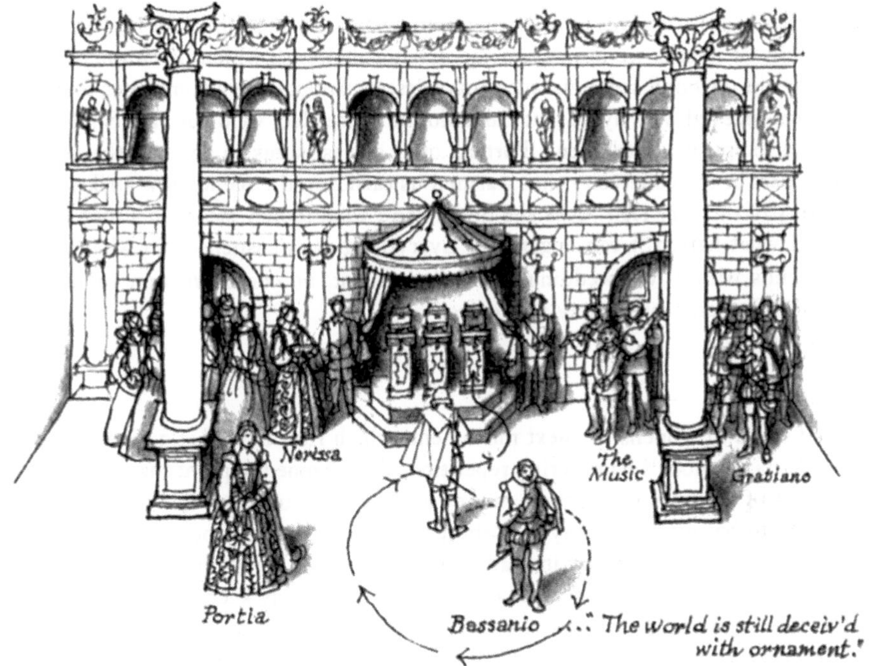

6 Bassanio makes his choice of casket. A possible staging of Act 3, Scene 2, by C. Walter Hodges

course that in the end Antonio is saved by Portia and not by her money. Meanwhile the involvement is there, and Shakespeare builds on it, and on the other spontaneous involvement we feel with the lovers' happiness in one another, by calling up all his poetic skills to communicate a joy so intense that those who experience it scarcely dare to name it. This is the effect of Portia's breathless aside, 'O love, be moderate…' (111–14), of the lingering conceits with which Bassanio praises Portia's likeness because he dares not yet trust himself to face her, and of his image of the bewildered runner at the winning post. Finally both acknowledge their happiness with a symbolic gesture – the giving and receiving of the ring – and with speeches that are the apex of the scene's eloquence: the happy abandon of Portia's speech 'You see me, Lord Bassanio' (149–74),[1] and Bassanio's rapturous 'wild of nothing, save of joy' (182).

The descent from these dizzy heights is achieved through the cheerful ribaldry of Gratiano: a deft modulation by which Shakespeare avoids the melodramatic effect of disaster impinging suddenly upon triumph. For we sense disaster in the very appearance of Salerio, probably a soberly-dressed official.[2] The dark and heavily-

[1] Ellen Terry felt this empathy of the audience when she first acted Portia: 'I knew that I had "got them" at the moment when I spoke the speech beginning "You see me…"' (*The Story of My Life*, 1908, p. 105).

[2] For the question of whether Salerio is the same character as Salarino, see Textual Analysis, pp. 191–5 below.

jewelled Jessica visibly reminds us of Shylock and of the alleged grounds for his hatred, and in the tally of wrecks we hear again the dry hostility with which he enumerated these ventures in the bond scene. In such ways destructive passion again comes to the fore. However relieved we may be that Bassanio has succeeded, we dread that Shylock will continue to spurn a settlement. Portia's offer of vast sums to appease the Jew, though it is part of the generosity that warmed us earlier in the scene, now strikes us as the naïvety of the very rich: does she understand what money *means* to a man like Shylock and what hatred it can engender? Everything is in suspense. So when the movement ends with a real wedding procession at last, no consummation follows; Bassanio and Gratiano must away to Venice.

DR BALTHAZAR

In the brief scene that opens the next movement, which runs from Act 3, Scene 3 to the end of Act 4, Shylock's hammering repetitions drive home the point that he is not to be baulked of his revenge. Portia's money is thus of no use, and her best course would appear to be to take to prayer as she proposes to do at the beginning of 3.4. So it comes as a shock to find her instead scampering off to Venice in male disguise, apparently for no better reason than that she and Nerissa may keep an eye on their husbands. We feel we are being forced back, reluctantly in the face of Antonio's peril, into the second act's atmosphere of intrigue comedy. Shakespeare of course is playing adroitly with our responses, much as Portia herself has been playing with Bassanio's in describing herself as an 'unlessoned girl, unschooled, unpractised' (3.2.159). The mime of a braggart youth which she performs with such relish (3.4.60–76) is a fresh instance of that anticipatory irony which draws off irrelevant reactions from a dramatic episode before it occurs. Shakespeare is making sure that we take Portia seriously when she appears in legal robes.

Before that happens, and in order to give the players of Portia and Nerissa ample time to change, Shakespeare interposes a scene which we can, if we wish, think of as his own breathing space, an interlude he could entrust to the patter of Will Kemp (who almost certainly played Lancelot) before the ardours of the trial scene. Yet the happy security of 3.5 makes a real dramatic point. Dinner, over which Jessica and Lorenzo will talk gentle nonsense, is nearly ready, and meanwhile the Fool – for Lancelot has taken on that function – provides a flow of entertainment much as the family television set would today: not of high quality, but a reassuring part of the domestic scene. Jessica is enjoying the home she has never had before and is reunited with her old companion Lancelot, whose jokes about Jews she can fend off (which is why he makes them) with a serene confidence: 'my husband...hath made me a Christian' (3.5.15). The scene effaces Tubal's image of Jessica squandering her father's money, and so subdues, even if it does not suppress, any notion we may have at the start of the trial that her marriage has given Shylock good cause for 'a lodged hate'. In further preparation for the confrontation of Portia and Shylock, Jessica is made to praise Portia in quasi-religious language, as 'heaven here on earth' (3.5.64). Our responses to the trial scene will continue to be those awakened by a 'pleasant comedy', as they have been in these two scenes in Belmont, but they will also be quickened by the sense of the momentous that belongs to morality drama.

The entry of the Duke and the magnificoes makes a brave show, but they are powerless to override the law, which is all on the side – or so he believes – of Shylock. If images of a bird or beast of prey come to mind at the sight of the lone, malevolent figure facing Antonio and his group of friends, they reinforce the duality of our responses in the first part of this scene. Shylock's savagery appals us, but we relish the grotesque, masterful debating skill which turns back upon the Christians the insults in which they have denied him all humanity. Now the response of this 'most impenetrable cur' (3.3.18) to the invitation to behave 'with human gentleness and love' (4.1.25) is to deflect the argument from the moral and human to the behaviouristic and animal, and to equate Antonio with some such object of revulsion as a gaping pig. At this, the argument narrows down to Bassanio's angry protests and Shylock's retorts, till Antonio intervenes out of his instinct to protect his friend. Thanks to the 'quietness of spirit' that he has already brought to his losses, Antonio can be as resigned to Shylock as he is to such forces of nature as winds and high seas. But still these images deny humanity to Shylock, and so open the way to his most damaging indictment of Venice: it is a slave-owning society. Ostensibly the argument is 'You own men, why should I not own a man's flesh?' but we recognise and can scarcely fail to appreciate the Jew's real targets; the racial exclusiveness which denied human rights to non-Christian captives, and the greed which exploited their labour.

Relief from this welter of responses comes with the entry of an easily-recognised Nerissa; some of the confidence of comedy is restored. Shylock does not press home his advantage, but shrinks to a sadistic figure crouched over his knife. Portia is thus given the ascendancy from the moment of her quietly ceremonial entry. She retains it for the next two hundred lines, shaping the scene into a rhetorical symmetry that would have been immediately apparent to an Elizabethan audience. In contrast to the essentially aural effects of 3.2 with its 'dulcet sounds' of music, its euphonious verse, and its dramatic changes of key, this scene has an architectural quality to which directors often respond by pyramidal visual effects. It is not perhaps wholly fanciful to relate this to Shylock's scales, a misappropriated emblem of justice. Shakespeare has an actor's eye for the dramatic potentialities of props: knife, money bags, deed, and balance all in turn hold our interest at a tense moment of the action.

In the exchanges which continue with minimal interruptions for the next ninety lines or so, Portia, unlike the Christians (the Duke apart), speaks to Shylock as a human being. Her first appeal to him is as a believer who, worshipping the same God as herself (a point the Christians choose to ignore), knows mercy to be a divine precept. Only when her appeal is rebuffed in Shylock's 'My deeds upon my head!' does she appeal to his financial instincts: can he not be satisfied with a gain of a hundred per cent or – here she raises the offer, since it is after all her own money – two hundred per cent? Her last appeal is the most basic; in asking for a doctor to be present she is striving to make Shylock, as a man, grasp the non-human savagery of what he intends.

To call these exchanges an unnecessary prolongation of Antonio's agony is to

7 'Tarry a little.' A possible staging of Act 4, Scene 1, by C. Walter Hodges

overlook the fact that Portia is systematically offering Shylock every chance to be merciful. But since we do not, unlike Portia, know what sanctions the law of Venice holds against Shylock's attempt to take his forfeiture, the confidence which was encouraged by the conventions of comedy and by Portia's eloquence begins to fade, and our feelings increasingly seek out the silent Antonio. There is thus a great theatrical build-up for Antonio's farewell of Bassanio; indeed, when it comes, its near-tragic eloquence is so powerful,[1] perhaps as a result of Shakespeare's difficulties with the character which have been touched on earlier (p. 24 above), that a rapid, even over-rapid, return to the mode of intrigue comedy has to be made. Portia and Nerissa take tart exception to their husbands' readiness to sacrifice their wives for their friend. But with a reference to Jessica's match, in which one relationship has actually been destroyed in favour of another, Shylock complains that time is being wasted; and Portia, picking up a reverberation from the world of dalliance with her 'Tarry a little', steps back into the world of reckoning and authoritatively changes the whole direction of the trial.

Now we watch the scale slowly turn in Antonio's favour, as Portia lays in the balance a succession of legal points against Shylock. The triangular symmetry of the scene is completed as these legal requirements are set against Portia's pleas for mercy in reversed order. Her last plea, that Antonio be prevented from bleeding to death, is matched by the proviso about shedding no blood; the offer of triple repayment matches the condition that only an exact pound may be taken; and the plea to Shylock to show mercy as he hopes to attain it is matched with the revelation that his life is now forfeit so that he must himself beg mercy from the Duke. Portia's eloquence in praise of mercy, which fell on deaf ears when it was spoken, now bears fruit in the Duke's pardon of Shylock and – at 'What mercy can you render him, Antonio?' (374) – in the generosity of Antonio, who restores half of his enemy's wealth to him at a time when he believes himself bankrupt.

During this elaborate dénouement, the responses of the audience which were powerfully unified in the central part of the scene, from Portia's entry to Shylock's 'I take this offer then' (313), begin to diversify and to fragment. For some, Portia's prolonged exposition of the case against Shylock sounds uncomfortably like a game of cat-and-mouse. And in Antonio's insistence that Shylock's wealth be inherited by 'the gentleman / That lately stole his daughter' there seems to be a deliberate reminder that there are other misuses of money beside usury. Above all, the forced conversion genuinely distresses a modern audience. Nor can we completely dismiss this last response as anachronistic. Granted that Shylock now has a chance, like Jessica,

[1] It has even been read as a religious allegory of redemption, for example by Israel Gollancz (*Allegory and Mysticism in Shakespeare*, 1931, p. 32), who quotes John Fletcher on the Crucifixion (1613):

He died indeed, not as an actor dies,
To die today, and live again tomorrow,
In show to please the audience, or disguise
The idle habit of enforcèd sorrow:
  The Cross his stage was, and he played the part
  Of one that for his friend did pawn his heart.

The lines could certainly have been suggested by a performance of Shakespeare's play, but the point they make is one of difference, not similarity.

of getting to heaven, that the way is open for family reconciliation, and that Antonio is making sure Shylock can ruin no more debtors, there are still signs that Shakespeare himself is not wholly happy about the conversion. The proposal comes not from Portia, who is seldom subject to critical irony, but from Antonio, of whom the dramatist has a far less steady image. Indeed in the 1981 Royal Shakespeare Company production, Sinead Cusack knelt beside Shylock as if her 'Art thou contented, Jew?' (389) was a way of sympathetically begging him to accede to the Christians' demands. There are signs of Shakespeare's uneasiness too in the abruptness with which Shylock signals his agreement and leaves. A humiliated character in a Shakespeare play, unless he is irrepressible like Falstaff or Parolles, is usually silent, because the dramatist knew how quickly an audience's sympathies veer towards the underdog. In this instance, because Shylock has really been treated as a dog outside the court, the swing is likely to be rapid. Gratiano's jeers seldom please an audience and if, as has been suggested earlier (p. 16 above), Shakespeare consciously breaks the dramatic illusion at lines 394–6, he catches our feelings on the rebound simply by calling a halt to our imaginative involvement. Shylock's power is gone, and there is no need for a lingering and spectacular exit. Shylock as the joint creation of Shakespeare and any gifted and understanding actor of the part will always be the dominant figure in our ultimate recall of the play.

This fourth movement culminates in a procession off the stage of the dignitaries and officials, all visibly relaxed and happy. It is not a wedding procession, but it leaves the two husbands face to face with their unrecognised wives to act out a kind of wedding ritual. Each husband bestows a ring on his wife, as he must have done before the altar at Belmont, but now each, as the audience well knows, is giving away his wife's keepsake. As doctor and clerk set the intrigue afoot here and in the next scene (retained as part of the same scene by Rowe) we adjust our expectations to a different type of comedy, knowing that at last we are to be offered the Carnival *inganni*, or deceptions and misunderstandings, that we looked for when Portia and Nerissa sped to Venice to assume their disguises.

THE RENEWING OF LOVE

The change of mood in the last act of *The Merchant of Venice* has troubled many readers. This may be in part because their idea of the play is based on a kind of folk memory of productions in which the actor-manager playing Shylock had the final curtain fall on his exit. But if the play had ended there, we would feel deprived of two expected features of a Shakespearean comedy: the ups and downs of courtship for which there was no scope in the casket story, and the traditional wedding-night ending of which we have been kept in mind by the conclusion of each of the play's earlier movements. The affair of the rings allows the wooing to begin afresh. Bassanio must now plead and Portia must remain obdurate until the battle of the sexes ends with a graceful capitulation of her power. Only then, when audience expectations have been fully satisfied in this way, can the lovers, in accordance with Elizabethan custom, be ceremoniously escorted to bed.

There is much to celebrate in Belmont: Portia's return, Antonio's safety, the lovers' reunion. Yet from very early in the act there occur sudden quick disturbances of our feelings, sudden almost subliminal recollections of the fear and pain of past events. It must strike us that the legendary lovers with whom Lorenzo and Jessica half-jestingly identify were all unhappy. This thought is countered, however, by the allusion to Medea, not here spoken of as Jason's deserted lover but as the enchantress who restored Jason's father to life – much as Portia has saved the elderly friend of her modern Jason, Bassanio. Moreover the incantatory language of the whole passage can be felt as a kind of exorcism, the ritual driving-out of bad spirits on the wedding night such as is performed at the end of *A Midsummer Night's Dream*. Discordant passions are thus set at a distance; if Jessica, like a little shrew, slanders her love, he is bound to forgive it her because in Belmont, in the words of an Elizabethan song, 'the falling out of faithful friends renewing is of love'. Music and Lorenzo's talk of music together celebrate the harmony of lover with lover, man with his natural setting, heaven with earth.

We could not be farther away from Shylock. He is never named in this scene nor spoken of as Jessica's father, but distanced and depersonalised as 'the wealthy Jew' (15) from whom she stole (here a disturbing double meaning flashes past) and as 'the rich Jew' (292) who has under duress made Lorenzo and Jessica his heirs. But at the point where the lovers' contentment seems most inviolable, Lorenzo's words (83–8) about the man who has no music in himself suddenly bring Shylock back to us as a person: the originator, certainly, of 'treasons, stratagems, and spoils', but also the victim of Jessica's spoils and Lorenzo's stratagems. Uneasy recollections darken the scene, and at 'affections dark as Erebus' (87) the moon, as if on cue, goes behind a cloud. Once again though, the uneasiness is short-lived. Portia restores a sense of moral security in her sententious return, fresh from her own good deed in a naughty world. And our sense of celebration is maintained through all the stages leading to Bassanio's return, right up to the sounding of the 'tucket' which Elizabethans would have recognised as the prelude to a royal entry. There is however to be no pomp and rhetoric. Bassanio and Portia continue their love talk as if disaster had never impinged on Act 3, and then quietly draw Antonio into the charmed circle.

Gratiano's angry bark now jars this concord, and the quarrel over the rings escalates fast. Since we are in the know, we can be confident that all will return to laughter: a security reinforced by the word-game of Bassanio's protests and Portia's counter-protests (192–208) and by the absurd oaths of Portia and Nerissa, which now replace the dangerous oath taken by Portia's suitors and the deadly oath taken by Shylock. But unreal as the quarrel is, it is real to Antonio. 'Th'unhappy subject of these quarrels' (238), he stands anxious, isolated, and vulnerable, embodying emotions we were tempted to believe could be forgotten. Again, the disturbance is fleeting. Portia appoints Antonio a role in the dénouement and then, when the truth is out, gives him a letter of good news that cancels the disastrous news of his own letter in the third act. Finally Nerissa completes the reversal of the play's events by handing Lorenzo a document very different from the fateful bond of the trial scene.

So Antonio's unhappiness and Shylock's hatred are relegated to the past. But the faint discords interspersed among the harmonies of the last act have shown them to be permanent elements of the play, and the last problem facing directors is whether or not these discords should be suggested in the final exeunt, which was an important part of Elizabethan dramaturgy. Some have sought to do so by, for example, leaving Antonio alone to tear up the news of his restored fortune.[1] Jonathan Miller kept us in mind of Shylock by giving Jessica a slow, solitary exit to the strains of a Jewish lament for the dead. But this, though splendidly theatrical, imposes as much upon the play's ending as would the belated arrival of Shylock in the pink of health and laden with presents. The play has exacted responses as complex as those we bring to real life. But at the point at which it returns us to real life and so defines itself as an artefact, we look for a resolution in full harmony. It may be that Lorenzo and Jessica relinquish with a gesture their posts as châtelaines and usher Portia, Bassanio, and Antonio into the house, leaving Gratiano to toss his last jest at the audience before chasing in Nerissa. Even if Antonio is not in the wedding procession, he is not left out of Belmont. Clifford Leech recalls how in Denis Carey's 1953 production Antonio slowly followed the couples, with a suggestion of his persistent melancholy – 'then, with a shrug, fitted himself to the mood of rejoicing, twirled his stick, and moved more briskly. It complicated the final mood for an instant, but the complications were basically Shakespeare's.'[2]

The afterlife of *The Merchant of Venice*

The Merchant of Venice shares with *Hamlet* the distinction of having been more often performed than any other of Shakespeare's plays. There is a very high probability that at the moment these words are read the play is being rehearsed or presented somewhere in the world. Its stage history is thus a rich one, and several famous actors have made their reputation in the part of Shylock. Though every group of actors and its director have necessarily to impose an overall unity of interpretation on what we have seen to be a very subtle play, the rapidity with which production follows production should serve to keep the idea of the play flexible and manifold in the minds of today's theatre-going public. But in the past *The Merchant of Venice* has been highly vulnerable to changing theatrical and social pressures, some of which have so far distorted it that several separate rescue operations in this century have been needed to get it back to some semblance of the play Shakespeare wrote. Its stage history has been rich, but it has not always been happy.

The play in fact had virtually no stage history for its first hundred and fifty years. After two performances before James I at Shrovetide, 1605, it vanished from the English stage, though actors who emigrated to Germany kept a few of its lines alive in German in a chaotic comedy called *Der Jud von Venedig*.[3] The right to perform *The Merchant of Venice* was assigned to the Theatre Royal after the Restoration, but its romantic treatment of love was not to the taste of the time, and readers held it to

[1] As described by Tyrone Guthrie, *In Various Directions*, 1965, p. 101.

[2] 'Stratford 1953', *SQ* 4 (1953), 461–6, quotation from p. 462.

[3] Ernest Brennecke, *Shakespeare in Germany 1590–1700*, 1964, gives a translation.

want 'that probability and verisimilitude, which is absolutely necessary to all the representations of the stage'.[1] But in 1701 the swing of public taste in favour of sentimental drama encouraged George Granville to adapt the play, in verse that horribly mangles the language of the original, as *The Jew of Venice*. In this, Shylock was a comic character, though the extra lines which Granville provided suggest that the Jew was played less as a 'low comedy' part than as a sort of Fagin. This presentation, like the promise in the Prologue to 'punish a stockjobbing Jew', is in keeping with the prejudices of the aristocratic adapter and his audience. The traditional antipathy of Court to City was now the hostility of Tory to Whig, and the Whig Revolution of 1688 had had the strong support of orthodox Jews, first- or second-generation immigrants whose new London synagogue numbered several members of the Exchange among its congregation.[2]

By 1741, Shakespeare's reputation stood high enough for Charles Macklin to restore the original play to the stage. He was to act Shylock for the next half-century, thus establishing the tradition of the play as a star vehicle. In that Shylock, for all his dramatic prominence, does not have a long part and makes only five appearances, Macklin's concentration on him was already a slight distortion. During the next century-and-a-half it was to lead to grosser ones as not only were characters irrelevant to the portrayal of Shylock dropped, but whole scenes, notably Act 5, were on occasion left out of the play. Even greater distortions were to result from the various ways actors responded to changing public attitudes towards the Jewish presence in European society. Macklin, to his credit, kept the play virtually intact, and presented a Shylock who could be said to be there in the text in so far as he was the menacing enemy envisaged by the Venetians. Contemporary accounts of Macklin's performance evoke a sullen, malevolent, implacable Jew, terrifying the audience by his ferocity in 3.1 and by his portentous silences in the trial (illustration 8). A foreign visitor confessed 'it is not to be denied that the sight of this Jew suffices to awaken at once, in the best-regulated mind, all the prejudices of childhood against these people'.[3] The apologetic tone of this comment made in 1775 shows that eighteenth-century reasonableness and sentiment were beginning to replace fanaticism and prejudice in an audience's response to Shylock. By the end of the century, a Jew had appeared in the London theatre as the eponymous hero of a play, and a critic had imagined a future adaptation of *The Merchant of Venice* in a Jewish national homeland, with Shylock's opponents overwhelmed by remorse.[4] The way was being prepared for the great romantic Shylock of Edmund Kean.

On Kean's first night at Drury Lane in 1814, a sparse and apathetic audience was suddenly brought to life by his playing of the bond scene. It was clear that the old hostility of Christendom towards Barbary had given place to a romantic fascination

[1] Charles Gildon, 'Remarks on the Plays of Shakespeare', Rowe, VII (1710), p. 321.

[2] Toby Lelyveld deals fully with the social history of Shylock in *Shylock on the Stage*, 1960. See also John Russell Brown's invaluable essay, 'The realization of Shylock', in *Early Shakespeare*, ed. J. R. Brown and B. Harris, 1961, pp. 186–209.

[3] Quoted in translation by Furness, p. 374.

[4] T. O. [i.e. Richard Hole], 'An apology for the character and conduct of Shylock', *Essays by a Society of Gentlemen at Exeter*, 1796, pp. 552–73.

8 Charles Macklin as Shylock, 1776

with the exotic. 'His thoughts take wings to the East', wrote Hazlitt of a later performance:

> his voice swells and deepens at the mention of his sacred tribe and ancient law, and he dwells delighted on any digression to distant times and places, as a relief to his vindictive and rooted purposes.[1]

The wide emotional compass that Kean was able to command made the Tubal scene, with its contrasts of rage and grief, the high point of his performance. Such lights and shades were not just virtuosity; thanks largely to his speaking as genuine soliloquies speeches which had been treated as 'asides', Kean was able to convince so perceptive a listener as G. H. Lewes that Shylock indeed suffered.[2] Moreover his Shylock was palpably intelligent, especially in his sardonic retorts to the Duke and Portia. The collapse of this intelligent and vulnerable being was horrible to watch; the reaction of the spectator who, in Heine's hearing, exclaimed 'the poor man is wronged' was only a little more extreme than that of the audience as a whole.[3] Shylock left the courtroom with the audience on his side.

It was magnificent – but was it Shakespeare? Henry Irving appears to have doubted that it was, since he described Shylock, in conversation, as a bloody-minded monster.[4]

[1] *Examiner* 16 March 1828, in *Works*, ed. P. P. Howe, 1930, XVIII, 377.

[2] *On Actors and the Art of Acting*, 1875, pp. 8–9.

[3] Ida Benecke, *Heine on Shakespeare: A Translation*, 1895, pp. 125–6. The notes on the play are, revealingly, classed under 'Tragedies'.

[4] William Winter, *Shakespeare on the Stage*, 1912, p. 175. Alan Hughes devotes a chapter to Irving's production in *Henry Irving, Shakespearean*, 1981.

But after Kean's triumph he could not play him as such. By Irving's time, however, there was less call for a 'protest' Shylock. The civil disabilities of being a Jew had been abolished, England had a popular Jewish prime minister, and the Rothschilds dominated the finances of Europe. In this late-Victorian business world it made good sense (in Shylock's meaning of the adjective) to try to understand the Jewish viewpoint and what was thought to be the characteristic Jewish temperament. Whereas Kean had created his Shylock from within, identifying himself with the experience of being disadvantaged and despised, Irving's Shylock was initially built up from alternation of stately bearing with volatile passion that he had observed in Jewish traders in the Levant. His elderly, Oriental Jew (illustration 10) dominated the bond scene by his poise and presence, but the outburst of 3.1 proved more difficult; in the end Irving abandoned the attempt to be, like Kean, 'hissing hot', and played the Tubal scene mainly for pathos. The peak of his performance was the trial scene. Here his Shylock spoke and moved with deliberation, coldly vengeful in his expectation of success, controlled and dignified – though physically shattered – in his defeat.[1] The overall effect of a man more sinned against than sinning was strengthened by the insertion of an extra scene. After Jessica, in 2.6, had been serenaded by singers in a gondola and swept out by Lorenzo in a whirl of Carnival figures, the curtain fell, and quickly rose again on an empty stage. Shylock made a slow entrance across the canal bridge which nearly spanned the stage, and knocked twice on the door of his house. There was a long silence, and the curtain fell.

Gondolas and canal bridges were essential to the spectacular magnificence of these nineteenth-century productions. The Victorians were as fascinated by Venice as the Elizabethans had been, but they no longer visited the city in order to study and admire its constitution and trade. Instead, as true 'picturesque' travellers of the period, they feasted their eyes on its architecture and tried, in their stage sets, to reproduce it as faithfully as painters had done from Carpaccio to Guardi.[2] Such spacious magnificence called for the presence of crowds of 'supers'. In Irving's trial scene these included a group of Jews who urged Shylock, in dumb show, to accept Bassanio's offer. When they left the court, yells of execration outside indicated the harm that had been done to race relations in Venice.

The spectacular effects must all have been enjoyable and the best of them, those of Irving and the Bancrofts, were certainly beautiful as well. But they aimed at a peepshow style of stage illusion which, like Kean's delivery of asides as soliloquies, made impossible the rapport between actor and audience that had been the heart of the theatrical experience in Shakespeare's non-illusory playhouse. A further damaging consequence of Victorian stage spectacle was that it necessitated a brutal cutting of the text. Bassanio was robbed of much of his fine eloquence in 3.2 and of the verbal

[1] Winter, pp. 195–6.

[2] Charles Kean's lavish production at the Princess's Theatre, 1858, is described by George C. D. Odell, *Shakespeare from Betterton to Irving*, 1920, II, 353–4. Charles Kean's own acting edition, 1858, gives full details. On the Bancrofts' scenery for their 1875 production, see William E. Kleb, 'Shakespeare in Tottenham-Street: an "aesthetic" *Merchant of Venice*', *Theatre Survey* 16 (1975), 97–121. Richard Foulkes writes on 'The staging of the trial scene in Irving's *The Merchant of Venice*', in *ETJ* 28 (1976), 312–17.

9 Edmund Kean as Shylock, by George Hayter

life given to his character by Portia's lines about 'young Alcides'. Bowdlerisation rendered the talk between Portia and Nerissa insipid, and the excision of her scenes with Lancelot left Jessica with little to say. To economise on scene-shifting, whole scenes were transposed, and this led to a further shuffling of passages of text: many of Shakespeare's transitions between Venice and Belmont, rich in dramatic effect, disappeared; Morocco's two scenes were run into a truncated whole; Arragon vanished; and the build-up of anxiety over Antonio's ventures was lost in the fusion

10 Henry Irving as Shylock, by Bernard Partridge

of 2.8 and 3.1. Edwin Booth ended the play with Shylock's departure and several later actors, including for a time Irving, did the same. Charles Kean, though he kept the last act, denuded it of its best poetry.

By about 1900, a kind of synthetic *Merchant of Venice* had replaced Shakespeare's play in playgoers' minds. It was above all a character study of Shylock, who emerged from its events as a tragic hero, even 'a heroic saint';[1] with the exception of Portia the

[1] Ellen Terry, *The Story of My Life*, p. 163.

rest of the characters might as well have been painted on the scenery, the splendour of which competed with Shylock's heart-rending last exit as the dominant memory of the play. This version was cuttingly summarised by William Poel in his parody of the first quarto's title page: 'The tragical history of the Jew of Venice, with the extreme injustice of Portia towards the said Jew in denying him the right to cut a just pound of the Merchant's flesh, together with the obtaining of the rich heiress by the prodigal Bassanio'.[1] Poel's own 1898 production for the Elizabethan Stage Society was a first brave attempt to restore the play's original character. But it had little immediate effect, perhaps because of Poel's own error of judgement in playing Shylock as a ludicrous figure in a red wig and big false nose. Academic actors, believing this to be the Elizabethan Shylock, have since tried the same style with no more success. Shylock, as Rowe saw, and the less aware Venetians in the play fail to see, is no laughing matter.

Though productions in the grand star-centred and 'upholstered' manner (illustration 13) continued well into the twentieth century, its early decades, those of the 'Shakespeare revolution', saw radical changes in the play's presentation. The actor-manager was making way for patterns of company organisation approximating more nearly to those of Shakespeare's own day; illusion was giving place to symbolic décors, thrust stages, and even theatre-in-the-round. Between the world wars, the Old Vic offered Londoners several productions of *The Merchant of Venice* in which it was evident that the company as a group had rediscovered the subtlety and variety of the whole play. The Shylock of Lewis Casson (1927), for example, was a mean, warped figure drawn to a scale that enabled the director to give proportionate interest to other characters, especially in the Belmont scenes. The final break with the *Merchant of Venice* of the actor-managers may be said to have occurred at Stratford in 1932, the first season of the new Shakespeare Memorial Theatre.[2] In April, the Old Bensonians arranged as a tribute to Frank Benson a special matinée of the play as he had produced and acted in it on many tours: first, a run of scenes in Venice, then all the scenes in Belmont, then the trial and the curtain down on Benson's exit in the part of Shylock. Five months later, Komisarjevsky laid this last Victorian ghost and challenged the whole solemn and archaeological tradition by treating the play as pure Carnival. His production opened to a scamper of pierrots against a scenic background which sent up all 'pictureque' productions by its crazy bridges and leaning towers. Shylock was a Jewish comedian from the music halls, Portia a china doll who donned a vast wig and spectacles for the trial. The Duke went to sleep. It was not Shakespeare's play, but it was a piece of much-needed iconoclasm.

Yet just at the point in time when the play was relieved of the theatrical pressures which had distorted it in the nineteenth century, social pressures such as had since the time of Kean affected the portrayal of Shylock were suddenly increased. 'I am a Jew' now evoked an uneasiness which deepened as the harassment of European Jews turned into persecution and finally into genocide. Whatever his interpretation of the role, the actor of Shylock had to take into account the distress and guilt of a whole

[1] William Poel, *Shakespeare in the Theatre*, 1913, p. 48.
[2] J. C. Trewin, *Illustrated London News*, 4 April 1953.

11 Setting (Act 2) by William Telbin for Charles Kean's production, 1858

12 Setting by Theodore Komisarjevsky and Lesley Blanch for Theodore Komisarjevsky's 1932 production

generation of playgoers. The problem could be evaded by gracefully fantasticated productions, of which there were several in the next quarter-of-a-century; or it could be frankly confronted, as was done by Jonathan Miller in his National Theatre production of 1970. Miller bypassed sixteenth-century notions of an accursed race and the ungodliness of usury by going to the economic roots of modern capitalism and setting the play in late-nineteenth-century Venice, the seedy city of T. S. Eliot's Bleistein-with-a-cigar whose enemies held that 'The Jew is underneath the lot.' Laurence Olivier played Shylock as a confident *arriviste* who needed Jessica's flight to discover in his own nature a deep racial trauma and a compensating hatred which led him to claim his monstrous forfeiture. Portia and her allies were his hereditary enemies, whose strength emerged in a trial scene that was un-stagily played in an ordinary room. Portia's mercy speech as it was delivered across the table (a psychological barrier which has been part of this scene from the eighteenth century onward) was remote, unearthly, and completely detached from the world as it could be understood by either Shylock or Bassanio.[1] The trial's reversal came as a series of blows so crushing that Shylock had to be supported to say 'I am content' in tones of desperation, and the long silence at his exit was broken by an appalling off-stage howl that left the victors visibly shaken. Jessica in this production was as much a victim of race prejudice as her father; she found in her marriage to a boorish Lorenzo that 'All things that are / Are with more spirit chasèd than enjoyed', and the Kaddish at the play's close was a lament for her fate no less than for Shylock's.

Miller's production was a resourceful attempt to relate an admiration for the play to disturbing historical events. In so doing, it had to impose, by many cuts and biases, an overall view of the play which is bound to seem restricting after the experience of multeity afforded by repeated readings. The reply to this is in part that made by Miller himself,[2] that a production can reveal only so much of the structure of a play, much as sections cut for microscopy reveal a plant's structure in only two planes, so that our picture of its overall form has to be assembled from many sections. To this it can be added that a director's overview, however partial, at least ensures that all the performers are acting the same play, which was not always the case in the past. The story goes that Macklin hid from his company until the first night his intention to play Shylock 'straight'; Kitty Clive apparently continued to play Portia for laughs, and one is left wondering what happened in the exchanges between the two characters. Irving and Ellen Terry also struck some playgoers as being at cross purposes. Ellen Terry had made a triumphant start as Portia in the Bancroft production of 1875, in which she not only looked as if she had stepped out of a canvas by Frederick Leighton,[3] but acted in Act 3 as if she were unashamedly in love with Bassanio and in Act 4 as if she really hoped Shylock could be brought to show mercy. But when she played

[1] Patrick J. Sullivan, 'Strumpet wind – the National Theatre's *Merchant of Venice*', *ETJ* 26 (1974), 31–44. For a protest over this production see John Russell Brown, 'Free Shakespeare', *S.Sur*. 24 (1971), p. 129.

[2] Helen Krich Chinoy, 'The director as mythagog: Jonathan Miller talks about directing Shakespeare', *SQ* 27 (1976), 7–14.

[3] Kleb, 'Shakespeare in Tottenham-Street', p. 114.

13 The trial scene in Arthur Bourchier's production, 1908. Arthur Bourchier as Shylock, Irene Vanbrugh as Portia

opposite Irving her conviction that Shylock was a martyr undermined her own performance; she saw Portia's mercy speech as a mere baiting of the trap, and delivered it to charm the stage and house audience rather than to move Shylock.

The roles of Portia and Antonio have been profoundly affected by a further social pressure, that exerted by the sexual revolution in twentieth-century society. The social liberation of women has probably helped audiences better to understand Portia as approximating in some ways to the sixteenth-century 'virago', or active woman, and actresses to portray her in the courtroom with some of the straightforwardness of an Elizabethan boy actor. By the nineteenth century, 'virago' was a term of abuse, and actresses could not conceive of a woman lawyer as anything but an anomaly. Ellen Terry accordingly had Portia deliver her judgement as the result of a 'lightning-like inspiration'.[1] Peggy Ashcroft mercifully broke with this tradition, and gave us in 1938 and in 1953 a Portia who had studied her case; if she seemed a little surprised at her own audacity, this only made her a better foil to the inflexible Shylock than some of the severely feminist Portias of recent productions. For the sexual revolution has also led to such distortions as Portia balefully hissing out 'Your wife would give you little thanks for that' (4.1.285) in a passion of jealousy over a relationship which directors from the 1960s onwards have increasingly tended to show as overtly homosexual. When byplay between Antonio and Bassanio involving 'a lot of kissing' distracts an

[1] *Ibid.*, p. 116.

audience from the verbal duel between Portia and Shylock, the play is being wrenched quite as much askew as ever it was in the nineteenth century.[1]

No such upstaging was possible or even conceivable in the theatre-in-the-round *Merchant of Venice* at The Other Place, Stratford, in 1978, which many consider the finest production of recent years. John Barton as director was determined to restore an equal balance of interest between Bassanio, Shylock, and Portia.[2] Chekovian costume, with Belmont still in mourning, helped the actors to suggest the melancholy that is one undercurrent of the play. Another, the implicit criticism of an arrogant and self-gratulatory society, was put across by having the young Venetians played as turn-of-the-century hearties. But Bassanio as played by John Nettles was made of better stuff, worthy of the affection of David Bradley's Antonio, who was wise, mature, and protective. He was not in love with Bassanio, but he loved him and Bassanio was the better for his love, as he was for Portia's. Marjorie Bland involved us in all the turmoil of Portia's feelings in Belmont while at the same time conveying an awareness of the moral fibre which sustained her absolute fairness to Shylock throughout the trial. Patrick Stewart's interpretation of Shylock was undominating and unsentimental. Shylock was a survivor in a hostile society against which he nursed a secret desire for vengeance; hence his obsession with money as the means of survival, and his clowning

[1] Sinead Cusack, 'Portia', in *Players of Shakespeare*, ed. Philip Brockbank, 1985, p. 37.
[2] Patrick Stewart, 'Shylock', *ibid.*, pp. 11–28.

14 Patrick Stewart as Shylock in the Royal Shakespeare Company's production, 1978

before the Gentiles as the manner of it. Among several props of which the production made a truly Shakespearean use the most unforgettable was Shylock's tin of cigarette stubs: tobacco he would live to smoke another day. When he dropped it after the judgement, it was significantly Portia who picked it up for him, so that he still had it for future use when he left the courtroom with an ingratiating laugh at Gratiano's joke about baptism. It was a performance of superb insight, showing how much the play can still yield to the attentive reader.

Recent critical and stage interpretations, by Charles Edelman

In his fine book *Theatre Criticism*, Irving Wardle notes that 'plays qualify as classics because there is always something new to say about them'.[1] The continued worldwide interest in *The Merchant of Venice* since this edition was published in 1987 proves the aptness of Wardle's observation: both critics and performers have provided a range of new interpretations, leading to an exciting diversity in the ways the play can be perceived.

Critical approaches

The *Merchant* has always been resistant to a uniform thematic approach, and most recent criticism concentrates on one or more specific aspects of the play. A topic receiving much attention over the past twenty years is the sexuality of the male characters: nowadays, productions that do not at least imply homosexual or bisexual relationships amongst Antonio, Bassanio and their friends are the exception rather than the rule. Some maintain that this is wrenching the play out of its historical context – 'homosexual' is a nineteenth-century word – but as Bruce R. Smith shows in his magisterial *Homosexual Desire in Shakespeare's England: A Cultural Poetics*, to the Elizabethans homosexuality was not a matter of placing people into clearly defined groups. The concept included a range of erotic desires and behaviours, and homosexual *desire*, as distinct from homosexual acts, was deeply embedded in the poetic discourse of early modern England. Alan Sinfield argues, 'whether Antonio's love is what we call sexual is a question which . . . is hard to frame, let alone answer': even so, Smith, Sinfield and Steve Patterson, in his article 'The bankruptcy of homoerotic amity in Shakespeare's *The Merchant of Venice*', are able to offer revealing insights into the play.[2]

To the extent that we endorse such readings, Portia becomes, like Shylock, an 'outsider' or intruder, threatening the closed power structures of a male-dominated Venice: as Catherine Belsey notes, the *Merchant* 'presents a sexual politics which is beginning to be the focus of feminist criticism and the cultural history of gender'.[3] Portia is by far the play's largest part, but she was never considered one of Shakespeare's important heroines until the late nineteenth century. In their fascinating discussions of Portia as perceived by Victorian actresses, critics and the reading public (particularly female readers), Julie Hankey and Linda Rozmovits describe how she was adopted by both sides of the 'Woman Question': to conservatives the epitome of noble womanhood, to radicals the 'New Woman', educated, self-assured, and successful in the male domain of the Law.[4]

[1] Irving Wardle, *Theatre Criticism*, 1992, p. 75.

[2] Bruce R. Smith, *Homosexual Desire in Shakespeare's England: A Cultural Poetics*, 1991; Alan Sinfield, 'How to read *The Merchant of Venice* without being heterosexist', in *Alternative Shakespeares*, ed. Terence Hawkes, v. 2, 1996, 122–39; Steve Patterson, 'The bankruptcy of homoerotic amity in Shakespeare's *The Merchant of Venice*', *SQ* 50 (1999), 9–32. See also Jonathan Goldberg, ed., *Queering the Renaissance*, 1994; Mario DiGangi, *The Homoerotics of Early Modern Drama*, 1997.

[3] Catherine Belsey, 'Love in Venice', in Martin Coyle, ed., *New Casebooks: The Merchant of Venice*, 1998, p. 140.

[4] Julie Hankey, 'Victorian Portias: Shakespeare's borderline heroine'. *SQ* 45 (1994), 426–48; Linda Rozmovits, *Shakespeare and the Politics of Culture in Late Victorian England*, 1998. Rozmovits also covers other aspects of the play's reception in Victorian England.

Setting the *Merchant* in the context of the 'Woman Question' is both original and stimulating. Nevertheless, what Karl Marx called 'the Jewish question' continues to dominate, as it always has, critical discussion. With his customary assurance, Harold Bloom states, 'one would have to be blind, deaf, and dumb not to recognize that Shakespeare's grand, equivocal comedy *The Merchant of Venice* is nevertheless a profoundly anti-Semitic work',[1] but readers wanting to investigate this matter for themselves are afforded a wealth of recent material on the Jews of Shakespeare's time: what sort of people they were, where and how they lived, their importance (or lack of it) to the Elizabethans, and how they were depicted in the drama and other literary texts.

Despite its title, not much of James Shapiro's *Shakespeare and the Jews* is about Shakespeare or *The Merchant of Venice*: the subject is what the English thought about Jews, from the middle ages through to the parliamentary debate over the 'Jew Bill' in 1763. To Shapiro, the English 'were obsessed with Jews in the sixteenth and seventeenth centuries';[2] they were the essential 'other', against whom the English defined themselves.

Shapiro presents a wealth of documentary evidence to support this claim – sermons, ballads, medieval legends, along with references to plays, poems and narrative fiction – but very little of it derives from Elizabethan England. Scholarship long ago exploded the myth that there were no Jews in Shakespeare's England, but as Steven Greenblatt argues, this does not mean they were numerous (they were not); that anti-Jewish feelings were prominent in the consciousness of the ordinary English playgoer at a performance of *The Merchant of Venice* is far from proven. Martin Yaffe cites Thomas Aquinas, Francis Bacon and others to show how Antonio's demand that Shylock become a Christian did not necessarily earn unanimous approval from the original audience, and Joan Ozark Holmer, by referring to other contemporary documents, offers persuasive evidence that 'the nature of sixteenth-century Christian thought on Jews and the significance of Jewish history for Elizabethan Christians are more complex . . . than is usually granted when these subjects are addressed as pertinent background for *The Merchant of Venice*'.[3]

Other long-accepted truisms about Shakespeare's play have been called into question. Stephen Orgel argues with some force that any connection with the trial and execution of Ruy Lopez[4] is 'both dubious and far-fetched', and in 'Which is the Jew that Shakespeare knew?', I attempt to cast doubt on the existence of any stereotypical Jewish stage villain to which Shylock supposedly conformed.[5] That 'Jews were com-

[1] Harold Bloom, *Shakespeare: The Invention of the Human*, 1998, p. 171.

[2] James Shapiro, *Shakespeare and the Jews*, 1996, p. 88.

[3] Stephen Greenblatt, 'Marlowe, Marx, and Anti-Semitism', in *Learning to Curse*, 1990, 40–58 (see also Greenblatt's review of Shapiro's book in the *New York Times Book Review*, 11 August 1996); Martin Yaffe, *Shylock and the Jewish Question*, 1997; Joan Ozark Holmer, *The Merchant of Venice: Choice, Hazard, and Consequence*, 1995, p. 19. Holmer's wide-ranging book seeks to find an artistic unity to the *Merchant* in its 'richly refined ideology about love, and human choices for and against love' (p. 3).

[4] See p. 7, above.

[5] Stephen Orgel, 'Shylock's tribe', in *Shakespeare and the Mediterranean: the Selected Proceedings of the International Shakespeare Association World Congress, Valencia, 2001*, ed. Tom Clayton, Susan Brock and Vicente Fores, forthcoming; Charles Edelman, 'Which is the Jew that Shakespeare knew? Shylock on the Elizabethan stage', *S.Sur.* 52 (1999), 99–106. See also Peter Berek, 'The Jew as Renaissance Man', *Renaissance Quarterly* 51 (1998), 128–62.

monly identified as usurers and financial brokers in early modern England'[1] is also open to serious doubt: as Garry Wills notes, 'the usurer, a common figure in the drama of Shakespeare's age, is normally a Christian', and one person who loaned out large sums of money at interest, and sued when he was not repaid, was one William Shakespeare of Stratford.[2]

In his most engaging essay about a dramatist named 'Wilhelm S' and 'the anti-Semitic play he wrote when in Nazi Germany', Laurence Lerner reminds us that 'the appeal to history can alter our reading of a text only if some kind of direct access to the past is possible; if it produces the same kind of arguments as already rage about the plays, we may find ourselves reasoning in a circle'.[3] Indeed, interpreting a play by what a community at large may have thought about a social, ethical or moral issue has the unfortunate result of making it less, not more interesting, for it implies that the Elizabethan theatre was a place where dominant ideologies were always confirmed, never subverted or questioned. But as John Drakakis observes in his 'materialist account' of the *Merchant*, the theatre itself was 'outwith the boundaries of official ideology . . . at the same time being symbolically central to its definition'. To Drakakis, Shylock might be seen as a 'repressive puritan, who presents a challenge to the orthodoxies of restraint and pleasure to which the theatre itself would claim allegiance'.[4]

The Merchant of Venice is also about money: huge amounts of it are borrowed, stolen, offered, spent, lost, recovered and bequeathed. This brings us to yet one more 'other' in the play, the vast commercial empire of the Republic of Venice. That Shakespeare exploits the 'Myth of Venice', both here and in *Othello*, is an established critical tradition, but the contacts England had with Venice were so long-standing, extensive and diverse that for many the 'myth' must have been supplanted by the reality. J. R. Mulryne writes, 'it may be that Shakespeare saw behind the costly veneer of the myth to something closer to the human and cultural conditions of sixteenth-century Venice'.[5]

One of those 'human and cultural conditions', and a prominent one, was Venice's Jewish population, whose presence and *protection* were vital to the Republic's interests; a subject that demands further investigation is the extent to which Shylock may be based not on some medieval bogey-man, but on his real-life Venetian counterparts. While not dealing with the play directly, several essays in *The Jews of Early Modern Venice*[6] add intriguing perspectives from which to regard not only Shylock, Jessica and Tubal, but also the Christian Venetians who associate with them.

[1] Shapiro, p. 98.

[2] Garry Wills, 'Shylock without usury', *New York Review of Books*, 18 January 1990, 22–5; E. A. J. Honigmann, '"There is a world elsewhere", William Shakespeare, businessman', in *Images of Shakespeare: Proceedings of the Third Congress of the International Shakespeare Association, 1986*, ed. Werner Habicht, D. J. Palmer and Roger Pringle, 1988. See also Norman Jones, *God and the Moneylenders*, 1989, and Katherine Duncan-Jones, *Ungentle Shakespeare: Scenes from his Life*, 2001.

[3] Laurence Lerner, 'Wilhelm S and Shylock', *S.Sur 48* (1995), 61–8.

[4] John Drakakis, 'Historical difference and Venetian patriarchy', in *New Casebooks: The Merchant of Venice*, ed. Martin Coyle, 1998; see also Michael Ferber, 'The ideology of *The Merchant of Venice*', *English Literary Renaissance* 20 (1990), 431–64.

[5] J. R. Mulryne, 'History and myth in *The Merchant of Venice*', in *Shakespeare's Italy: Functions of Italian Locations in Renaissance Drama*, ed. Michele Marrapodi, A. J. Hoenselaars, Marcello Cappuzzo and L. Falzon Santucci, 1993, 87–99. See also Murray Levith, *Shakespeare's Italian Settings and Plays*, 1989, and David C. McPherson, *Shakespeare, Jonson, and the Myth of Venice*, 1990.

[6] Robert C. Davis and Benjamin Ravid, ed., 2001.

The play on the stage

The Merchant of Venice has one of the richest performance histories of any play, not only in England, but wherever Shakespeare's works are performed. The breadth and variety of this topic are shown by the titles of two particularly interesting studies, Fan Shen's 'Shakespeare in China: *The Merchant of Venice*',[1] and Joel Berkowitz's 'A true Jewish Jew: three Yiddish Shylocks'.[2]

John Gross's *Shylock: Four Hundred Years in the Life of a Legend* gives an account of the development of the play's central character, from speculations about what the first Shylock might have been like down to Antony Sher in 1987. Although not a short book, the vastness of the topic does not allow for a comprehensive approach, or for long discussion of any particular performance. Simon Williams and Wilhelm Hortmann, in their studies of Shakespeare on the German stage, show that the play's fortunes there are as noteworthy and varied as in England; Maria Verch's essay is especially valuable for its description of one of the great Shylocks, Fritz Kortner.[3] Of equal interest are Avraham Oz's essay on the *Merchant* in Israel, and Penny Gay's description of some significant Australian productions; James C. Bulman, in *Shakespeare in Performance: The Merchant of Venice*, focuses on several English productions, and provides a lucid analysis of each.[4]

In the 1980s and '90s, the scope and diversity of theatrical interpretations of the *Merchant* were truly extraordinary, offering new and exciting ways of understanding the play. The following discussion of some major productions of recent years is not chronological; instead I have tried to 'classify' them by some similarity in directorial emphasis.[5]

Confronting the audience

Two Royal Shakespeare Company productions of the 1980s were noteworthy in tackling 'Shylock head on as an unsympathetic figure',[6] while at the same time presenting the Christians as equally, or more, deserving of condemnation. Most critics dismissed John Caird's 1984 effort due to its distractingly over-elaborate scenery, but Michael

[1] *Asian Theatre Journal* 5 (1988), 23–37.

[2] *Theatre Survey* 37 (1996), 75–88.

[3] John Gross, *Shylock: Four Hundred Years in the Life of a Legend*, 1992; Simon Williams, *Shakespeare on the German Stage, Volume I: 1586–1914*, 1990; Wilhelm Hortmann, *Shakespeare on the German Stage: The Twentieth Century*, 1998; Maria Verch, '*The Merchant of Venice* on the German stage since 1945', *Theatre History Studies* 5 (1985), 84–94. See also Cedric C. Brown, 'Shakespeare and race relations: Shylock in English, German and Austrian theatre and culture', in *Cultural Negotiations: Sichtweisen des Anderen*, ed. Cedric C. Brown and Therese Fischer-Seidel, 1998, 19–34.

[4] Avraham Oz, 'Transformations of authenticity: *The Merchant of Venice* in Israel', in *Foreign Shakespeare*, ed. Dennis Kennedy, 1993, 56–75, also in Oz's *The Yoke of Love: Prophetic Riddles in The Merchant of Venice*, 1995; Penny Gay, ed., *The Merchant of Venice*, 1995; see also John Golder and Richard Madelaine, ed., *O Brave New World: Two Centuries of Shakespeare on the Australian Stage*, 2001; James C. Bulman, *Shakespeare in Performance: The Merchant of Venice*, 1991, second edition forthcoming.

[5] Much of what follows is taken from my introduction to *Shakespeare in Production: The Merchant of Venice*, 2002. Readers seeking more information about these and other performances may find it there, and in Peter Holland's incisive *English Shakespeares: Shakespeare on the English Stage in the 1990s*, 1997.

[6] Irving Wardle, *The Times*, 11 April 1984.

Billington looked beyond this point to see 'a perfectly serious view of the play which treats Shylock as a ghetto victim and the Christians as a more than usually repulsive set of opportunists'. Ian McDiarmid's Shylock was 'a despised alien, still sensitive to insults; witness the flick of pain that passes across his face when told "the devil can cite Scripture to his purpose" . . . a man who comes to realise his power as the play proceeds and who is noisily exultant in the court understanding that Venice's status rests upon its law'.[1]

In an articulate and revealing description of his approach to the part, McDiarmid notes, 'Shylock's wealth and his daughter represented his internal life, "ducats and my daughter!" and his "precious, precious jewels!". When they were stolen by the Christians, I conjectured, it was as if his identity and his heart had been removed at one stroke, his flesh torn away, his inside ripped out. At hand, to assuage the agony, was a sure provider of short-term relief – revenge.'[2]

Three years later Antony Sher followed McDiarmid on to the Royal Shakespeare Theatre stage, in Bill Alexander's production, with an exotic, Levantine Shylock, speaking in a Turkish accent. Sher remarked in an interview,

> There have been a lot of productions set in the turn of the century – or in the last century – where he's dressed in a frock coat like everybody else and is an assimilated Jew. To me, that is nonsense, because clearly he sticks out like a sore thumb in society . . . What we were doing with that was trying to extend the racism and by just making him a very unassimilated foreigner, very foreign, rather than very Jewish, we hoped to slightly broaden the theme of racism. We also wanted to make the racism as explicit and as brutal as described in the text.[3]

Sher's 'unassimilated foreigner' status was emphasised by having the Venetians more viciously hostile than in any production previously seen at Stratford: Shylock was beaten, stoned and spat upon, and Jessica was openly derided. The racism extended to Deborah Findlay's Portia, whose 'attitude to her unsuccessful suitors was disturbing rather than amusing'.[4]

Alexander also emphasised homosexual relationships to a greater extent than in any previous RSC *Merchant*: 'Antonio was obviously to be understood as a depressive homosexual, and Bassanio's reciprocation of his affection did not preclude the thought that their relationship might have been physical as well as emotional'.[5] The 'Salads' were seen to be lovers as well – Gregory Doran, who played Solanio, relates, 'we paralleled the central relationship [of Antonio and Bassanio] and pointed up the way the two follow its vagaries, hang upon its changes of mood, and thereby fuel the cold embers of their own affair. At one point we had the sentimental Salerio[6] attempt to

[1] Michael Billington, *The Guardian*, 11 April 1984.
[2] Ian McDiarmid, 'Shylock in *The Merchant of Venice*', in *Players of Shakespeare 2*, ed. Russell Jackson and Robert Smallwood, 1988.
[3] Gerard Raymond, 'Portrait of the actor as a young artist', *Theater Week*, 5 September 1988.
[4] Stanley Wells, 'Shakespeare performances in London and Stratford-upon-Avon, 1986–7', *S.Sur. 41* (1988), 159–81. Findlay assesses her own performance and the production in general in 'Portia in *The Merchant of Venice*', *Players of Shakespeare 3*, ed. Russell Jackson and Robert Smallwood, 1993.
[5] Wells, *ibid.*
[6] Salarino in this edition.

kiss his young toy-boy. It seemed a valuable moment, neither gratuitous nor provocative, but it was hell on schools' matinees.'[1]

No less aggressive or confrontational a Shylock than McDiarmid or Sher was provided by Ron Leibman in Barry Edelstein's 1995 production for the New York Shakespeare Festival. Like Alexander, Edelstein emphasised what by 1995 had become customary – gay relationships and rampant Venetian anti-Semitism – but no one could have expected what Leibman brought to Shylock: 'exhibiting beard, gaberdine, yarmulke . . . and attributes of the orthodox',[2] he delivered long speeches in a sustained and ferocious rage. By showing total disregard for, and therefore gaining, the audience's sympathy, Leibman created a Shylock 'at once repellent and appealing'.[3] The moment of his forced conversion was a triumph of sorts – he tore the yellow badge from his gaberdine and stared at Antonio as if to ask, 'What will you do when there are no more Jews to hate?'

In Andrei Serban's *Merchant* for the American Repertory Theatre in 1998, Will LeBow played Shylock in the mode of comedian Lenny Bruce, savagely mocking both the Venetians and himself. While Leibman spoke 'hath not a Jew eyes . . .' as 'machine-gun fire',[4] LeBow popped 'up and down behind a miniature screen, a smile painted on his face and revenge burning in his eyes';[5] respect for Venetian justice was shown by his eating peanuts throughout the trial scene. This 'shtick-comedian' Shylock offended many, as it was clearly intended to, but Serban's production, like those of Caird, Alexander and Edelstein, revitalised the play by dealing with its contentious themes in a coherent and thought-provoking way.

Thoroughly modern Merchants

Since Tyrone Guthrie first presented a *Merchant* in contemporary clothes at Israel's Habimah Theatre in 1959, directors have employed a modern setting to highlight various aspects of the text. That the play, like our contemporary world, seems to revolve around money, was brought out with force and clarity by two recent productions, one German and one English. Peter Zadek's, opening at the Vienna Burgtheater in 1988,[6] 'subordinated questions of anti-Semitism to an examination of capitalist morality',[7] placing the action in the steel and glass office towers of today's Wall Street, with Gert Voss as 'a middle-aged . . . broker, designer dressed and equipped with an attaché case and pocket computer, [who] momentarily overreached himself in a whimsical deal, losing status, fortune and daughter in the process, but gave every indication of being back on the floor shortly'.[8]

[1] Gregory Doran, 'Solanio in *The Merchant of Venice*', in *Players of Shakespeare 3*, ed. Russell Jackson and Robert Smallwood, 1993.
[2] Margaret Loftus Ranald, *Shakespeare Bulletin*, Spring 1995.
[3] Robert Brustein, *The New Republic*, 3 April 1995.
[4] Jeremy Gerard, *Variety*, 7 February 1995.
[5] Patti Hartigan, *Boston Globe*, 19 December 1998.
[6] With the same actors in the major roles, this production continued for a number of years, and reached a wide European audience – in Paris, Berlin and, in 1995, as part of a Berliner Ensemble tour to Edinburgh.
[7] Michael Billington, *The Guardian*, 18 April 1991.
[8] Hortmann, p. 259.

15 Ron Leibman as Shylock and Byron Jennings as Antonio in Barry Edelstein's production, New York Shakespeare Festival, 1995. Courtesy of the photographer, Michal Daniel

Blond and Aryan-looking, Voss was the opposite of Sher, 'largely indistinguishable, except in his energy, trenchancy and edginess, from his Gentile fellow-operators on the Rialto . . . so like the others in look and bearing that, when Portia first meets him with Antonio in court, it is Antonio she takes to be the Jew'.[1] As one might expect in this environment, 'Bassanio turned up in Belmont with his business cronies who offered shrewd market advice about which casket to plump for . . . at the end, far from being devastated by his losses, [Shylock] wrote out promissory notes and made a dignified exit, presumably to ring up his Swiss bank manager'.[2]

When Zadek's *Merchant* toured to the Edinburgh Festival in 1995, it seemed 'old-hat' to some reviewers who had already seen David Thacker's very similar 1993 Stratford production. Thacker's Venice was transformed into London's 'City', where 'news came from the Rialto by telephone, fax, and computer network, and Shylock could assure himself that Antonio was "sufficient" by referring to the laptop on his desk'.[3] David Calder began as a financier Shylock indistinguishable from his Christian counterparts, accepted on the surface, yet subject to genteel but omnipresent prejudice. Unlike Voss, however, the loss of Jessica transformed Calder into the Jew of the anti-Semite's imagination, Savile Row suit replaced by a black Jewish gaberdine, his head now covered by a yarmulke. As Shylock's office-boy, Christopher Luscombe demonstrated 'amazing proof that Lancelot Gobbo, long thought the least funny of Shakespeare's clowns, can be deliriously funny'.[4]

Situated at the centre of Mediterranean commerce, sixteenth-century Venice was perhaps the world's most multi-cultural city, and in 1994, Peter Sellars sought to find a modern counterpart in 'the teeming, multicultural world of 1994 Venice Beach, California'.[5] By casting African-Americans as Shylock, Jessica and Tubal, Asian-Americans as Portia and the other Belmont characters, and Latinos as the Venetians, he hoped 'to touch the texture of life in contemporary America; the metaphor and the reality of anti-Semitism . . . extended to include parallel struggles and their related issues'.[6]

Much of the performance was seen via television monitors, the pictures originating from cameras held by the actors: sometimes the monitors showed relevant images, such as the beating of Rodney King and the violence in Los Angeles that followed it (Portia's mercy speech was undercut by a Presidential press conference). The production received near-universal disapproval from the critics, due not so much to the concept, but to Sellars' execution of it. Everything moved at a snail's pace for over four hours, negating the powerful Shylock of Paul Butler, who communicated 'the awful endlessness of someone being expected to turn the other cheek to blow after blow after blow'.[7]

[1] Roger Savage, *TLS*, 8 September 1995.
[2] Billington, *ibid.*
[3] Russell Jackson, 'Shakespeare performed: Shakespeare at Stratford-upon-Avon', 1993–94, *SQ* 45 (1994), p. 340.
[4] Holland, p. 199; see also Christopher Luscombe, 'Launcelot Gobbo in *The Merchant of Venice* and Moth in *Love's Labour's Lost*', *Players of Shakespeare 4*, ed. Robert Smallwood, 1998.
[5] Richard Zoglin, *Time*, 31 October 1994.
[6] Peter Sellars, quoted in W. B. Worthen, *Shakespeare and the Authority of Performance*, 1997.
[7] Benedict Nightingale, *The Times*, 18 November 1994.

As Zadek, Calder and Sellars sought to interrogate the commercial or racial discourse of the play through a contemporary setting, Jude Kelly's highly praised production for the West Yorkshire Playhouse in 1994 brought gender politics to the fore by placing the action in the early twentieth century. Of all *Merchants* of the '80s and '90s, Kelly's came closest to making Portia the central character, Nichola McAuliffe portraying her 'with overtones of Hedda Gabler, an angry prisoner to her father's will who practised pistol shooting in her home, put bullets into a portrait of her father and played Russian Roulette'.[1]

This was a Portia at first imprisoned by her father's will, then having to battle an insular group of gay men not about to release one of their own to her willingly. Michael Cashman's Antonio resembled Aschenbach of *Death in Venice*, 'wearing steel-rimmed glasses, loitering in an art gallery at the opening; elegant and decadent and slightly gone to seed'.[2] Portia's saving of Antonio's life was accomplished 'not without a spasm of malice' against him, and when Bassanio, with Antonio's urging, treats her as 'one of us' with the gift of her ring, 'she is aghast – and teeters right back into full despair'.[3]

Standing apart from this triangle, Gary Waldhorn's Shylock was a victim of the European anti-Semitism that was growing alarmingly at this time; pelted with stones by ghetto children when attempting to deliver the deed of gift, Portia showed 'a saddened comprehension of their resentment'.[4] John Peter wrote in the *Sunday Times* of 20 March 1994, 'I cannot believe that anyone who understands this production could think this an anti-Semitic play: it emerges, rather, as one of painful, heard-earned humanity'.

The 1930s

Two very successful productions chose the 1930s, for a setting. At Stratford, Ontario, in 1996, Marti Maraden placed the action early in the decade, 'that time', as she explained, 'before the evil is full-blown – when people you think of as very civilized and intelligent are saying thoughtless things about people whom they perceive to be alien, to have an otherness'.[5] Maraden's Venice was a wintry place, the men costumed in 'overcoats, hats, and scarfs to enhance the atmosphere of frigidity'; by contrast, 'Belmont seemed warm and light, with lovely female attendants sketching by a pool, while Portia and Nerissa chatted under graceful Renaissance arches'.[6] Elegantly attired in a pin-striped suit, a homburg covering his yarmulke, Douglas Rain was as quiet and refined a Shylock as Leibman was loud and aggressive, but in one aspect their performances were strikingly similar: 'there was not a single moment when he asked for the audience's sympathy . . . in the trial scene, he was quiet, contained, abso-

[1] Elizabeth Schafer, *Ms-Directing Shakespeare: Women Direct Shakespeare*, 1998, p. 123.
[2] *Ibid.*, p. 120.
[3] Alastair Macaulay, *Financial Times*, 26 March 1994.
[4] Lisa Hopkins, *Shakespeare Bulletin*, Summer 1994
[5] Quoted by John Bemrose in *Maclean's*, 17 June 1996.
[6] Richard Hornby, 'The other Stratford', *Hudson Review* 49 (1996), p. 472.

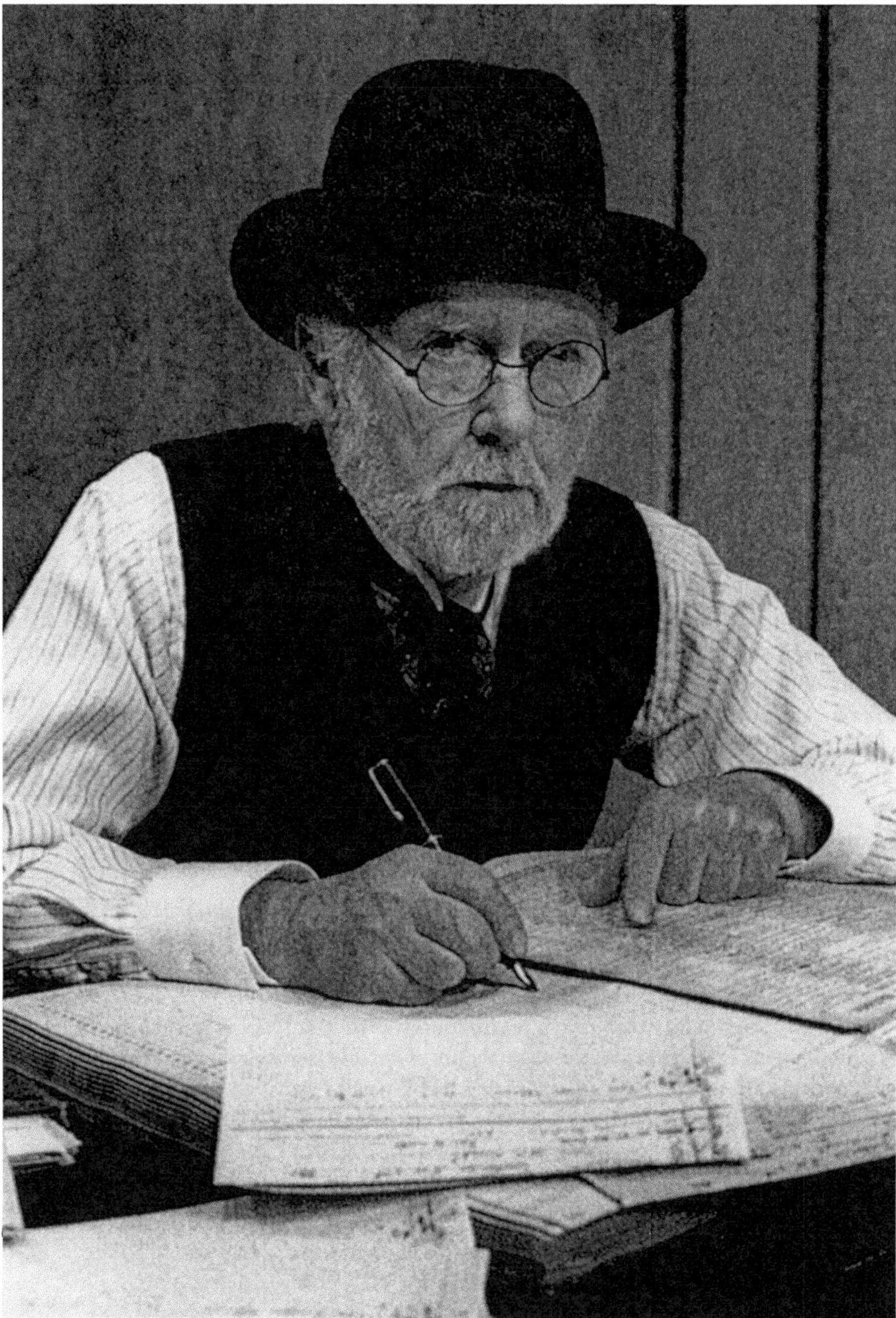

16 Douglas Rain as Shylock in Marti Maraden's production, Stratford Festival of Canada, 1986. Photograph by Cylla von Tiedemann. Courtesy of the Stratford Festival Archives and Douglas Rain

lutely sure that he was right. He argued his case with Portia – he was always willing to argue – but nothing could shift him.'[1]

With some subtle and inventive stage business, Maraden paralleled the defeat of Shylock with indications of the increasing hostility Italian Jews suffered at this time. The opening scene was set in an outdoor café, with ordinary Venetians enjoying the winter sunshine, but later, 'when Solanio did his impersonation of Shylock raging in the streets, the café patrons included, for the first time, two young men in black shirts, who found Solanio's take-off on the Jew highly amusing and gave him a round of applause'.[2] When Tubal entered, all empty chairs were tipped up against the tables – Jews were no longer welcome at this restaurant – creating a far more powerful effect in its quiet nastiness than the spitting and beatings of other productions.

Unusually for the 1990s, no homosexual relationship between Bassanio and Antonio was foregrounded, so Susan Coyne's Portia did not need to compete with Antonio for Bassanio's affections in the way that Nichola McAuliffe did. But Coyne was very much the disaffected woman of the 1930s, chain-smoking and contemptuous of her black suitor. Like McAuliffe, she learned a great deal from her excursion to Venice, and she was visibly upset when Antonio demanded that Shylock be baptised, this disquiet only increasing when, after the trial, the blackshirts recognised her in the street and applauded her.

Trevor Nunn's production for the Royal National Theatre, opening in June of 1999 in the intimate Cottesloe Theatre, also brought us into the 1930s, less Venice than the Berlin of Christopher Isherwood's stories. The Venetian scenes were mostly in the centre of a traverse stage, 'elegant café tables on a black and white chequered floor, much drinking of champagne, the noisy young men of the Christian community in an impressive range of well-cut suits and blacks such as Lancelot Gobbo doing the menial jobs'.[3]

Henry Goodman, his conservative suit not completely covering a prayer shawl, was an outstanding Shylock, but the production's greatest strength was in the quality of the ensemble. David Bamber's Manchester-accented Antonio was 'a brooding, middle-aged depressive who had long sublimated his secret love for Bassanio into being a self-absorbed businessman', his 'dull, centre-parted hair [and] behind-the-fashion suit contrasted splendidly with the dashing playboy elegance of Alexander Hanson's beautifully coiffured Bassanio'.[4]

The uniform quality of Nunn's production was most apparent in that the Belmont scenes were as interesting as those in Venice. Derbhle Crotty was the ideal Portia for the 1930s, 'tall, tense and elegant, with a wary, prickly sense of humour'.[5] In a complete reversal of how the Morocco scenes are usually played, Portia 'found herself surprisingly wrong-footed by the exotic poetic earnestness of Chu Omambala's splendid Morocco',[6] a dashing prince who had Portia desperately hoping he would choose the right casket, and becoming tearful when he did not.

[1] Alexander Leggatt, *Shakespeare Bulletin*, Winter 1997.
[2] Leggatt, *ibid.*
[3] Robert Smallwood, 'Shakespeare performances in England, 1998'. *S.Sur. 52* (1999), pp. 267–8.
[4] John Peter, *Sunday Times*, 27 June 1999; Smallwood, *ibid.*, p. 268.
[5] Peter, *ibid.*
[6] Smallwood, *ibid.*

To some reviewers, this production was too much of a good thing: although many lines were deleted, the amount of stage business inserted led to a performance over three hours in length. Whether or not this criticism is justified, there can be little doubt that Nunn's *Merchant* brought spectators into the play as deeply as did in any production since Charles Macklin played Drury Lane in 1741.

NOTE ON THE TEXT

This edition is based on the first quarto (Q1), which was printed in 1600, probably straight from Shakespeare's manuscript. Spellings have been modernised in accordance with the conventions of the series, speech headings have been regularised, and a few clarifying stage directions have been added. The punctuation has been kept as light as possible. Where a word carried a different stress from that in use today, or where the metre requires a vowel to be pronounced which today would be elided, a grave accent is used thus: aspèct, renownèd.

Q1 is a clean text in that it reveals very few signs of possible confusion in the manuscript and has very few errors. Some of its rare errors were put right in one or both of the two other early editions, the second quarto (Q2) and the First Folio (F). Q2 bears the date 1600 on its title page, but was in fact printed in 1619 from a copy of Q1. Its variants are thus at two removes from Shakespeare's manuscript. A number of them have however considerable interest in that they indicate what struck a contemporary reader of Q1 as unclear or difficult. F (1623) was also printed from a copy of Q1 which it on occasion corrects or emends. It also incorporates directions for musical effects and makes small changes in the text to avoid profanity and a slighting reference to the Scots. These insertions and changes are valuable because they tell us something about the play as it was performed in the reign of James I.

The few occasions on which I have departed from Q1 are recorded in the collation at the foot of each page of text. The authority for the reading which has been adopted comes immediately after the square bracket. Where Q2 or F or both have introduced what appear to be deliberate changes affecting the meaning, Q1 is followed in the text but the Q2 and F variants are recorded in the collation for their literary or theatrical interest. To have included all the variants on the names 'Salarino', 'Solanio' and 'Salerio' would have given undeserved prominence to the problem of whether Shakespeare intended three characters or two, and what names he wanted them to have. Variants on the three names have therefore been removed to a table in the Textual Analysis (see p. 192 below), where these and other problems are discussed.

My text is indebted to Rowe and subsequent editors chiefly in such matters as line arrangement and the placing of stage directions. The number of readings taken from these later editors is very small indeed, and it will be seen from the Commentary that even the best of them, such as Johnson's 'tombs' for 'timber' at 2.7.69, have to be considered conjectural.

Except for the words quoted before the square bracket (the 'lemma') which exactly correspond to the form of the words in the text, the original spellings of the early editions have been retained in the collation, with the simplification that when there occur differences between editions of spellings of the same word, or of abbreviations of the same speech heading, only the earliest is given. The Elizabethan convention of printing i and I to represent initial j and J, and u to represent medial v, has not been followed in the collation, though it is observed in the Textual Analysis.

The Merchant of Venice

LIST OF CHARACTERS

THE DUKE OF VENICE
THE PRINCE OF MOROCCO, *a suitor to Portia*
THE PRINCE OF ARRAGON, *suitor also to Portia*
BASSANIO, *an Italian lord, suitor likewise to Portia*
ANTONIO, *a merchant of Venice*
SOLANIO, SALARINO, GRATIANO, LORENZO, } *gentlemen of Venice, and companions with Bassanio*
SHYLOCK, *the rich Jew, and father of Jessica*
TUBAL, *a Jew, Shylock's friend*
PORTIA, *the rich Italian lady*
NERISSA, *her waiting-gentlewoman*
JESSICA, *daughter to Shylock*
GOBBO, *an old man, father to Lancelot*
LANCELOT GOBBO, *the Clown*
STEPHANO, *a messenger*
JAILER
SALERIO, *a messenger from Venice*
LEONARDO, *one of Bassanio's servants*
BALTHAZAR, SERVINGMAN, MESSENGER, } *members of Portia's household*
A SERVINGMAN *employed by Antonio*
ATTENDANTS
MAGNIFICOES OF VENICE
COURT OFFICIALS

Notes

This is substantially the list given in Q3 (1637). The definite articles in the Shylock and Portia references suggest that these characters were already known by hearsay to the seventeenth-century reader. After JAILER the Q3 list adds 'and Attendants' and ends. Except for the magnificoes and court officials, the names which complete the list correspond to speech headings in the copy text, Q1.

SALARINO He may very probably be the same character as 'Salerio'. See Textual Analysis, p. 191 below.

LANCELOT For the possible variants of this name, see note at 2.2.0 SD below.

members of Portia's household The Messenger of 2.9.86 may be identical with Stephano who appears at 5.1.24, but Balthazar is unlikely to be the servingman addressed as 'sirrah' at 1.2.109.

ATTENDANTS . . . OFFICIALS These are walking-on parts.

THE MERCHANT OF VENICE

1.[1] *Enter* ANTONIO, SALARINO, *and* SOLANIO

ANTONIO In sooth I know not why I am so sad.
It wearies me, you say it wearies you;
But how I caught it, found it, or came by it,
What stuff 'tis made of, whereof it is born,
I am to learn.
And such a want-wit sadness makes of me,
That I have much ado to know myself.
SALARINO Your mind is tossing on the ocean,
There where your argosies with portly sail
Like signors and rich burghers on the flood,
Or as it were the pageants of the sea,

Title] F; The comicall History of the Mer*chant of Venice* Q1, Q2 *subst.* Act 1, Scene 1 1.1] *Rowe subst.; not in* Q1–2; *Actus Primus.* F 5–6] *As two lines* Q3; *as one line* Q1–2, F

Title Only one other play before 1600, Greene's *Alphonso of Aragon*, is called a comical history (i.e. story). Most comedies were described as 'a pleasant comedy' or 'a conceited [i.e. witty] comedy'. 'History' may be used here to emphasise the romance nature of the play.

Act 1, Scene 1

1.1 There are no act and scene divisions in the quartos, though F divides the play into acts. Scene divisions were introduced by eighteenth-century editors.

0 SD SALARINO Most recent editors follow NS in changing this to Salerio. See Textual Analysis, p. 191 below.

0 SD SOLANIO He is at first called Salanio, and Q2 keeps this form throughout. See Textual Analysis, p. 183 below.

1 In sooth Truly. We are to suppose Antonio is replying to a question that has just been put to him.

1 sad Antonio's sadness, making him taciturn in contrast to the volubility of his friends, is often theatrically expressed as a contrast between his stillness and their movement and gestures

5 I...learn I have yet to learn. The short line suggests a moment's pensiveness, perhaps a sigh.

6–7 And...myself Probably 'sadness has made me so absent-minded that I hardly know who I am'; otherwise, 'sadness has so deadened me that I find it difficult to understand the cause of my melancholy'. *Nosce teipsum*, 'know thyself', was a familiar adage.

9 argosies Privately-owned cargo vessels, also called carracks or round ships, which in the sixteenth century replaced the state-owned trading galleys of Venice. The name derives from Ragusa (now Dubrovnik) where many of them were built. See *OED* sv.

9 portly stately; perhaps with the additional meaning 'bellying'.

10 signors The word has a specifically Venetian flavour, as the *Signoria* was a small group of hereditary noblemen who had an important part in the government of Venice.

11 pageants Either floats in street processions or decorated barges in water processions such as were a feature of Venetian festivals (see illustration 3, p. 26). See Alice Venezky, *Pageantry on the Shakespearean Stage*, 1951, p. 102.

Do overpeer the petty traffickers
That curtsey to them, do them reverence,
As they fly by them with their woven wings.
SOLANIO Believe me, sir, had I such venture forth,
The better part of my affections would
Be with my hopes abroad. I should be still
Plucking the grass to know where sits the wind,
Piring in maps for ports, and piers, and roads;
And every object that might make me fear
Misfortune to my ventures, out of doubt
Would make me sad.
SALARINO My wind cooling my broth
Would blow me to an ague when I thought
What harm a wind too great might do at sea.
I should not see the sandy hourglass run
But I should think of shallows and of flats,
And see my wealthy Andrew docked in sand,
Vailing her high top lower than her ribs
To kiss her burial. Should I go to church

13 curtsey] F; cursie Q1–2 19 Piring] Q1; Piering Q2; Peering F; Prying Q3 27 Andrew docked] *Rowe subst.*; *Andrew* docks Q1–2, F; *Andrew*'s decks *conj. Collier*; *Andrew*, decks *Delius*[2]

12 **overpeer** look down upon; used both literally and figuratively.

13 **curtsey** Q1's 'cursie' is a sixteenth-century variant. The small cargo ships lower their topsails as a mark of respect (A. F. Falconer, *Shakespeare and the Sea*, 1965, p. 22); or, they bob about in the wash of the argosies. Either way they resemble humble tradesmen bowing to passing dignitaries.

14 **they** the argosies; they are likened to flying birds for their speed and to rich burghers for the billowing splendour of their appearance.

15 **venture forth** i.e. goods and ships at sea in an uncertain commercial enterprise. 'Venture' is a key word of the play.

16 **The better part** Most.

16 **affections** feelings, concern (the usual meaning in Shakespeare).

17 **still** constantly; as often in Shakespeare, e.g. 1.1.135.

18 **Plucking** i.e. in order to toss it in the air, and so discover the direction of the wind.

19 **Piring** Looking closely. A different word from 'Peering' (Q2), which makes a jingle with 'piers', so the actor may prefer to use Q3's 'prying'.

19 **roads** anchorages.

20 **object** Used in its etymological sense of 'something thrown in one's way'. See *OED* sv *sb* 2.

21 **out of doubt** certainly; or, less probably, 'because of my uncertainty'.

23 **blow...ague** bring on a shivering fever; used as a metaphor of anxiety. Malaria, as its name implies, was thought to be caused by bad air.

26 **But...think** Without thinking. 'But' often means 'except' in Elizabethan English.

26 **flats** shoals.

27 **wealthy Andrew** i.e. a ship as richly laden as the San Andrés, or Andrew, captured in Cadiz harbour in 1596. See p. 1 above.

27 **docked** Rowe's emendation of 'docks' (Q1–2), which is a probable misreading of 'dockt' in Elizabethan handwriting. A ship could be deliberately docked in ooze or soft sand (see *OED* sv v^2 2), but the oddity of the term for a ship that has run aground and capsized led Delius to prefer the emendation 'decks'. This, however, assumes an improbable misreading, and requires the further intervention of a comma after 'Andrew'. The image foreshadows the disaster related by Salarino at 3.1.2–5.

28 **Vailing** Bowing down. Salarino imagines the ship lowering her topsail or top mast, to kiss the ground.

28 **ribs** i.e. the timbers curving between the keel and the decks.

And see the holy edifice of stone
And not bethink me straight of dangerous rocks,
Which touching but my gentle vessel's side
Would scatter all her spices on the stream,
Enrobe the roaring waters with my silks,
And (in a word) but even now worth this,
And now worth nothing? Shall I have the thought
To think on this, and shall I lack the thought
That such a thing bechanced would make me sad?
But tell not me: I know Antonio
Is sad to think upon his merchandise.

ANTONIO Believe me, no. I thank my fortune for it,
My ventures are not in one bottom trusted,
Nor to one place; nor is my whole estate
Upon the fortune of this present year:
Therefore my merchandise makes me not sad.

SOLANIO Why then, you are in love.

ANTONIO Fie, fie!

SOLANIO Not in love neither? Then let us say you are sad
Because you are not merry; and 'twere as easy
For you to laugh and leap, and say you are merry
Because you are not sad. Now by two-headed Janus,
Nature hath framed strange fellows in her time:
Some that will evermore peep through their eyes,
And laugh like parrots at a bagpiper;
And other of such vinegar aspèct,

32 **gentle** Both 'delicate' and 'noble'.

33–4 **spices...silks** For centuries these had been brought from the Levant and from Alexandria in Venetian trading ships and re-exported to western Europe. See, for example, F. C. Lane, *Venice: A Maritime Republic*, 1973, pp. 285–94.

35 **but even now** only just now.

35 **this** i.e. the wealth represented by silks and spices.

42 **bottom** ship's hull; hence, a ship. The proverb 'Venture not all in one bottom' is also echoed in *1H6* 4.6.33: 'To hazard all our lives in one small boat' (Tilley A209).

46, 47 SH SOLANIO Q2 gives these speeches to Salarino as the more talkative of the pair. See Textual Analysis, p. 188 below.

46 **Fie, fie!** The break in the metre possibly but not necessarily represents an embarrassed pause. NS suggests that Shakespeare wrote 'o no. Fie, fie' and that 'o no' was read as the last part of Antonio's name in the speech heading.

47–8 **sad...merry** A catchphrase to brush off enquiries, as in *TGV* 4.2.28–9.

49 **laugh and leap** A catchphrase (Tilley / Dent L92a.1).

50 **Janus** The Roman god of openings faced both ways at once. Shakespeare associates these two faces with the sad and merry masks of tragedy and comedy.

52 **peep...eyes** i.e. because their eyes are narrowed by laughter.

53 **laugh...bagpiper** A parrot might pick up a laugh and then reproduce it when sad music was playing. Falstaff claims to be as melancholy as 'a Lincolnshire bagpipe' in *1H4* 1.2.76.

54 **other** others. This old plural continued in use into the seventeenth century.

54 **vinegar aspèct** sour looks.

That they'll not show their teeth in way of smile
Though Nestor swear the jest be laughable.

Enter BASSANIO, LORENZO, *and* GRATIANO

Here comes Bassanio, your most noble kinsman,
Gratiano, and Lorenzo. Fare ye well;
We leave you now with better company.

SALARINO I would have stayed till I had made you merry,
If worthier friends had not prevented me.

ANTONIO Your worth is very dear in my regard.
I take it your own business calls on you,
And you embrace th'occasion to depart.

SALARINO Good morrow, my good lords.

BASSANIO Good signors both, when shall we laugh? Say, when?
You grow exceeding strange; must it be so?

SALARINO We'll make our leisures to attend on yours.

Exeunt Salarino and Solanio

LORENZO My Lord Bassanio, since you have found Antonio
We two will leave you, but at dinner time
I pray you have in mind where we must meet.

BASSANIO I will not fail you.

GRATIANO You look not well, Signor Antonio.
You have too much respect upon the world:
They lose it that do buy it with much care.
Believe me, you are marvellously changed.

ANTONIO I hold the world but as the world, Gratiano:

57 Here] *NS; Sola.* Here Q1–2, F *subst.*

56 **Nestor** The Homeric Greek hero was as often mocked as commended for his age and gravity in the Elizabethan theatre: 'old Nestor, whose wit was mouldy ere your grandsires had nails on their toes' (*Tro.* 2.1.104–6).

57 **kinsman** This is the only time we hear of the friends being related. In *Il Pecorone*, the major source for Shakespeare's play (see p. 2 above), Ansaldo was Giannetto's godfather.

61 **prevented** forestalled.

64 **occasion** opportunity.

66 **laugh** i.e. meet and jest together.

67 **strange** distant, unfriendly.

67 **must it be so?** Either 'must you be so distant?' or 'must you go?'

68 **We'll...yours** i.e. Salarino and Solanio will make a point of being free at a time when Bassanio is at leisure too.

69–117 On the possibility of this being an inserted portion of Shakespeare's manuscript, see Textual Analysis, p. 183 below.

72 **I...you** This half-line is perhaps completed by a gesture of leavetaking between Lorenzo and Bassanio, while Gratiano is waylaying Antonio.

74 **respect upon** regard for.

75 **They lose...care** 'Those who take the world too seriously find they have lost the capacity to enjoy it' (Rosser). Some editors hear an echo of Matt. 16.25, but the thought there is really very different.

A stage where every man must play a part,
And mine a sad one.

GRATIANO Let me play the Fool.
With mirth and laughter let old wrinkles come,
And let my liver rather heat with wine
Than my heart cool with mortifying groans.
Why should a man whose blood is warm within
Sit like his grandsire cut in alabaster?
Sleep when he wakes? And creep into the jaundice
By being peevish? I tell thee what, Antonio –
I love thee, and it is my love that speaks –
There are a sort of men whose visages
Do cream and mantle like a standing pond,
And do a wilful stillness entertain,
With purpose to be dressed in an opinion
Of wisdom, gravity, profound conceit,
As who should say, 'I am Sir Oracle,
And when I ope my lips, let no dog bark!'

87 it is] F; tis Q1–2 93 Sir] *Pope*; sir Q1–2; sir an F

78 **A stage...part** This Elizabethan commonplace was to be the motto of the Globe Theatre (*Totus mundus agit histrionem*). Here, as in its expansion by Jaques (*AYLI* 2.7.139–66), it takes fresh life from its context; Antonio's friends are overacting.

79 **Let...Fool** Murray J. Levith (*What's in Shakespeare's Names*, 1978, p 79) points out that Florio's Italian dictionary (1611) defines *Gratiano* as 'a gull, a fool or clownish fellow in a play or comedy'. In the *commedia dell' arte* he was a comic doctor.

80 **old** Both 'typical of old age' and (the intensive use, as at 4.2.15) 'any amount of'.

82 **mortifying** Both 'penitential' and 'causing death'. Sighs were supposed to shorten life.

84 **Sit...alabaster** Be as motionless as the effigy of his grandfather sculpted in white stone. 'Sit' is probably equivalent to 'keep still', because figures on Elizabethan tombs stand, kneel, or lie, but do not sit.

85 **jaundice** This disease was held until well into the nineteenth century to be of psychosomatic origin. It is so described in *Tro.* 1.3.2.

88–9 **whose...pond** i.e. their faces are masked ('mantled') by impassivity, as milk is with cream or stagnant ('standing') pondwater with algae. The second image recurs in *Lear* 3.4.133 and *Temp.* 4.1.182.

90–2 **do...wisdom** maintain an obstinate silence, in order to be adorned with a reputation for wisdom.

92 **conceit** concept, thought (as usual in Shakespeare).

93 **As...say** As if they were to say.

93 **Sir Oracle** F takes 'sir' to be a mode of address, and reads 'sir an oracle', thus spoiling both the metre and the joke. But Shakespeare, like his contemporaries, uses 'Sir' as a mock title: 'Sir Assurance' (*Shr.* 5.2.65), 'Sir Smile' (*WT* 1.2.196), and 'Sir Prudence' (*Temp.* 2.1.286).

94 **let no dog bark** Possibly figurative – 'let no inferior person interrupt me with nonsensical chatter'. However, dogs were trained to bark at anyone of beggarly appearance (so *R3* 1.1.23: 'dogs bark at me as I halt by them'); and in a play so much concerned with Jew and non-Jew Shakespeare may have remembered Exod. 11.7 (GB): 'But against none of the children of Israel shall a dog move his tongue, neither against man nor beast, that ye may know that the Lord putteth a difference between the Egyptians and Israel.' On the many biblical quotations and echoes in the play, see Appendix, p. 196 below.

O my Antonio, I do know of these
That therefore only are reputed wise
For saying nothing; when I am very sure
If they should speak, would almost damn those ears
Which, hearing them, would call their brothers fools.
I'll tell thee more of this another time.
But fish not with this melancholy bait
For this fool gudgeon, this opinion.
Come, good Lorenzo. Fare ye well awhile;
I'll end my exhortation after dinner.

LORENZO Well, we will leave you then till dinner time.
I must be one of these same dumb wise men,
For Gratiano never lets me speak.

GRATIANO Well, keep me company but two years moe,
Thou shalt not know the sound of thine own tongue.

ANTONIO Farewell; I'll grow a talker for this gear.

GRATIANO Thanks, i'faith, for silence is only commendable
In a neat's tongue dried, and a maid not vendible.

Exeunt [*Gratiano and Lorenzo*]

ANTONIO It is that anything now.

110 Farewell] Q2; Far you well Q1, F 112 tongue] Q2, F; togue Q1 112 SD *Gratiano and Lorenzo*] *Theobald subst.; not in* Q1–2, F 113 It is that anything now.] Q1–2, F; Is that any thing now? *Rowe;* Is that anything new? *conj. Johnson*; It is that: – anything now. *Collier;* It is that. Anything now? *Delius;* Ay! is that anything now? *conj. Lettsom*

95 of these i.e. some of the sort of men referred to in 88.

96–7 That...nothing A proverb (Tilley / Dent F531) originating in the Bible: 'a very fool when he holdeth his tongue is counted wise' (Prov. 17.28, BB; compare Job 13.3). In *Shakespeare's Biblical Knowledge*, 1935, Richmond Noble has traced this and many other expressions to their scriptural source.

97 when Rowe emends to 'who', to supply a subject for 'would' in the next line. But the omission of a subject suggests rapid, colloquial speech.

98–9 damn...fools i.e. cause their hearers to call them fools, and so incur the condemnation of Matt. 5.22: 'whosoever shall say unto his brother ...thou fool shall be in danger of hell fire' (BB).

101–2 fish...opinion i.e. don't use your melancholy as the bait for an easily caught reputation (of silent wisdom). Writers of the period, up to and including Izaak Walton, stress the gullibility of the gudgeon.

108 moe i.e. more in number, a different word from 'more' meaning more in size or quality. The eighteenth-century emendation to 'more', though incorrect, is more easily understood by a modern audience.

110 Farewell Q1's 'Far you well' was probably contracted in performance to the dissyllabic 'Farwell' of Q2.

110 for this gear If 'gear' is 'discourse, talk' (*OED sb* 11a), the phrase means 'on account of all you've said'. But Antonio may be indicating that he now wants to talk privately with Bassanio, in which case 'gear' is 'matter, affair' (*OED sb* 11c) and the phrase then approximates to 'for this once'.

111–12 silence...vendible i.e. lack of activity is only proper to a sexually impotent old man or a sexually unmarketable woman. Phoebe, in *AYLI* 3.5.60, is 'not for all markets'.

112 neat's tongue dried cured ox tongue (and so a withered penis incapable of excitement).

113 It is...now If 'that anything' is Antonio's way of referring to Gratiano's haphazard and bawdy definition of silence, the sentence means 'Peace at last!' Most editors follow Rowe in dropping 'It' in order to make the sentence a question: 'What was all that about?'

BASSANIO Gratiano speaks an infinite deal of nothing, more than any man in all Venice. His reasons are as two grains of wheat hid in two bushels of chaff: you shall seek all day ere you find them, and when you have them they are not worth the search.

ANTONIO Well, tell me now what lady is the same
To whom you swore a secret pilgrimage
That you today promised to tell me of.

BASSANIO 'Tis not unknown to you, Antonio,
How much I have disabled mine estate
By something showing a more swelling port
Than my faint means would grant continuance.
Nor do I now make moan to be abridged
From such a noble rate, but my chief care
Is to come fairly off from the great debts
Wherein my time, something too prodigal,
Hath left me gaged. To you, Antonio,
I owe the most in money and in love,
And from your love I have a warranty
To unburden all my plots and purposes
How to get clear of all the debts I owe.

ANTONIO I pray you, good Bassanio, let me know it,
And if it stand as you yourself still do
Within the eye of honour, be assured
My purse, my person, my extremest means
Lie all unlocked to your occasions.

BASSANIO In my schooldays, when I had lost one shaft,
I shot his fellow of the selfsame flight

115 reasons sensible meanings.

119 secret pilgrimage Another vestige of Shakespeare's main source, *Il Pecorone*, in which Giannetto conceals his quest of the Lady of Belmont. The lover as pilgrim was a commonplace that Shakespeare exploited fully in Romeo's first meeting with Juliet (*Rom.* 1.5.92–106).

121–33 Some of the difficulty of this speech comes from Bassanio's embarrassment, which renders his language stiff and unidiomatic.

122–4 How much I have depleted my fortune by flaunting a rather ('something') more extravagant lifestyle than my limited means would allow me to keep up.

125–6 make moan...rate complain about being forced to cut back my expenditure, which was on the grand scale.

127 come fairly off extricate myself honourably.

128 time past.

129 gaged owing.

131 And...warranty i.e. and your love authorises me.

132 unburden disclose.

135–6 And if it...honour i.e. and if it can be looked on as honourable, as you yourself have always been.

138 occasions needs. The *-ion* ending is often dissyllabic in Elizabethan verse.

139–43 The notion of shooting a second arrow as a means of recovering the first was proverbial (Tilley A325), though this is the first recorded use of it in English. Elizabethan writers found it laughably ingenuous; it is possible that the play's first audience did too.

140 flight i.e. the arrow's weight, size, and power of flight.

The selfsame way, with more advisèd watch
To find the other forth; and by adventuring both
I oft found both. I urge this childhood proof
Because what follows is pure innocence.
I owe you much, and like a wilful youth
That which I owe is lost; but if you please
To shoot another arrow that self way
Which you did shoot the first, I do not doubt,
As I will watch the aim, or to find both
Or bring your latter hazard back again
And thankfully rest debtor for the first.

ANTONIO You know me well, and herein spend but time
To wind about my love with circumstance;
And out of doubt you do me now more wrong
In making question of my uttermost
Than if you had made waste of all I have.
Then do but say to me what I should do
That in your knowledge may by me be done,
And I am prest unto it: therefore speak.

BASSANIO In Belmont is a lady richly left,
And she is fair, and – fairer than that word –
Of wondrous virtues. Sometimes from her eyes
I did receive fair speechless messages.
Her name is Portia, nothing undervalued
To Cato's daughter, Brutus' Portia.

141 **advisèd** careful.

142 **find...forth** i.e. find out. In *Err.* 1.2.37 a drop of water is described as falling into the ocean 'to find his fellow forth'.

142 **adventuring** risking. If the metre is intentionally irregular, Shakespeare is using it to make Bassanio sound hesitant. But the irregularity may be a sign of 'foul papers'; see Textual Analysis, p. 183 below.

143 **proof** experience; as in *Cym.* 3.3.27: 'Out of your proof you speak.'

144 **innocence** ingenuousness.

145 **like...youth** i.e. because I have behaved like a headstrong young man.

147 **self** selfsame.

149–50 **or...Or** either... Or.

150 **hazard** A key word of the play, linking the choice of caskets with Antonio's risks.

152 **spend but time** only waste time.

153 **To wind...circumstance** In going such a roundabout way to make use of my affection for you.

155 **In...uttermost** By doubting that I will give you all the help I can.

159 **prest** ready; from Middle French *prest*, modern *prêt*, perhaps conflated with the past participle 'prest' (now 'pressed'), meaning 'driven, or incited'.

160 **richly left** who has been left a fortune.

161 **fairer...word** 'what is more to the point' (Rosser). Riches, beauty and virtue are here placed in an ascending order of desirability.

162 **Sometimes** At one time, formerly.

165 **Portia** Shakespeare was soon to stress, in *Julius Caesar*, the virtue of the historical Portia: 'Think you I am no stronger than my sex, / Being so father'd and so husbanded?' (2.1.296–7). Her father was the high-minded tribune Cato Uticensis, and her husband 'the noblest Roman of them all', Brutus.

Nor is the wide world ignorant of her worth;
For the four winds blow in from every coast
Renownèd suitors, and her sunny locks
Hang on her temples like a golden fleece,
Which makes her seat of Belmont Colchos' strand,
And many Jasons come in quest of her.
O my Antonio, had I but the means
To hold a rival place with one of them,
I have a mind presages me such thrift
That I should questionless be fortunate.

ANTONIO Thou know'st that all my fortunes are at sea;
Neither have I money nor commodity
To raise a present sum; therefore go forth,
Try what my credit can in Venice do,
That shall be racked even to the uttermost
To furnish thee to Belmont to fair Portia.
Go presently enquire, and so will I,
Where money is, and I no question make
To have it of my trust or for my sake.

Exeunt

[1.2] *Enter* PORTIA *with her waiting-woman* NERISSA

PORTIA By my troth, Nerissa, my little body is aweary of this great world.

NERISSA You would be, sweet madam, if your miseries were in the same abundance as your good fortunes are; and yet for aught I see, they are as sick that surfeit with too much as they that starve with

Act 1, Scene 2 1.2] *Rowe subst.; not in* Q1–2, F

169–71 golden fleece...Colchos' strand...Jasons In one of the oldest quest stories, Jason led a party of Greek heroes called the Argonauts through many hazards in order to bring back the Golden Fleece from the shores ('strand') of Colchis on the Black Sea.

174 thrift In its two meanings of 'profit' and 'success' (the meaning 'economy' is not found at the period), this is to be another important word in the play's language.

177 commodity merchandise.

178 present sum ready money.

180 racked stretched.

182 presently at once; the word carries this meaning in its six further occurrences in this play.

184 To have...sake 'on my credit or for friendship sake' (NS).

Act 1, Scene 2

0 SD WAITING-WOMAN i.e. a companion and confidante. She should not be played as the stage version of a Victorian lady's maid.

1–2 little body...great world The antithesis is the familiar Elizabethan one between a human being as microcosm and the physical universe as macrocosm.

1 aweary Portia's melancholy matches Antonio's and so serves to link Belmont with Venice; see p. 27 above.

nothing. It is no mean happiness, therefore, to be seated in the mean – superfluity comes sooner by white hairs, but competency lives longer.

PORTIA Good sentences, and well pronounced.

NERISSA They would be better if well followed.

PORTIA If to do were as easy as to know what were good to do, chapels had been churches, and poor men's cottages princes' palaces. It is a good divine that follows his own instructions; I can easier teach twenty what were good to be done, than be one of the twenty to follow mine own teaching. The brain may devise laws for the blood, but a hot temper leaps o'er a cold decree – such a hare is madness the youth, to skip o'er the meshes of good counsel the cripple. But this reasoning is not in the fashion to choose me a husband. O me, the word 'choose'! I may neither choose who I would, nor refuse who I dislike, so is the will of a living daughter curbed by the will of a dead father. Is it not hard, Nerissa, that I cannot choose one, nor refuse none?

NERISSA Your father was ever virtuous; and holy men at their death have good inspirations. Therefore the lottery that he hath devised in these three chests of gold, silver, and lead, whereof who chooses

6 mean] Q1–2; smal F 14 be] F; to be Q1–2

7 mean F avoids the repetition of 'mean' by using 'small', and so loses the pun. The platitude was proverbial (Tilley v80).

7–8 superfluity...longer Nerissa, herself probably a poor relation of Portia's, insists that 'excess of fortune and extravagance in living age us prematurely, and we live longer if we have only a sufficiency'. 'But' offsets the gain of white hairs with the gain of long life.

9 sentences maxims.

9 pronounced delivered.

11–13 If to do...instructions Portia tries out some 'sentences' of her own, the first modelled on 'If wishes were horses, beggars would ride'; the second one, 'Practise what you preach', is used by Ophelia in reply to her brother's moralisings, *Ham.* 1.3.47–51.

15–16 The brain...decree Portia's recognition that her choices, like those of any young woman, are more likely to be dictated by passion than reason has the effect on the audience of making her father's scheme seem less implausible.

16 hot temper ardent temperament. The temper, or disposition, was due to the individual's admixture of the four fluids, or humours, in his body; the blood was a hot humour.

16–17 such...madness Compare the proverbial 'mad as a March hare'. The leaps performed by hares in spring are a form of sexual behaviour.

17 meshes i.e. of a net to catch hares; used as an image of the attempts made to restrain the natural impulses of others on the part of those who no longer feel them for themselves.

18–19 But...husband Portia means 'no amount of talking will find a husband for her' (Brown).

20–1 will...will Portia first puns on the meanings 'wishes' and 'sexual longings', and then on the meanings 'imposed control' and 'testament'.

24 inspirations Such as those of the dying John of Gaunt: 'Methinks I am a prophet new inspir'd' (*R2* 2.1.31).

24 lottery Merchant detects a pun on 'allottery' meaning 'portion' as in *AYLI* 1.1.73, 'the poor allottery my father left me'.

25 these This may well indicate that the caskets are on the stage, having been revealed by the drawing back of a curtain at the start of the scene.

25 chests The same word is used on Q1's title page, and suggests the substantial objects depicted in one of the illustrations to Hanmer's edition (illustration 5, p. 32), which may be based on early stage practice. In Elizabethan English a 'casket', as in American English today, could be sizeable.

his meaning chooses you, will no doubt never be chosen by any rightly but one who you shall rightly love. But what warmth is there in your affection towards any of these princely suitors that are already come?

PORTIA I pray thee over-name them, and as thou namest them I will describe them – and according to my description, level at my affection.

NERISSA First, there is the Neapolitan prince.

PORTIA Ay, that's a colt indeed, for he doth nothing but talk of his horse; and he makes it a great appropriation to his own good parts that he can shoe him himself. I am much afeared my lady his mother played false with a smith.

NERISSA Then is there the County Palatine.

PORTIA He doth nothing but frown, as who should say, 'And you will not have me, choose.' He hears merry tales and smiles not; I fear he will prove the weeping philosopher when he grows old, being so full of unmannerly sadness in his youth. I had rather be married to a death's head with a bone in his mouth than to either of these. God defend me from these two!

26 will no doubt] Q1, F; no doubt you wil Q2 **27** you] Q1, F; *not in* Q2 **33** Neapolitan] Q2; Neopolitane Q1, F **38** Palatine] Q2; Palentine Q1, F

26 his meaning i.e. the one he intended.

26 will...chosen 'Lottery' is the subject of 'chosen'. In reading 'no doubt you will never be chosen by any rightly, but one who shall rightly love', Q2 attempts to break up a long, loose sentence but in so doing changes the sense. Nerissa is reassuring Portia that her father's choice and her *own* feelings will coincide.

27 rightly...rightly The first means 'correctly', the second 'truly'.

28, 31–2 affection inclination, feeling.

30 over-name enumerate, run through. The dialogue that follows is very similar to the scene between Julia and her waiting-woman in *TGV* 1.2, which may have been a great success on the stage.

31 level at take aim at. Portia asks Nerissa to guess at her state of feeling in each case – unless the phrase is used here to mean 'aim truly', and so 'infer'.

33 Neapolitan Portia's suitors are national stereotypes. The southern Italians were famous for their horsemanship.

34 colt raw and uncouth young man.

35 a great...parts a great addition to his own accomplishments.

38 County Palatine He corresponds to the Elizabethan stereotype of the Spaniard. Shakespeare may have meant to include a Spanish suitor in Portia's survey, when he either remembered or decided that a Spanish prince was to figure in the play, and substituted this unspecific title which was held by various Hungarians, Poles, Germans, and Burgundians. 'County' may owe its second syllable to the Italian or Old French *conte*, or to confusion with the term 'county palatine' meaning a province within an empire or realm, in which a nobleman held exclusive jurisdiction and royal privileges. 'The County Paris' is a character in *Rom.*

39 as...say as if to say.

39 And If; a common Elizabethan meaning, usually clear from the context as at 73 below.

40 choose i.e. have it your own way. See *OED* sv 8b. In *Three Ladies of London* (1584), a play about a flesh bond (see p. 22 above), a character says 'And thou wilt do it, do it, and thou wilt not choose' ($C1^v$).

41 weeping philosopher Heraclitus of Ephesus (*c.* 500 B.C.), considered a melancholy recluse because he relinquished a throne. Juvenal contrasts him with Democritus, the laughing philosopher.

42 unmannerly (1) impolite, (2) unbecoming (to his youth).

NERISSA How say you by the French lord, Monsieur Le Bon?

PORTIA God made him, and therefore let him pass for a man. In truth I know it is a sin to be a mocker, but he! – why, he hath a horse better than the Neapolitan's, a better bad habit of frowning than the Count Palatine: he is every man in no man. If a throstle sing, he falls straight a-capering; he will fence with his own shadow. If I should marry him, I should marry twenty husbands. If he would despise me, I would forgive him; for if he love me to madness, I shall never requite him.

NERISSA What say you then to Falconbridge, the young baron of England?

PORTIA You know I say nothing to him, for he understands not me, nor I him: he hath neither Latin, French, nor Italian, and you will come into the court and swear that I have a poor penny-worth in the English. He is a proper man's picture, but alas who can converse with a dumbshow? How oddly he is suited! I think he bought his doublet in Italy, his round hose in France, his bonnet in Germany, and his behaviour everywhere.

NERISSA What think you of the Scottish lord his neighbour?

PORTIA That he hath a neighbourly charity in him, for he borrowed a box of the ear of the Englishman and swore he would pay him again when he was able. I think the Frenchman became his surety and sealed under for another.

45 Bon] *Capell; Boune* Q1–2, F 48 Neapolitan's] Q2; Neopolitans Q1, F 49 Palatine] Q2; Palentine Q1, F 49 throstle] *Pope;* Trassell Q1–2, F 53 shall] Q1–2; should F 63 Scottish] Q1–2; other F

45 **by** about, of.

49 **is...no man** imitates everyone and has no character of his own.

49 **throstle** The song thrush. Q1–2 and F have 'trassell', which might be a dialect form, or the result of the compositor reading *o* as *a*. Bottom sings about the throstle in *MND* 3.1.127.

52 **if** even if.

54 **Falconbridge** Shakespeare took this name from his own *King John*, in which Falconbridge is the quintessential Englishman.

58 **come...swear** i.e. bear witness; a catch-phrase.

58–9 **have a poor...in the** i.e. speak very little; another catchphrase.

59 **proper man's picture** i.e. the very epitome of a handsome man – with a hint that he is not quite real.

60 **suited** dressed. The eclectic taste of the English was a stock joke of the age: 'I have seen an English gentleman so diffused in his suits, his doublet being for the wear of Castile, his hose for Venice, his hat for France, his cloak for Germany' (Greene, *Farewell to Folly* (1591), quoted by Merchant).

61 **round hose** padded breeches.

63 **Scottish** Discreetly changed to 'other' in F, since under James I it was dangerous to satirise the Scots; the authors of *Eastward Ho!* were imprisoned for doing so in 1605.

64 **neighbourly charity** An echo of Rom. 13.10: 'Charity worketh no ill to his neighbour' (BB).

64 **borrowed** (1) received, (2) took as a loan (with no date set for repayment: see previous note). Brown detects a possible allusion to troubles on the Border in 1596 and 1597, after which 'pledges' of compensation were exacted from some Scots. But the image may just have arisen because Shakespeare's mind was running on the flesh-bond story.

66–7 **I think...another** i.e. the Frenchman also let the Englishman strike him, merely swearing to retaliate, much as a surety adds his seal to that of

NERISSA How like you the young German, the Duke of Saxony's nephew?

PORTIA Very vilely in the morning when he is sober, and most vilely in the afternoon when he is drunk. When he is best he is a little worse than a man, and when he is worst he is little better than a beast. And the worst fall that ever fell, I hope I shall make shift to go without him.

NERISSA If he should offer to choose, and choose the right casket, you should refuse to perform your father's will if you should refuse to accept him.

PORTIA Therefore, for fear of the worst, I pray thee set a deep glass of Rhenish wine on the contrary casket, for if the devil be within, and that temptation without, I know he will choose it. I will do anything, Nerissa, ere I will be married to a sponge.

NERISSA You need not fear, lady, the having any of these lords. They have acquainted me with their determinations, which is indeed to return to their home, and to trouble you with no more suit unless you may be won by some other sort than your father's imposition, depending on the caskets.

PORTIA If I live to be as old as Sibylla, I will die as chaste as Diana unless I be obtained by the manner of my father's will. I am glad this parcel of wooers are so reasonable, for there is not one among them but I dote on his very absence; and I pray God grant them a fair departure.

NERISSA Do you not remember, lady, in your father's time, a Venetian, a scholar and a soldier, that came hither in company of the Marquis of Montferrat?

90 pray God grant] Q1–2; wish F

the principal debtor. There is unlikely to be any specific reference to the 'auld alliance' between Scots and French, which at this time was in abeyance.

73 fall befall, happen.

73 make shift contrive.

75 offer attempt.

79 Rhenish Rhineland wine was highly thought of; see 3.1.33.

79 contrary wrong, as in *John* 4.2.198, where slippers are 'falsely thrust upon contrary feet'.

85 sort means, way.

87 Sibylla Shakespeare would have known about the Cumaean sibyl, or prophetess, who was granted as many years of life as she could hold grains of sand in her hand, from his reading of Ovid's *Metamorphoses* 14, 121–81. Pooler suggests that the way the word is used in the *Dies Irae* hymn – *teste David cum Sibylla* ('both David and the sibyl bear witness') – led to its being treated as a proper name, as here and in *Shr.* 1.2.70.

87 Diana Goddess of chastity, as *MND* 1.1.89–90 makes clear: 'on Diana's altar to protest / For aye austerity and single life'.

90 pray...grant The change in F to 'wish' is in compliance with the 1606 Act against profanity in plays.

93 scholar and a soldier The Renaissance idea of the many-sided man.

93–4 Marquis of Montferrat Shakespeare could have picked up this name from the *Decamerone* of Boccaccio. Or he may have known that the contemporary holder of the title, Vicenzio Gonzaga I, Duke of Mantua, had led a campaign in Hungary against the Turks in 1595.

PORTIA Yes, yes, it was Bassanio! – as I think so was he called.

NERISSA True, madam; he of all the men that ever my foolish eyes looked upon was the best deserving a fair lady.

PORTIA I remember him well, and I remember him worthy of thy praise.

Enter a SERVINGMAN

How now, what news?

SERVINGMAN The four strangers seek for you, madam, to take their leave; and there is a forerunner come from a fifth, the Prince of Morocco, who brings word the prince his master will be here tonight.

PORTIA If I could bid the fifth welcome with so good heart as I can bid the other four farewell, I should be glad of his approach. If he have the condition of a saint, and the complexion of a devil, I had rather he should shrive me than wive me.

Come, Nerissa; sirrah, go before:
Whiles we shut the gate upon one wooer, another knocks at the door

Exeunt

95 so was he] Q1, F; he was so Q2 99 SD] *As in* F; *follows 100 in* Q1–2 100] Q1–2; *not in* F 101 for] Q1–2; *not in* F

95 as I think Portia attempts to cover up her eagerness. In substituting a smoother wording, 'as I think he was so called', Q2 loses the naturalness of her confusion.

100 How...news F's omission of this is probably an error, but some editors think the question too peremptory for Portia.

101 four But we have been told about six suitors. Joseph Hunter, *New Illustrations...of Shakespeare*, 1845, suggested that the scene had been revised to include the Englishman and the Scot. But such inconsistency is characteristic of 'foul papers'. See Textual Analysis, p. 183 below.

107 condition character, disposition; as in *LLL* 5.2.20: 'A light condition in a beauty dark'.

107 devil Devils traditionally were black. Portia seems about to make some pious remark about virtue mattering more than looks.

107–8 I had...wive me I would rather have him for a confessor than a husband. To shrive was to give absolution.

109–11 Come...door Not printed as verse in Q1–2 and F, but most editors feel it to be a rough closing couplet.

[1.3] *Enter* BASSANIO *with* SHYLOCK *the Jew*

SHYLOCK Three thousand ducats, well.

BASSANIO Ay, sir, for three months.

SHYLOCK For three months, well.

BASSANIO For the which, as I told you, Antonio shall be bound.

SHYLOCK Antonio shall become bound, well.

BASSANIO May you stead me? Will you pleasure me? Shall I know your answer?

SHYLOCK Three thousand ducats for three months, and Antonio bound.

BASSANIO Your answer to that?

SHYLOCK Antonio is a good man –

BASSANIO Have you heard any imputation to the contrary?

SHYLOCK Ho no, no, no, no: my meaning in saying he is a good man is to have you understand me that he is sufficient. Yet his means are in supposition: he hath an argosy bound to Tripolis, another to the Indies; I understand moreover upon the Rialto he hath a third at Mexico, a fourth for England, and other ventures he hath squandered abroad. But ships are but boards, sailors but men;

Act 1, Scene 3 1.3] *Rowe subst.; not in* Q1–2, F 1, 3, 5 well.] Q1–2, F; well? *Pooler, conj. Hudson* 4] *As prose, Pope; as two lines divided after* you, Q1–2, F 6–7] *As prose, Pope; as two lines divided before* Shall Q1–2, F 8–9] *As prose, Pope; as two lines divided after* months, Q1–2, F

Act 1, Scene 3

0 SD SHYLOCK This is not known to occur as a Jewish name in Shakespeare's day. The nearest biblical approximation is 'Shiloh' (Gen. 49.10), which incongruously means 'Messiah'. A possible source is Joseph Ben Gurion's *History...of the Jews' Commonweal*, translated in 1595, which records that when a Roman captain called Antonius was defending Askalon one of the Jewish leaders who went to parley with him was called Shiloch (p. 85). See 44 n. below.

1 SH SHYLOCK The variations in speech headings between 'Shylock' and 'Jew' are part of the evidence for the play having been printed from Shakespeare's manuscript: see Textual Analysis, p. 170 below. In this scene the variations do not appear to have any substantive significance.

1 **ducats** Gold ducats, literally coins 'of the duke', were first struck in Venice in the thirteenth century. The name was evocative of great wealth, like Swiss francs or Krugerrands today.

1, 3, 5 **well.** Some editors and many actors have made these lines interrogative. But Shylock is more likely to respond to Bassanio's eagerness with a studied deliberation.

4 **bound** compelled to repay by a written undertaking. There is a sinister undertone of the meaning 'captive'.

6 **May you stead me?** Can you help me?

6 **pleasure** oblige.

11 **good** Shylock means 'financially sound', but in a conflict of values typical of the play Bassanio takes the word to mean 'honourable'.

14 **sufficient** i.e. security enough in normal circumstances.

15 **in supposition** to be assumed, hypothetical.

15–17 **Tripolis...England** On this range of ventures, impossible for a real Venetian merchant of the time, see p. 13 above. Tripoli (Tarabulus esh Sham) in Lebanon was a major port for the trade in oriental goods.

16 **Rialto** The Exchange of Venice, and its adjoining piazza. Florio's Italian dictionary (1611) defines it as 'An eminent place in Venice where merchants commonly meet'.

18 **squandered** This may simply mean 'scattered', without any hint of contempt (*OED v* 1a); but Shakespeare's only other use of the verb, 'squand'ring glances of the fool' in *AYLI* 2.7.57, implies folly; so Shylock may, from the viewpoint of a prudent financier, be glancing at the want of prudence in Antonio's undertakings.

there be land rats, and water rats, water thieves and land thieves – I mean pirates – and then there is the peril of waters, winds and rocks. The man is notwithstanding sufficient. Three thousand ducats: I think I may take his bond.

BASSANIO Be assured you may.

SHYLOCK I will be assured I may; and that I may be assured, I will bethink me – may I speak with Antonio?

BASSANIO If it please you to dine with us –

SHYLOCK Yes, to smell pork, to eat of the habitation which your prophet the Nazarite conjured the devil into. I will buy with you, sell with you, talk with you, walk with you, and so following; but I will not eat with you, drink with you, nor pray with you. What news on the Rialto? Who is he comes here?

Enter ANTONIO

BASSANIO This is Signor Antonio.

SHYLOCK [*Aside*] How like a fawning publican he looks!
I hate him for he is a Christian;
But more, for that in low simplicity
He lends out money gratis, and brings down
The rate of usance here with us in Venice.

24, 27, 33 SH SHYLOCK] Q2; *Jew* Q1, F 33 SD] *Rowe; not in* Q1–2, F

20 pirates Piracy, largely by Balkan refugees from the Turkish invasions, reached horrifying proportions in the Adriatic at this time. The word thus had the associations of 'terrorist' today, and it is a pity if the actor detracts from its menace by pronouncing it 'pi-rats' to chime with 'land rats, and water rats'; the spelling of Q1–2 and F, 'Pyrats', is widespread enough to have no special significance. The prosaic explanation of a figure of speech is typical of Shylock's very individual speech habits; compare 2.5.33, and see Brian Vickers, *The Artistry of Shakespeare's Prose*, 1968, pp. 82–8.

23, 24 assured Bassanio means 'reassured', but Shylock twists the meaning to 'financially secure'.

24–5 I will bethink me – A dash has been used, in place of the comma of the early texts, to suggest a half-formed thought of some ingenious kind of security. But the sentence could be complete, and decisive – 'I will give the matter my careful consideration.' The actor has a choice.

28 Nazarite Jesus of Nazareth. The word is used with reference to Nazareth in both BB and GB (e.g. 'He should be called a Nazarite', Matt. 2.23) and it was not until the AV (1611) that 'Nazarene' was used in order to avoid confusion with the Jewish sect called Nazarites.

28 conjured...into The Synoptic Gospels relate that devils driven out of two madmen by Jesus entered into a herd of pigs. See Matt. 8.28 to end.

32 This is Not a formal introduction, but simply 'It's'. The short line may indicate that Bassanio goes over to reassure the startled Antonio, who did not expect to find him with Shylock.

33 fawning publican The adjective is meant to recall the publican – that is, tax gatherer – in the parable told in Luke 18.9–14; his humility (compare 'low simplicity' in 35) is contrasted with the arrogance of the Pharisee who, like Shylock, prides himself on his observance of the law. Noble, however, thinks that 'Shylock meant to stigmatise Antonio as the creature of the ruling class... Antonio bullied Jews, just as had the publicans' (p. 164).

35 low simplicity humble foolishness.

36 gratis without taking interest.

37 usance Shylock prefers 'usance' to 'usury' as, in Thomas Wilson's phrase, 'a more cleanly name' (*Discourse upon Usury* (1572), ed. R. H. Tawney, 1925, p. 228).

If I can catch him once upon the hip,
I will feed fat the ancient grudge I bear him.
He hates our sacred nation, and he rails
Even there where merchants most do congregate
On me, my bargains, and my well-won thrift
Which he calls interest. Cursed be my tribe
If I forgive him!

BASSANIO Shylock, do you hear?

SHYLOCK I am debating of my present store,
And by the near guess of my memory
I cannot instantly raise up the gross
Of full three thousand ducats. What of that?
Tubal, a wealthy Hebrew of my tribe,
Will furnish me. But soft, how many months
Do you desire? [*To Antonio*] Rest you fair, good signor!
Your worship was the last man in our mouths.

ANTONIO Shylock, albeit I neither lend nor borrow
By taking nor by giving of excess,
Yet to supply the ripe wants of my friend
I'll break a custom. [*To Bassanio*] Is he yet possessed
How much ye would?

42 well-won] Q1–2; well worne F 44 Shylock] Q2, F; Shyloch Q1 51 SD] *Follows* signor *in Rowe; not in* Q1–2, F 56 SD] *NS; following* would *in 58, Staunton; not in* Q1–2, F 56 Is...possessed] Q1, F; are you resolv'd Q2 57 ye would] Q1; he would have Q2; he would F

38 **upon the hip** at a disadvantage; Iago claims to have Cassio 'on the hip' in *Oth.* 2.1.305. As this is a wrestling metaphor, N. Nathan thinks Shakespeare is remembering the story of Jacob wrestling with the angel in Gen. 32, which comes a little after the story of Jacob and Laban (*NQ* 197 (1952), 74; see 63–80 below).

42 **well-won** F's emendation, if it is one, to 'well-worne' may just conceivably be right. In the sense of 'long accustomed', it implies that the taking of interest was a time-honoured practice.

43, 67, 68 **interest** Shylock recoils from the crude association of this word with unnatural profit. See 37 n.

43 **my tribe** Presumably one of the twelve tribes of Israel, from which all Jews traced their descent. Shakespeare is attempting a kind of local colour, but the oath rings false to Jewish ears.

44 **Shylock** Q1's spelling here, 'Shyloch', may result from Shakespeare's initial uncertainty about the name. See 1 SH n. above.

45 **debating...store** considering what ready cash I have.

47 **gross** full sum.

49 **Tubal** By involving him in the deal, Shakespeare shows that the Jews in Venice follow the injunction of Deut. 23.20 in lending freely to each other and taking interest only of non-Jews. On the name see 3.2.284 n.

50 **soft** wait a moment.

50 **months** months' credit.

52 **Your...mouths** i.e. we were just talking about you. Shylock's delay in greeting Antonio suggests his fear and revulsion.

54 **of excess** anything over and above the sum in question; i.e. interest.

55 **ripe** pressing.

56–7 **Is he...would?** Has he been told how much you want? Antonio has turned abruptly away in distaste from the moneylender. Q2's editor failed to see this and emended the lines so that Antonio continues to speak to Shylock. The F reading probably makes the same mistake, and emends so that Antonio asks Shylock if Bassanio knows yet how much money he is going to need – an improbable question.

SHYLOCK Ay, ay, three thousand ducats.
ANTONIO And for three months.
SHYLOCK I had forgot, three months; [*To Bassanio*] you told me so.
Well then, your bond; and let me see – but hear you,
Methoughts you said you neither lend nor borrow
Upon advantage.
ANTONIO I do never use it.
SHYLOCK When Jacob grazed his uncle Laban's sheep –
This Jacob from our holy Abram was
(As his wise mother wrought in his behalf)
The third possessor; ay, he was the third –
ANTONIO And what of him, did he take interest?
SHYLOCK No, not take interest, not as you would say
Directly interest. Mark what Jacob did:
When Laban and himself were compromised
That all the eanlings which were streaked and pied
Should fall as Jacob's hire, the ewes being rank
In end of autumn turnèd to the rams,
And when the work of generation was
Between these woolly breeders in the act,
The skilful shepherd pilled me certain wands

59 SD] *Brown; not in* Q1–2, F 76 pilled] *Knight;* pyld Q1–2; pil'd F; peel'd *Pope*

58 And…months Brown suggests the missing half-line indicates a pause. Shylock does not want to appear too compliant.

59 you told me so This oblique, almost over-the-shoulder remark to Bassanio underlines how quickly the scene is developing into a confrontation between Antonio and Shylock.

62 advantage i.e. to the lender's advantage, or profit.

62 I…use it Antonio may mean more than 'That is not my custom.' 'Use it' may mean 'take usury', a sarcastic formation on the lines of 'wive it' (*Shr.* 1.2.75) or 'prince it' (*Cym.* 3.3.85).

63–80 When Jacob…were Jacob's Gen. 27 relates how Rebecca deceived her blind husband Isaac into mistaking her son Jacob for his half-brother Esau. She put rough kidskins on Jacob's hands, so that his father mistook his touch for that of Esau, blessed him, and made him his heir. Jacob fled from Esau's consequent anger and served his uncle Laban for seven years in order to gain the hand of his daughter Rachel. In Gen. 30 the story is told of Jacob's sheep. Laban agreed to his keeping all the parti-coloured animals in their flock. Jacob acquired huge numbers of sheep by means of the trick Shylock describes here, which was based on the belief that offspring resemble whatever the mother sees at their conception.

64 Abram N. Nathan suggests that Shakespeare intentionally used the original name (Gen. 11.26), which meant 'sterile', rather than the name 'Abraham' given to the patriarch in Gen. 17.2, which meant 'father of many nations' (*NQ* ns 17 (1970), 127–8).

70 compromised agreed.

71 eanlings new-born lambs; from the verb 'ean' meaning 'to give birth'. See also 79 below.

72 hire wages.

72 rank on heat.

74 work of generation mating.

76 pilled…wands partly stripped the bark off some twigs. The old form 'pilled' is retained here because it is found in Gen. 30.37 in the Tudor translations of the Bible, though it is reasonable the actor should modernise to 'peeled' with the Revised Version. 'Me' is the ethic dative, which adds nothing to the meaning but 'personalises' Shylock's speech.

And in the doing of the deed of kind
He stuck them up before the fulsome ewes,
Who then conceiving, did in eaning time
Fall parti-coloured lambs, and those were Jacob's.
This was a way to thrive, and he was blest;
And thrift is blessing if men steal it not.

ANTONIO This was a venture, sir, that Jacob served for,
A thing not in his power to bring to pass,
But swayed and fashioned by the hand of heaven.
Was this inserted to make interest good?
Or is your gold and silver ewes and rams?

SHYLOCK I cannot tell, I make it breed as fast.
But note me, signor –

ANTONIO Mark you this, Bassanio,
The devil can cite Scripture for his purpose.
An evil soul producing holy witness
Is like a villain with a smiling cheek,
A goodly apple rotten at the heart.
O what a goodly outside falsehood hath!

SHYLOCK Three thousand ducats, 'tis a good round sum.
Three months from twelve, then let me see, the rate –

ANTONIO Well, Shylock, shall we be beholding to you?

SHYLOCK Signor Antonio, many a time and oft
In the Rialto you have rated me
About my monies and my usances.
Still have I borne it with a patient shrug

77 **in the doing...kind** during mating.

78 **fulsome** *OED* bases its definition 'lustful' (sv 2c) on this passage.

80 **Fall** Drop.

81 **blest** In Gen. 31 Jacob claims that he acted as he did on God's guidance ('The God of my father hath been with me', 31.5), because Laban had been cheating him out of his wages.

82 **thrift** profit, increase; compare 1.1.174.

83 **venture** speculation involving some uncertainty. Antonio, like the Reformation commentators, condones Jacob's stratagem as an act of faith 'showing that he looked to God, whose hand alone could dispose of this so abstruse and hidden a thing in the course of nature' (William Whately, quoted Neil Carson, 'Hazarding and cozening in *The Merchant of Venice*', *ELN* 9 (1972), 168–77, p. 175).

83 **served for** i.e. he continued to work for Laban while carrying out his scheme. A common objection to usury was that its production involved no toil.

86 **inserted** Probably 'brought into our talk'; less probably, 'put into the biblical story'.

88 **I cannot tell** A polite formula for maintaining a difference of opinion.

89 **note me** Either Shylock claims attention by this phrase, as Antonio disdainfully turns aside to Bassanio; or he has withdrawn into his calculations.

94 **goodly** The emendation of Rowe and some other eighteenth-century editors to 'godly' avoids a repetition from the previous line, but it has no textual authority.

99 **rated** berated. The word pivots Shylock from his matter-of-fact calculations of 'the rate' (96) into his dramatic outburst.

100, 108, 111, 121 **monies** Strictly 'sums of money', but often used in Elizabethan English where we should use the singular. Later writers adopted it as a typical Jewish usage, in imitation of Shylock.

For suff'rance is the badge of all our tribe.
You call me misbeliever, cut-throat dog,
And spit upon my Jewish gaberdine,
And all for use of that which is mine own.
Well then, it now appears you need my help.
Go to, then, you come to me, and you say,
'Shylock, we would have monies' – you say so,
You that did void your rheum upon my beard,
And foot me as you spurn a stranger cur
Over your threshold: monies is your suit.
What should I say to you? Should I not say
'Hath a dog money? Is it possible
A cur can lend three thousand ducats?' Or
Shall I bend low, and in a bondman's key,
With bated breath and whisp'ring humbleness,
Say this:
'Fair sir, you spat on me on Wednesday last,
You spurned me such a day, another time
You called me dog: and for these courtesies
I'll lend you thus much monies.'

ANTONIO I am as like to call thee so again,
To spit on thee again, to spurn thee too.
If thou wilt lend this money, lend it not
As to thy friends, for when did friendship take
A breed for barren metal of his friend?

103 cut-throat] Q1–2, F; cut-throat, *Hudson, conj. Thirlby* 117] *As separate line, Steevens*[3]; *as part of 118*, Q1–2, F **126** for] Q1–2; of F

102 suff'rance...tribe Sufferance means 'forbearance', but there is perhaps some play on the meaning 'suffering' because the 'badge' or distinguishing mark which Venetian Jews were compelled to wear was a yellow O, which could be interpreted as a cry. See F. C. Lane, *Venice: A Maritime Republic*, 1973, p. 300, and compare the analogous use of the letter H with a play on 'ache' (*Ant.* 4.7.8).

103 dog Particularly insulting to Shylock, to whom as a Jew dogs were unclean.

104 gaberdine A loose outer garment, not distinctively Jewish. In *Temp* 2.2.38 Trinculo creeps under Caliban's gaberdine.

105 use With a nuance of 'putting to use, taking interest upon'. There is a possible echo of Matt. 20.15, which had become proverbial (Tilley 099): 'Is it not lawful for me to do as I will with my own?' (GB).

109 void your rheum spit.

111 suit request.

115 key tone of voice.

117 Say this The pause gives time for a mock obeisance, and throws emphasis on to the concluding lines of the speech.

126 A breed...metal i.e. an increase in a sum of money, as if it were able to reproduce. The idea originated with Aristotle's play upon the Greek word for 'interest' which means 'offspring': 'And this term interest, which means the birth of money from money, is applied to the breeding of money because the offspring resembles the parent. Wherefore of all modes of getting wealth this is the most unnatural' (*Politica*, trans. B. Jowett, in *Works*, ed. W. D. Rouse, 1908, 1258b).

126 for F changes the preposition, but 'for' is quite natural. Compare its common use in such phrases as 'a daughter for Margaret'.

But lend it rather to thine enemy,
Who if he break, thou mayst with better face
Exact the penalty.

SHYLOCK Why look you how you storm!
I would be friends with you, and have your love,
Forget the shames that you have stained me with,
Supply your present wants, and take no doit
Of usance for my monies, and you'll not hear me.
This is kind I offer.

BASSANIO This were kindness.

SHYLOCK This kindness will I show.
Go with me to a notary, seal me there
Your single bond, and, in a merry sport,
If you repay me not on such a day,
In such a place, such sum or sums as are
Expressed in the condition, let the forfeit
Be nominated for an equal pound
Of your fair flesh, to be cut off and taken
In what part of your body pleaseth me.

ANTONIO Content, in faith! I'll seal to such a bond,
And say there is much kindness in the Jew.

BASSANIO You shall not seal to such a bond for me;
I'll rather dwell in my necessity.

ANTONIO Why, fear not, man, I will not forfeit it.
Within these two months, that's a month before
This bond expires, I do expect return
Of thrice three times the value of this bond.

SHYLOCK O father Abram, what these Christians are,

128 **break** go bankrupt.

133 **doit** A very small Dutch coin of little value.

135, 136 **kindness** In picking up this word, which Bassanio uses in its normal sense, Shylock is made to pun grimly on the meaning 'natural inclination', which also supplies an ominous overtone to the word in 146. Similar ambiguities in the use of 'kind' and 'kindly' occur in *King Lear*.

138 **single bond** i.e. an unconditional bond. But Shylock immediately pretends that a condition has occurred to him by way of a joke.

138 **merry sport** This may either echo or be echoed by line 49 of the ballad *Gernutus*: 'But we will have a merry jest.' See p. 5 above. In Irving's production, Shylock tapped Antonio confidingly on the chest at these words, and Antonio recoiled from his touch. Olivier preserved Irving's gesture, but used it five lines later, at 'your fair flesh'.

141 **condition** i.e. the terms of the bond.

142 **nominated for** named as.

142 **equal** exact. This insistence on exactness is to prove Shylock's undoing.

142–4 **an equal...me** This closely follows *Il Pecorone*: 'una libra di carne d'addosso di qualunque luogo e' volesse' (a pound of flesh from whatever place you wish).

148 **dwell...necessity** continue to lack means (for my venture). The rhyme helps the emphasis of Bassanio's words.

Whose own hard dealings teaches them suspect
The thoughts of others! Pray you tell me this:
If he should break his day what should I gain
By the exaction of the forfeiture?
A pound of man's flesh, taken from a man,
Is not so estimable, profitable neither,
As flesh of muttons, beefs, or goats. I say
To buy his favour, I extend this friendship.
If he will take it, so; if not, adieu,
And for my love, I pray you wrong me not.

ANTONIO Yes, Shylock, I will seal unto this bond.

SHYLOCK Then meet me forthwith at the notary's.
Give him direction for this merry bond,
And I will go and purse the ducats straight,
See to my house left in the fearful guard
Of an unthrifty knave, and presently
I'll be with you. *Exit*

ANTONIO Hie thee, gentle Jew.
The Hebrew will turn Christian, he grows kind.

BASSANIO I like not fair terms and a villain's mind.

ANTONIO Come on, in this there can be no dismay,
My ships come home a month before the day.
Exeunt

170 SD] Q1–2, F; *placed at end of line, Capell* 170–1 Hie...kind] *As in* Q3; ...turne / Christian...Q1–2, F
171 The] Q1–2; This F

154 **dealings...teaches** Plural subjects with a singular form of the verb are not uncommon in Shakespeare (Abbott 333).

160 **muttons, beefs** sheep, oxen. The distinction between the native English word for the animal and the French one for its meat was not rigid in the sixteenth century.

163 **for my love** for my sake.

168 **fearful** untrustworthy.

169 **unthrifty** careless.

169 **knave** Not as disparaging as in modern English. Its primary meaning was still 'servant', as in *Oth.* 1.1.45.

170 **gentle** A pun on 'Gentile' as at 2.6.52.

173 **dismay** i.e. cause for dismay.

2.[1] *[A flourish of cornets.] Enter [the Prince of]* MOROCCO, *a tawny Moor all in white, and three or four followers accordingly; with* PORTIA, NERISSA, *and their train*

MOROCCO Mislike me not for my complexion,
The shadowed livery of the burnished sun,
To whom I am a neighbour and near bred.
Bring me the fairest creature northward born,
Where Phoebus' fire scarce thaws the icicles,
And let us make incision for your love
To prove whose blood is reddest, his or mine.
I tell thee, lady, this aspèct of mine
Hath feared the valiant; by my love I swear
The best-regarded virgins of our clime
Have loved it too. I would not change this hue,
Except to steal your thoughts, my gentle queen.
PORTIA In terms of choice I am not solely led

Act 2, Scene 1 2.1] *Rowe subst.; not in* Q1–2; *Actus Secundus.* F 0 SD *A...cornets*] *Malone subst.; not in* Q1–2; *Flo. Cornets / follows / train / in* 0 SD.3, F 0 SD *the Prince of*] *Capell; not in* Q1–2, F 0 SD MOROCCO] *Capell;* Morochus Q1–2, F 1 SH MOROCCO] Q1 *subst.; Moroc.* Q2; *Mor.* F

Act 2, Scene 1

0 SD.1 ***A...cornets*** This musical stage direction from F is a theatrical addition. A flourish was a short call or phrase, probably extemporised. Cornets at the time were thin, curved woodwind instruments, as in C. Walter Hodges's drawing (illustration 4, p. 28 above). They signified the entry of an important person.

0 SD.1 ***tawny*** i.e. light-skinned, as distinct from a 'blackamoor', or sub-Saharan Negro. See Eldred Jones, *Othello's Countrymen*, 1965, pp. 68–9.

0 SD.2 ***white*** Shakespeare, who may have known that white was a ceremonial colour in Islam, visualises a theatrically effective contrast between the strangers and the rich colours worn by Portia's 'train'.

0 SD.2 ***three or four*** This vagueness is typical of a dramatist's own manuscript.

0 SD.2 ***accordingly*** i.e. 'complexioned and dressed as Morocco' (Brown).

1 **complexion** The metre requires this to have four syllables. This may suggest Morocco's careful 'foreign' diction, in contrast to Portia's trisyllabic 'direction' (14) and 'affection' (22).

1–3 **Mislike...bred** Reminiscent of Song of Sol. 1.5 (BB): 'Marvell not at me that I am so black, for why? the sun hath shined upon me.'

2 **shadowed** dark; with some play on the word as applied to a way of weaving or dyeing textiles (*OED* sv 5), rather than the heraldic meaning 'outlined' proposed by NS and subsequent editors.

2 **livery** uniform; with a nuance of the original meaning 'something bestowed' (*OED sb* 1).

2 **burnished** bright like polished metal. A word from Shakespeare's 'high style'; he uses it to enliven Plutarch's description of Cleopatra's barge, as translated by North (*Ant.* 2.2.191).

3 **near bred** (1) reared nearby, (2) closely related. Morocco makes himself sound both subservient ('livery') in the courtly-love tradition and superhumanly connected with the sun god, Phoebus.

4 **fairest** most light-skinned.

6 **make incision** The image keeps the idea of the flesh bond, heard of only minutes ago, reverberating in our minds.

7 **reddest** 'Red blood is a traditional sign of courage' (Johnson).

9 **feared** terrified.

10 **best-regarded** most admired.

12 **queen** Like 2–3, this suggests both courtly-love subservience and royal condescension.

13 **terms of** Probably in the vague sense recognised by Onions and the *OED*, 'as a matter of, in respect of', as when Hamlet says 'in my terms of honour' (5.2.246).

By nice direction of a maiden's eyes.
Besides, the lottery of my destiny
Bars me the right of voluntary choosing.
But if my father had not scanted me,
And hedged me by his wit to yield myself
His wife who wins me by that means I told you,
Yourself, renownèd prince, then stood as fair
As any comer I have looked on yet
For my affection.

MOROCCO Even for that I thank you.
Therefore I pray you lead me to the caskets
To try my fortune. By this scimitar,
That slew the Sophy and a Persian prince
That won three fields of Sultan Solyman,
I would o'er-stare the sternest eyes that look,
Outbrave the heart most daring on the earth,
Pluck the young sucking cubs from the she-bear,
Yea, mock the lion when a roars for prey,

25 prince] Q1, F; Prince, Q2 **26** of] Q1–2, F; for *conj. Chew* **27** o'er-stare] Q1, F; out-stare Q2 **30** a] Q1; he Q2, F

14 nice over-discriminatory, 'choosy'; from Portia's words at 1.2.106–8 we suspect she is also using the term to mean 'fastidious'.

14 direction (1) guidance, (2) point towards which one turns.

17 scanted restricted (*OED v* 6).

18 hedged confined.

18 wit sagacity; with a possible pun on the obsolescent meaning 'testament' (Hilda Hulme, '*Wit, rage, mean*: three notes on *The Merchant of Venice*', *Neophilologus* 41 (1957), 46–50).

18–19 yield...who bestow my hand upon the man who.

20 then...fair would then have stood as good a chance (with some play on 'fair' as meaning 'light-skinned'). The audience, who have heard Portia's views on her previous suitors, recognise this as a back-handed compliment.

22 For my (1) Of gaining my, (2) Of deserving my.

24 scimitar Morocco perhaps draws and flourishes it, to the alarm of Portia's attendants.

25 Sophy The Shah of Persia. No Shah was slain in battle in the sixteenth century, so either Shakespeare has got his facts wrong or he is making Morocco a boastful liar.

25–6 That...Solyman A recollection of Kyd's *Soliman and Perseda* (1592): 'Against the Sophy in three pitchèd fields, / Under the conduct of great Soliman / Have I been chief commander of a host / And put the flint-heart Persians to the sword' (1.3.51–4). The Turks under Solyman the Magnificent, to whom the Moroccans owed allegiance, were at war with the Persians in the mid sixteenth century. The Turks were generally the victors, and no Persian prince won three battles, so there is some justification for S. C. Chew's conjecture 'for' in place of 'of' in 26 (*The Crescent and the Rose*, 1937, p. 255). With a comma after 'prince', as in Q2, 'scimitar' then becomes the antecedent of 'That'. This would make both the Sophy and the Persian prince victims of the well-tried blade. However, Shakespeare was probably more intent on creating dramatic effect by a doubly-sworn oath than on maintaining historical accuracy.

29 Pluck...bear The exploit was proverbial (Tilley S292), and probably based on the biblical image of ferocity: 'chafed in their minds, and are even as a bear robbed of her whelps in the field' (2 Sam. 17.8, BB). Both this line and the next recall another grandiloquent stage Moor, Muly Hamat in Peele's *Battle of Alcazar* (1594), who forced food from a lioness.

30 a This sixteenth-century form of the third person singular is modernised to 'he' in Q2 and F.

To win thee, lady. But alas the while,
If Hercules and Lichas play at dice
Which is the better man, the greater throw
May turn by fortune from the weaker hand.
So is Alcides beaten by his rage,
And so may I, blind Fortune leading me,
Miss that which one unworthier may attain,
And die with grieving.

PORTIA You must take your chance,
And either not attempt to choose at all
Or swear before you choose, if you choose wrong,
Never to speak to lady afterward
In way of marriage: therefore be advised.

MOROCCO Nor will not. Come, bring me unto my chance.

PORTIA First forward to the temple; after dinner
Your hazard shall be made.

MOROCCO Good fortune then,
To make me blest – or cursèd'st among men!

Cornets. Exeunt

31 thee] *Rowe*[2]*;* the Q1–2, F 35 rage] Q1–2, F*;* page *Theobald;* wag *NS;* rogue *Sisson;* wage *conj. Brown*
46 SD *Cornets*] F *(crowded into margin after 45); not in* Q1–2

31 thee Rowe's emendation is supported by Morocco's surprising (or perhaps foreign) use of the condescending or familiar second person singular at 8. Michael J.Warren prefers Q1's 'the lady' as typical of Morocco's deliberately 'heroic' style ('A note on *The Merchant of Venice* II.1.31', *SQ* 32 (1981), 104–5).

32 Hercules E. A. Honigmann ('Shakespeare's Plutarch', *SQ* 10 (1959), 27–33) points out that Plutarch, in his Life of Romulus, has an anecdote about Hercules playing dice with the guardian of his temple, and so winning 'a fair gentlewoman' (Plutarch's *Lives*, I, 52). On the same page of North's translation there is mention of the she-wolf which suckled Romulus, so Shakespeare's imagination may have moved from the 'she-bear' of 29, via Hercules' fight with a lion (30), to the same god's success in a lottery for a lady, such as Morocco is now engaged in.

32 Lichas Hercules' servant, who unwittingly brought him a poisoned shirt and was then thrown into the sea by him (Ovid, *Metamorphoses* 9, 152–229).

35 Alcides The Greek name for Hercules. The god's destructive frenzy caused by the poisoned shirt is likened to the destructive grief which will overwhelm Morocco if he fails to win Portia. Hilda Hulme however takes 'rage' to mean 'rash jest, wild folly'; that is, the folly of entering such a dicing contest. She quotes the Elizabethan saying that 'the best throw of the dice is to throw them away' ('*Wit, rage, mean*: three notes on *The Merchant of Venice*', *Neophilologus* 41 (1957), 46–50). There is no need to emend 'rage'.

42 be advised consider, be cautious.

43 Nor will not Either Morocco is agreeing to the condition that, if he chooses amiss, he shall never court any other lady; or he is simply throwing caution to the winds.

44 temple Morocco's 'pagan' term for a church. Oaths in the period were customarily taken at an altar.

46 SD Cornets Another musical direction added to F.

[2.2] *Enter* [LANCELOT GOBBO,] *the Clown, alone*

LANCELOT Certainly, my conscience will serve me to run from this Jew my master. The fiend is at mine elbow and tempts me, saying to me 'Gobbo, Lancelot Gobbo, good Lancelot', or 'Good Gobbo', or 'Good Lancelot Gobbo, use your legs, take the start, run away.' My conscience says 'No: take heed, honest Lancelot, take heed, honest Gobbo' – or (as aforesaid) – 'honest Lancelot Gobbo; do not run, scorn running with thy heels.' Well, the most courageous fiend bids me pack. 'Fia!' says the fiend, 'Away!' says the fiend. ''Fore the heavens, rouse up a brave mind', says the fiend, 'and run.' Well, my conscience, hanging about the neck of my heart, says very wisely to me, 'My honest friend Lancelot, being an honest man's son, or rather an honest woman's son' (for indeed my father did something smack, something grow to; he had a kind of

Act 2, Scene 2 2.2] *Rowe subst.; not in* Q1–2, F 0 SD LANCELOT GOBBO] *Capell; Launcelot / Rowe; not in* Q1–2, F 1 SH LANCELOT] *Rowe, throughout; Clowne* Q1–2, F 3, 4, 6 Gobbo] Q2; Iobbe Q1, F; Job F3 9 'Fore] *Collier*[2]; for Q1–2, F

Act 2, Scene 2

0 SD LANCELOT This name is always 'Launcelet' in Q1 (*au* being a typical Shakespearean spelling for nasalised *a*), and usually 'Lancelet' in Q2 and F. 'Lancelot' occurs only once in Q2 (2.2.70), but it is the form throughout Q3; it is adopted here as more conformable to the editorial tradition than 'Lancelet' and as possibly meant by Shakespeare to be the name of the medieval romance hero. 'Lancelet' could however mean 'a little knife', either in allusion to the Clown's cutting witticisms (Jürgen Schäfer, 'The orthography of proper names in modern-spelling editions of Shakespeare', *SB* 23 (1970), 1–19) or as a deliberate misnomer; there are signs the Clown is fat (2.2.56, 87–8; 2.5.3–4; 3.5.17–28). In the collation 'Launcelot' and 'Lancelot' are not distinguished.

0 SD *the Clown* i.e. the company's professional comedian who at the date the play was first performed would have been Will Kemp. His act was a broader, simpler kind of comedy than that of his successor Armin who played such roles as Feste.

1 serve...run 'support me in running' (Ludowyk), but with a play on the meaning 'be subservient' so that Lancelot is saying 'My conscience will do what I tell it to.' 1 Pet. 2.18–19 praises servants who 'in conscience' stay with a bad master, but the GB gloss shows that the matter was, as Lancelot makes it, debatable.

2 fiend 'Lancelot imagines himself the central character of a morality play' (Brown).

3, 4, 6 Gobbo Q1's spelling 'Iobbe', which F3 turns into 'Job', may reflect Shakespeare's initial uncertainty about what he wanted Lancelot to be called. A famous Venetian church is dedicated to S. Giobbe, i.e. Job. The name 'Gobbo' may derive from *il Gobbo di Rialto* (see p. 13 above, and illustration 2, p. 14) or, Merchant thinks, from the companies of performing dwarfs popular at the Medici court (Jacques Callot, *Varie figure gobbi* (Florence, 1616)). *Gobbo* means 'hunchback'; nothing in the play implies that either Gobbo is thus deformed, but compare note above on 0 SD LANCELOT.

7 scorn despise; with a play on the meaning 'kick aside', from the phrase 'scorn with thy heels'. In *Ado* 3.4.50–1 the dancing Margaret says 'I scorn that with my heels.'

7 courageous encouraging.

8 pack be gone.

8 Fia Go on; from Italian *via*. 'Fia', possibly an English dialect form, was used as an exhortation to horses and oarsmen.

10 hanging...heart An audience that believed it had outgrown the personifications of the morality plays would have enjoyed this anatomical mix-up.

13–14 smack...grow to...taste All three verbs are used for their sexual overtones. The verb 'smack' meant 'to kiss noisily' (*OED* smack *v* 2), while as a noun 'smack' meant 'flavour' or 'trait' and, by extension, 'a way with women'. In *Venus and Adonis* 540 'face grows to face', and *The Rape of Lucrece* 699 speaks of Tarquin's 'taste delicious'.

taste): well, my conscience says 'Lancelot, budge not!' 'Budge!' says the fiend.'Budge not!' says my conscience. 'Conscience', say I, 'you counsel well.' 'Fiend', say I, 'you counsel well.' To be ruled by my conscience, I should stay with the Jew my master who – God bless the mark! – is a kind of devil; and to run away from the Jew, I should be ruled by the fiend who – saving your reverence – is the devil himself. Certainly the Jew is the very devil incarnation, and, in my conscience, my conscience is but a kind of hard conscience to offer to counsel me to stay with the Jew. The fiend gives the more friendly counsel: I will run, fiend, my heels are at your commandment, I will run.

Enter OLD GOBBO *with a basket*

GOBBO Master young-man, you, I pray you, which is the way to Master Jew's?

LANCELOT [*Aside*] O heavens! This is my true-begotten father who being more than sand-blind, high gravel-blind, knows me not. I will try confusions with him.

GOBBO Master young-gentleman, I pray you, which is the way to Master Jew's?

LANCELOT Turn upon your right hand at the next turning, but at the next turning of all on your left. Marry, at the very next turning turn of no hand but turn down indirectly to the Jew's house.

GOBBO Be God's sonties, 'twill be a hard way to hit! Can you tell me whether one Lancelot that dwells with him, dwell with him or no?

16 well.' To be] Q1, F (*subst.*); ill. To be Q2 21 incarnation] Q1, F; incarnall Q2 27 SD] *Johnson; not in* Q1–2, F 29 confusions] Q1, F; conclusions Q2 35 Be] Q1–2, F; By F4

16 well Q2 spoils the joke by changing this to 'ill'.

19–20 saving your reverence This probably sounded affected, like its modern equivalent, 'if you'll pardon the expression'.

21 incarnation In trying to get rid of Lancelot's misuse of a word, the editor of Q2 produced his own nonce-word, 'incarnall' for 'incarnate'.

21 in my conscience An asseveration, like the modern 'in all conscience'.

22 offer presume.

27 true-begotten father Another deliberate confusion.

28 sand-blind half-blind; from the Old English prefix 'sam-'; but Lancelot, like Dr Johnson, thinks it has to do with sand-like specks before the eyes. Hence his invention 'gravel-blind' for the more extreme condition.

28 high absolutely; an intensifier.

29 confusions Once again, Q2 will not allow Shakespeare his joke and changes this to 'conclusions'. To try or prove conclusions is explained by *OED* as 'to experiment', and this appears to be the meaning in *Ham.* 3.4.195. But conclusions are also riddles, as in *Per.* 1.1.56.

32–4 Turn...house This joke, as old as Terence (compare *Adelphi* 4.2.573–83), is most effective if Lancelot turns his father about until he is immediately in front of the door to Shylock's house (from which Lancelot himself emerged at the start of the scene).

33 Marry By Mary. An asseveration which had lost its original meaning.

36 dwells...dwell The first means 'is a member of his household', the second 'lodges'.

LANCELOT Talk you of young Master Lancelot? [*Aside*] Mark me now, now will I raise the waters. Talk you of young Master Lancelot?

GOBBO No 'master', sir, but a poor man's son. His father, though I say't, is an honest, exceeding poor man and, God be thanked, well to live.

LANCELOT Well, let his father be what a will, we talk of young Master Lancelot.

GOBBO Your worship's friend and Lancelot, sir.

LANCELOT But I pray you, *ergo* old man, *ergo* I beseech you, talk you of young Master Lancelot?

GOBBO Of Lancelot, an't please your mastership.

LANCELOT *Ergo* Master Lancelot. Talk not of Master Lancelot, father, for the young gentleman, according to fates and destinies, and such odd sayings, the sisters three, and such branches of learning, is indeed deceased, or as you would say in plain terms, gone to heaven.

GOBBO Marry, God forbid! The boy was the very staff of my age, my very prop.

LANCELOT Do I look like a cudgel or a hovel-post, a staff or a prop? Do you know me, father?

GOBBO Alack the day, I know you not, young gentleman, but I pray you tell me, is my boy – God rest his soul! – alive or dead?

LANCELOT Do you not know me, father?

GOBBO Alack, sir, I am sand-blind, I know you not.

LANCELOT Nay indeed, if you had your eyes you might fail of the knowing me: it is a wise father that knows his own child. Well, old

38 SD] *Johnson, after* now,; *not in* Q1–2, F 56 Do...prop?] *As in* Q1–2, F; *as an aside, Collier* 59 God] F; G O D Q1–2

39 **raise the waters** conjure up a storm; i.e. bring tears to old Gobbo's eyes.

41–2 **well to live** well-to-do. The phrase occurs in North's Plutarch, in the Life of Aristides (Plutarch's *Lives*, III, 108).

45 **Your..sir** The polite formula for repudiating a title, as we might say 'Please call me John.' Costard disowns the name of Pompey with 'Your servant, and Costard' (*LLL* 5.2.571).

46 *ergo* therefore. Latin; much used in academic disputation. Brown quotes Nashe on Gabriel Harvey: 'he was called nothing but Gabriel Ergo up and down the college' (*Works*, ed. R. B. McKerrow, 1904–10, III, 66–7).

49 **father** Lancelot is not giving the game away. 'Father' was a courteous form of address to an older person.

51 **sisters three** The three sisters, in classical mythology, who spun and eventually cut the threads of people's lives. They were identical with the Fates and the Destinies, so this phrase is a tautology, twice over. By the 1590s allusions to them were felt to be comically trite, as is shown by Thisbe's apostrophe to them (*MND* 5.1.336–41).

54 **God forbid!** A similar joke occurs in Sir Andrew's challenge in *TN* 'God have mercy upon one of our souls! He may have mercy upon mine, but my hope is better' (3.4.166–8).

54 **staff...age** Young Tobias is this to his parents in BB (Tobit 5.23; 10.4) but the phrase is not used in GB.

56 **hovel-post** A post to hold up a shelter.

63 **wise father...child** Proverbial (Tilley C309). Dent quotes Barnaby Riche, *Irish Hubbub*

man, I will tell you news of your son. [*Kneels*] Give me your blessing; truth will come to light, murder cannot be hid long, a man's son may, but in the end truth will out.

GOBBO Pray you, sir, stand up; I am sure you are not Lancelot my boy.

LANCELOT Pray you, let's have no more fooling about it, but give me your blessing; I am Lancelot your boy that was, your son that is, your child that shall be.

GOBBO I cannot think you are my son.

LANCELOT I know not what I shall think of that; but I am Lancelot the Jew's man, and I am sure Margery your wife is my mother.

GOBBO Her name is Margery indeed. I'll be sworn if thou be Lancelot thou art mine own flesh and blood. Lord worshipped might he be, what a beard hast thou got! Thou has got more hair on thy chin than Dobbin my fill-horse has on his tail.

LANCELOT It should seem then that Dobbin's tail grows backward. I am sure he had more hair of his tail than I have of my face when I last saw him.

GOBBO Lord, how art thou changed! How dost thou and thy master agree? I have brought him a present. How 'gree you now?

LANCELOT Well, well; but for mine own part, as I have set up my rest to run away, so I will not rest till I have run some ground. My master's a very Jew. Give him a present? Give him a halter! I am

64 SD] *Collier; not in* Q1–2, F 65 murder] F; muder Q1; Murther Q2 80 of his] Q1–2, F; on his *Rowe* 80 of my] Q1–2, F; on my F3 81 last] Q2; lost Q1, F 83 'gree] Q1, F (gree); agree Q2

(1617): 'We were wont to say, it was a wise child that did know the own father, but now we may say it is a wise father that doth know his own child' (p. 16).

65 truth...long Brown notes that Kyd had already run together these two proverbs (Tilley M1315 and T591) in *The Spanish Tragedy* 2.6.58–60: 'The heavens are just, murder cannot be hid. / Time is the author both of truth and right, / And time will bring this treachery to light.'

69–70 give...blessing Shakespeare may have hit upon the comic 'business' that follows upon Lancelot kneeling for his father's blessing because he had made use, two scenes back, of Jacob tricking Isaac into giving him his blessing. See nn. on 1.3.63–80, and on 77 below.

71 child that shall be Possibly an echo of the liturgical formula ascribing glory to God 'as it was, is now, and ever shall be'. But Ludowyk reads it simply as Lancelot's promise to behave as a dutiful child.

75 thou Old Gobbo now shifts from the respectful 'you' to the familiar 'thou'.

76 worshipped...be This phrase is slipped in by Gobbo to avert his own profane use of 'Lord'.

77 beard Old Gobbo has grasped the hair at the back of Lancelot's head.

78 fill-horse dray horse. 'Fills', with the meaning 'shafts', is used teasingly by Pandarus to Cressida: 'and you draw backward we'll put you i'th'fills' (*Tro.* 3.2.45–6).

79 backward i.e. from long to short.

80 of...of Lancelot's deliberate use of 'of' in place of his father's 'on' suggests that 'on' is less urban or less fashionable. See Abbott 175.

84 set...rest ventured my final stake or reserve; 'rest' is a gambling term (*OED* Rest *sb*² 7a), but there is also a pun on the meaning 'residence, abode' (*OED sb*¹ 5).

86 very An intensifier, corresponding to the modern 'real'.

86 halter hangman's noose.

famished in his service; you may tell every finger I have with my ribs. Father, I am glad you are come; give me your present to one Master Bassanio, who indeed gives rare new liveries: if I serve not him, I will run as far as God has any ground. O rare fortune, here comes the man! To him, father, for I am a Jew if I serve the Jew any longer.

Enter BASSANIO *with* [LEONARDO *and*] *a follower or two*

BASSANIO You may do so, but let it be so hasted that supper be ready at the farthest by five of the clock. See these letters delivered, put the liveries to making, and desire Gratiano to come anon to my lodging.

[*Exit one of his men*]

LANCELOT To him, father.

GOBBO God bless your worship!

BASSANIO Gramercy; wouldst thou aught with me?

GOBBO Here's my son, sir, a poor boy –

LANCELOT Not a poor boy, sir, but the rich Jew's man that would, sir, as my father shall specify –

GOBBO He hath a great infection, sir, as one would say, to serve –

LANCELOT Indeed, the short and the long is, I serve the Jew, and have a desire, as my father shall specify –

GOBBO His master and he, saving your worship's reverence, are scarce cater-cousins –

LANCELOT To be brief, the very truth is that the Jew having done me

92 SD LEONARDO *and*] *Theobald subst.; not in* Q1–2, F 96 SD] Q2; *not in* Q1, F

87–8 **you...ribs** The traditional stage business of Lancelot placing his father's hand on the fingers of his own hand, which he has spread out to represent his ribs, probably fulfils Shakespeare's intention. As his resolve to 'try confusions' indicates, there is often method in Lancelot's muddles, requiring such supporting business. Compare 32–4 and 77 nn.

88 **me** on my behalf. The ethic dative.

89 **rare new liveries** In *Il Pecorone*, Giannetto, living the life of a wealthy gentleman at Ansaldo's expense, equips his servants with liveries ('vestir famigli').

90 **as far...ground** i.e. to the ends of the earth. Like 'as far as land will let me' in *R2* 1.3.252, this sounds proverbial (Tilley / Dent G252.1).

91 **a Jew** i.e. someone I could not possibly be; as in the modern 'or I'm a Dutchman'.

92 SD ***or two*** The vagueness typical of an authorial manuscript. Compare 2.1.0 SD and see Textual Analysis, pp. 181–2 below.

95–6 **and desire...lodging** Gratiano's arrival in front of Shylock's house at 145 below may result from Shakespeare compressing this part of the action as he writes – a not unusual feature of continuous dramatic composition. NS, however, suspects a loose end resulting from revision.

99 **Gramercy** The conventional polite response to Gobbo's form of greeting. Like the French *merci* it derives from the Old French *grant merci*, '[God] reward you.'

103 **infection** Gobbo's mistake for 'affection' meaning 'desire'.

107 **cater-cousins** Close friends who would customarily eat together, though not cousins-german, who were blood relations.

wrong doth cause me – as my father being I hope an old man shall frutify unto you –

GOBBO I have here a dish of doves that I would bestow upon your worship, and my suit is –

LANCELOT In very brief, the suit is impertinent to myself, as your worship shall know by this honest old man, and though I say it, though old man, yet poor man, my father –

BASSANIO One speak for both. What would you?

LANCELOT Serve you, sir.

GOBBO That is the very defect of the matter, sir.

BASSANIO I know thee well, thou hast obtained thy suit.
Shylock thy master spoke with me this day,
And hath preferred thee, if it be preferment
To leave a rich Jew's service to become
The follower of so poor a gentleman.

LANCELOT The old proverb is very well parted between my master Shylock and you, sir: you have the grace of God, sir, and he hath enough.

BASSANIO Thou speak'st it well; go, father, with thy son;
Take leave of thy old master, and enquire
My lodging out. [*To a follower*] Give him a livery
More guarded than his fellows'; see it done.

LANCELOT Father, in. I cannot get a service, no, I have ne'er a tongue in my head! [*Looks at palm of his hand*] Well, if any man in Italy

124, 131 SH LANCELOT] Q2; *Clowne* Q1, F **129** SD] *Johnson subst., after* livery; *not in* Q1–2, F **132** SD] *Hanmer subst., after* Well; *not in* Q1–2, F

110 frutify Probably used for 'fructify', since old Gobbo takes this as his cue to produce his gift.

111 dish of doves Not, as has been claimed, Italian local colour. Doves were bred for food in sixteenth-century England.

113 impertinent For 'pertinent'.

118 defect For 'effect' meaning 'purpose'.

121 preferred recommended. The question of when this took place troubles no one in the theatre. The reader may presume it to have happened at the notary's, when Bassanio would have again invited Shylock to his house.

124 old proverb The proverb 'The grace of God is gear enough' (Tilley G393) is based upon 2 Cor. 12.9: 'My grace is sufficient for thee.'

124 parted divided.

130 guarded braided or frogged. In *When You See Me, You Know Me*, a play acted about 1605, the actor playing Henry VIII's jester wore a long coat with yellow braid trimmings. But the reference to the livery of Lancelot's fellows suggests that what he reappears in resplendently at 2.4 is an exaggerated version of the uniform worn by Bassanio's servants, rather than a Fool's garb. This would not preclude his acting as a jester (indeed the exaggeration would sanction it) and Bassanio's praise in 127 seems to acknowledge his possibilities as the sententious type of Fool.

131–40 Father...twinkling Lancelot and his father move upstage towards the door of Shylock's house, while Bassanio and Leonardo confer downstage. This blocking helps establish an association of two localities, house and street, which will persist until the end of 2.6.

132–4 Well...fortune Like the rest of us, Shakespeare's characters sometimes start a sentence with one construction and end it with another.

have a fairer table which doth offer to swear upon a book! – I shall have good fortune. Go to, here's a simple line of life, here's a small trifle of wives: alas, fifteen wives is nothing, eleven widows and nine maids is a simple coming-in for one man. And then to 'scape drowning thrice, and to be in peril of my life with the edge of a featherbed: here are simple 'scapes. Well, if Fortune be a woman, she's a good wench for this gear. Father, come, I'll take my leave of the Jew in the twinkling.

Exeunt Lancelot [*and Gobbo*]

BASSANIO I pray thee, good Leonardo, think on this.
These things being bought and orderly bestowed,
Return in haste, for I do feast tonight
My best esteemed acquaintance. Hie thee, go.

LEONARDO My best endeavours shall be done herein.

Enter GRATIANO

GRATIANO Where's your master?
LEONARDO Yonder, sir, he walks. *Exit*
GRATIANO Signor Bassanio!
BASSANIO Gratiano?
GRATIANO I have a suit to you.
BASSANIO You have obtained it.
GRATIANO You must not deny me, I must go with you to Belmont.

135 eleven] Q2; a leven Q1, F 140 SD] *Rowe subst.*; *Exit Clowne* Q1–2, F 146 SD] *Theobald subst.*; *after 145*, Q1–2, F 149 a] Q2, F; *not in* Q1

133 **table** i.e. the palm of the hand, which would be laid on the Bible when taking an oath. Lancelot is studying the 'fortune' in the lines of his palm.

134 **Go to** An expression of impatience. Lancelot, who was only too glad of his father's help, now pretends that his father did not think he had a chance of getting the job.

134 **simple** unremarkable (used ironically).

135 **wives** Certain lines in the palm are supposed to indicate marriage and the status of the spouse. The sexual adventures in prospect for Lancelot (compare 3.5.30–5) are a parody of his new employer's love quest.

136 **simple coming-in** only a beginning; see *OED* Coming-in *sb* 7; probably with a second, bawdy meaning of 'enter sexually'.

137–8 **and...featherbed** Lancelot is still 'reading' his eventful future in his palm. Warburton says this is 'a cant phrase to signify the danger of marrying' and quotes from an unidentified French writer: 'j'aimerais mieux être tombée sur la point d'un oreiller, et m'être rompu le cou' – 'I would rather I had tripped over the corner of a pillow and broken my neck.' Danger (of infidelity) lurks in the most secure-seeming marriage.

138 **'scapes** adventures.

139 **gear** business, matter.

140 **twinkling** See Appendix, p. 186 below.

141 **this** Bassanio and Leonardo have resumed the conversation they were engaged in at the entry at 93.

142 **orderly bestowed** neatly stowed on board.

145 **herein** All the early texts give Leonardo an exit here. Shakespeare may have written one before deciding to telescope the action by bringing on Gratiano.

149 **You...it** granted before you ask it; a polite formula.

BASSANIO Why then, you must. But hear thee, Gratiano:
Thou art too wild, too rude, and bold of voice –
Parts that become thee happily enough,
And in such eyes as ours appear not faults;
But where thou art not known, why there they show
Something too liberal. Pray thee take pain
To allay with some cold drops of modesty
Thy skipping spirit, lest through thy wild behaviour
I be misconstered in the place I go to,
And lose my hopes.
GRATIANO Signor Bassanio, hear me:
If I do not put on a sober habit,
Talk with respect, and swear but now and then,
Wear prayer books in my pocket, look demurely,
Nay more, while grace is saying, hood mine eyes
Thus with my hat, and sigh and say 'amen',
Use all the observance of civility
Like one well studied in a sad ostent
To please his grandam, never trust me more.
BASSANIO Well, we shall see your bearing.
GRATIANO Nay, but I bar tonight, you shall not gauge me
By what we do tonight.
BASSANIO No, that were pity.
I would entreat you rather to put on
Your boldest suit of mirth, for we have friends
That purpose merriment. But fare you well,
I have some business.
GRATIANO And I must to Lorenzo and the rest;
But we will visit you at supper time.

Exeunt

151 **you...thee** Bassanio drops into the familiar second person singular for his admonitions.

152 **rude** uncouth, outspoken (not 'discourteous').

153 **Parts** Qualities (with a hint that such behaviour is put on, like an actor's part). Compare 1.1.78 n.

156 **liberal** free and easy.

157 **modesty** decorum.

158 **skipping** flighty, effervescent.

158 **spirit** Elided into a monosyllable.

159 **misconstered** misconstrued, misinterpreted. The Elizabethan spelling, like 'conster' for 'construe', indicates the word was pronounced with the stress on 'con'.

161 **habit** (1) costume, (2) behaviour.

162 **but** only.

164–5 **hood...hat** i.e. tilt my hat respectfully over my eyes. Elizabethan men kept their hats on indoors, even for meals.

166 **Use...civility** observe all civilities. The rather pompous language here is part of Gratiano's 'act'.

167 **one...ostent** someone who has thoroughly practised a staid outward behaviour.

170 **gauge** measure, judge.

[2.3] *Enter* JESSICA *and* [LANCELOT] *the Clown*

JESSICA I am sorry thou wilt leave my father so.
Our house is hell, and thou a merry devil
Didst rob it of some taste of tediousness.
But fare thee well: there is a ducat for thee.
And, Lancelot, soon at supper shalt thou see
Lorenzo, who is thy new master's guest;
Give him this letter, do it secretly.
And so farewell: I would not have my father
See me in talk with thee.

LANCELOT Adieu; tears exhibit my tongue. Most beautiful pagan, most sweet Jew, if a Christian do not play the knave and get thee, I am much deceived. But adieu; these foolish drops do something drown my manly spirit. Adieu! [*Exit*]

JESSICA Farewell, good Lancelot.
Alack, what heinous sin is it in me
To be ashamed to be my father's child!
But though I am a daughter to his blood
I am not to his manners. O Lorenzo,
If thou keep promise, I shall end this strife,
Become a Christian and thy loving wife. *Exit*

Act 2, Scene 3 2.3] *Capell subst.; not in* Q1–2, F 0 SD LANCELOT] *Rowe; not in* Q1–2, F 10 SH LANCELOT] Q2; *Clowne* Q1, F 11 do] Q1–2, F; did F2 12 something] Q1–2; somewhat F 13 SD] Q2, F; *not in* Q1

Act 2, Scene 3

2.3 Rowe, a practical man of the theatre, does not divide 2.2–6. The action of these five scenes can be made continuous, provided there are three entrances which can be localised in the manner of the old-style multiple staging found in *Err.* One entrance is already identified, from 2.2, as the door of Shylock's house; another may indicate the direction of Gratiano's lodging; and a third, probably the central curtained space, may serve as the entrance to Bassanio's house. Had Shakespeare written the masquing scene we are led to expect, the curtains would eventually have been drawn back to reveal a feast.

0 SD JESSICA The name 'Jischa' occurs in Gen. 11.29 (BB; GB has 'Iscah'). M. J. Landa, in *The Shylock Myth*, 1942, p. 40, refers to a twelfth-century document about a rich Jewess of Norwich called Jessica. See p. 8 above, for the relationship of Jessica to Marlowe's Abigail.

10 Adieu A high-flown word, unlike Jessica's 'farewell'.

10 exhibit In mistake for 'inhibit', but, as with Lancelot's other mistakes, we cannot be sure this is not intentional: it allows him to say, in effect, 'My tears express what I cannot utter.'

11 get F2 takes the word to mean 'beget' and substitutes 'did' for 'do'. The change has some support from a later remark of Lancelot's, 3.5.8–9, and is followed by many editors. But the meaning 'get hold of' points forward to the focus of interest and excitement in 2.3–6, Jessica's abduction.

19 this strife these divided feelings.

[2.4] *Enter* GRATIANO, LORENZO, SALARINO, *and* SOLANIO

LORENZO Nay, we will slink away in supper time,
Disguise us at my lodging, and return
All in an hour.
GRATIANO We have not made good preparation.
SALARINO We have not spoke us yet of torchbearers.
SOLANIO 'Tis vile unless it may be quaintly ordered,
And better in my mind not undertook.
LORENZO 'Tis now but four of clock; we have two hours
To furnish us.

Enter LANCELOT [*with a letter*]

Friend Lancelot! What's the news?
LANCELOT And it shall please you to break up this, it shall seem to signify.
LORENZO I know the hand; in faith, 'tis a fair hand,
And whiter than the paper it writ on
Is the fair hand that writ.
GRATIANO Love news, in faith!
LANCELOT By your leave, sir.
LORENZO Whither goest thou?
LANCELOT Marry, sir, to bid my old master the Jew to sup tonight with my new master the Christian.

Act 2, Scene 4 2.4] *Capell subst.; not in* Q1–2, F 3] *As separate line, Capell; as part of* 2, Q1–2, F 5 us] Q1–2, F; as F4 9 SD] *Placed as Johnson; follows* 9, Q1, F; *follows* 8, Q2 9 SD *with a letter*] F; *not in* Q1–2

Act 2, Scene 4

2.4 See n. on 2.3 above.

1 slink away The Elizabethan masque involved a spectacular entry, with music and torches, into a great hall; after parading round, the masquers led the ladies of the house on to the dance floor. In *Rom.* and *H8* the masquers come from outside, but in *Ado* they are guests who slink away to prepare their entry, as Lorenzo and his companions propose to do here.

5 spoke us Robin Hood suggests this is a reflexive form on the model of 'bethought us', and means 'discussed arrangements about'. This seems more probable than the meaning 'given orders, bespoken', of which this is the sole *OED* instance (*OED* Speak 11e). Several editors follow F4 in emending 'us' to 'as'; the confusion was a probable one in Shakespeare's handwriting.

6 quaintly ordered skilfully organised. Shakespeare the man of the theatre speaks through Solanio.

7 undertook An Elizabethan use of the past tense for the past participle, as in *JC* 2.1.50, 'I have took them up', and 1.2.48, 'I have much mistook your passion' (See Abbott 343).

10 break up unseal.

10–11 seem to signify i.e. appear to indicate what the news is.

12, 14 fair hand The first means 'elegant writing', the second 'beautiful hand': a faded conceit which provokes Gratiano's sarcasm.

15 By your leave Excuse me. A phrase to excuse one's departure.

LORENZO Hold here, take this. Tell gentle Jessica
I will not fail her; speak it privately.

Exit Lancelot

Go, gentlemen:
Will you prepare you for this masque tonight?
I am provided of a torchbearer.

SALARINO Ay marry, I'll be gone about it straight.

SOLANIO And so will I.

LORENZO Meet me and Gratiano
At Gratiano's lodging some hour hence.

SALARINO 'Tis good we do so.

Exeunt [Salarino and Solanio]

GRATIANO Was not that letter from fair Jessica?

LORENZO I must needs tell thee all. She hath directed
How I shall take her from her father's house,
What gold and jewels she is furnished with,
What page's suit she hath in readiness.
If e'er the Jew her father come to heaven,
It will be for his gentle daughter's sake;
And never dare misfortune cross her foot,
Unless she do it under this excuse
That she is issue to a faithless Jew.
Come, go with me; peruse this as thou goest.
Fair Jessica shall be my torchbearer.

Exeunt

20–2] *As three lines, Collier; as two lines divided after* privately Q1–2, F*; as two lines divided after* go *Capell* **20** privately.] Q2*;* privatly, Q1*;* privately: F **20** SD] *Placed as White; after 23,* Q1–2, F*; after* go *Capell* **20** SD *Lancelot*] *Rowe; Clowne* Q1–2, F **21** Go, gentlemen] *Rowe;* Goe gentlemen Q1–2, F*;* Go. – Gentlemen *Theobald;* Go. – / Gentlemen *Capell* **25–6** Meet...hence] *As Pope;* Meet...lodgings / Some...hence Q1–2, F **27** SD] *Capell subst.; Exit* Q1–2, F **39** SD] *Rowe; Exit* Q1–2, F

19 this A tip.

26 some hour about an hour.

34 gentle With a hint of the earlier pun on 'gentle' and 'Gentile' (1.3.170).

35 cross her foot obstruct her path. There is an implicit allusion to the traditionally unlucky omen of tripping over something when on a journey

37 faithless i.e. lacking the Christian faith, but with the more usual meaning of 'untrustworthy' (which the audience may feel comes oddly from Lorenzo in the circumstances).

[2.5] *Enter* [SHYLOCK] *the Jew and* [LANCELOT] *his man that was, the Clown*

SHYLOCK Well, thou shalt see, thy eyes shall be thy judge,
The difference of old Shylock and Bassanio –
What, Jessica! – Thou shalt not gourmandise
As thou hast done with me – What, Jessica! –
And sleep, and snore, and rend apparel out.
Why, Jessica, I say!
LANCELOT Why, Jessica!
SHYLOCK Who bids thee call? I do not bid thee call.
LANCELOT Your worship was wont to tell me I could do nothing without bidding.

Enter JESSICA

JESSICA Call you? What is your will?
SHYLOCK I am bid forth to supper, Jessica.
There are my keys. But wherefore should I go?
I am not bid for love, they flatter me;
But yet I'll go in hate, to feed upon
The prodigal Christian. Jessica my girl,
Look to my house. I am right loath to go;
There is some ill a-brewing towards my rest,
For I did dream of money bags tonight.
LANCELOT I beseech you, sir, go; my young master doth expect your reproach.

Act 2, Scene 5 2.5] *Capell subst.; not in* Q1–2, F 0 SD SHYLOCK] *Rowe; not in* Q1–2, F 0 SD LANCELOT] Q2; *not in* Q1, F 0 SD *his man that was, the Clown*] *NS, conj. Thirlby; Enter Jewe and his man that was the Clowne* Q1, F; *not in* Q2 1 SH SHYLOCK] Q2; *Jewe* Q1, F 6, 8, 19, 22, 38 SH LANCELOT] *Rowe; Clowne* Q1–2, F 8–9 Your...bidding] *As in* Q2; *as two lines divided after* me Q1, F 19–20] *As prose, Pope; as two lines divided after* master Q1, F; *as two lines divided after* go Q2

Act 2, Scene 5

2.5. See 2.3. n. above.

0 SD SHYLOCK After being 'Jew' here and in 1 SH, Shylock is given his name in the remaining speech headings of this scene, in which he figures as the householder and father rather than the moneylender.

0 SD *his man...Clown* Probably Shakespeare first wrote 'his man that was', meaning 'his former servant', and then added 'the Clown' to make clear that Lancelot is intended. See Textual Analysis, p. 181 below. It is less likely that Shakespeare meant 'his servant who used to be a country bumpkin'; in a stage direction 'Clown' could only mean the company's chief 'comic', even when he played a sophisticated Fool such as Feste. See 2.2.0 SD *the Clown* and n.

5 rend apparel out wear clothes out by tearing them.

16 Look to Take good care of.

18 money bags Dreams were supposed to go by opposites, so Shylock is afraid he is going to lose money – rightly, as it turns out.

18 tonight i.e. last night, as Romeo means when he says 'I dreamt a dream tonight' (*Rom.* 1.4.50).

SHYLOCK So do I his.

LANCELOT And they have conspired together – I will not say you shall see a masque; but if you do, then it was not for nothing that my nose fell a-bleeding on Black Monday last, at six a clock i'the morning, falling out that year on Ash Wednesday was four year in th'afternoon.

SHYLOCK What, are there masques? Hear you me, Jessica,
Lock up my doors, and when you hear the drum
And the vile squealing of the wry-necked fife,
Clamber not you up to the casements then
Nor thrust your head into the public street
To gaze on Christian fools with varnished faces;
But stop my house's ears – I mean my casements –
Let not the sound of shallow foppery enter
My sober house. By Jacob's staff I swear
I have no mind of feasting forth tonight:
But I will go. Go you before me, sirrah;
Say I will come.

LANCELOT I will go before, sir.
[*Aside to Jessica*] Mistress, look out at window for all this:
There will come a Christian by
Will be worth a Jewès eye [*Exit*]

SHYLOCK What says that fool of Hagar's offspring, ha?

39 SD] *Collier*[3] *subst.; not in* Q1–2, F 41 Jewès] *Keightley;* Jewes Q1–2, F; Jew's F4; Jewess' *Pope* 41 SD] *Rowe subst.; not in* Q1–2, F

24 nose fell a-bleeding There are many Elizabethan allusions to this ill omen. 'Lancelot's prognostications mock Shylock's dream about the moneybags' (NS).

24 Black Monday A traditional name for Easter Monday. All explanations of it are folklorist and unreliable.

29 wry-necked 'Fife' (like 'drum') could be used of the player as well as the instrument, so the image may simply be of a musician twisting his neck to play the fife, which is traverse-blown. Boswell quotes Barnaby Riche, *Irish Hubbub* (1619 edn), p. 57: 'A fife is a wry-necked musician, for he always looks away from his instrument.' Robert McDonnell, however, thinks that the sound of the fife is being likened to the high-pitched call of the bird called a wry-neck. If 'wry-necked' could thus mean 'untuneful' there would be some point in Riche's words, which are supposed to be a 'witty sentence' (*SQ* 15 (1964), 115–17).

32 with...faces wearing painted masks.

35 By Jacob's staff Though not a Jewish expression, this recalls Shylock's admiration for Jacob's 'thrift'. Jacob set out for Padan-arum with only a staff in his hand (Gen. 32.10), and returned a rich man. Brown quotes G. Babington's 1592 Commentary: 'A notable meditation morning and evening for rich merchants'.

41 Jewès eye The old inflected genitive is kept in this phrase, which was proverbial for something of high value. Gabriel Harvey has 'dear as a Jewes eye' (*Works*, ed. A. B. Grosart, 1884–5, II, 146). The source is more likely to be the biblical 'an eye for an eye' than stories of medieval atrocities against Jews.

42 Hagar's offspring This has a triple relevance. The Egyptian bondwoman Hagar fled Abraham's house complaining of harsh treatment (Gen. 16); Ishmael, her son by Abraham, was a mocker (Gen. 21.9), as Lancelot is at 19–20 and 22–6; consequently, Hagar and Ishmael became outcasts, as Shylock considers all Gentiles to be.

JESSICA His words were 'Farewell, mistress', nothing else.
SHYLOCK The patch is kind enough, but a huge feeder,
Snail-slow in profit, and he sleeps by day
More than the wildcat. Drones hive not with me,
Therefore I part with him, and part with him
To one that I would have him help to waste
His borrowed purse. Well, Jessica, go in;
Perhaps I will return immediately.
Do as I bid you, shut doors after you.
Fast bind, fast find:
A proverb never stale in thrifty mind. *Exit*
JESSICA Farewell, and if my fortune be not crossed,
I have a father, you a daughter, lost. *Exit*

[2.6] *Enter the masquers*, GRATIANO *and* SALARINO

GRATIANO This is the penthouse under which Lorenzo
Desired us to make stand.
SALARINO His hour is almost past.
GRATIANO And it is marvel he outdwells his hour,
For lovers ever run before the clock.
SALARINO O, ten times faster Venus' pigeons fly
To seal love's bonds new made than they are wont
To keep obligèd faith unforfeited!

52] *As in* Q2; *as part of* 51, Q1, F Act 2, Scene 6 2.6] *Capell subst.; not in* Q1–2, F 2 stand] Q1–2; a stand F

44 patch Probably a contemptuous term for something as insignificant as a scrap of cloth (*OED* sv *sb* 1), but with overtones of *sb* 2, 'fool'. Bottom speaks of a 'patched fool' (*MND* 4.1.209), and Caliban calls Trinculo a patch (*Temp.* 3.2.63).

46 wildcat A nocturnal animal which rests by day.

49 go in Shylock is hesitating anxiously at the door that we have come to identify during 2.2. and 2.3 as the entrance to his house. The door key becomes an important stage property.

52 fast...find A very common proverb from the fifteenth century onwards (Tilley B352).

Act 2, Scene 6

2.6 See 2.3 n. above.

0 SD *masquers* Fantastic costumes and vizards (Shylock's 'varnished faces'), with a torch or two, help build up the atmosphere of Carnival abandon and recklessness.

0 SD SALARINO Rowe and other editors substitute Solanio, on the assumption that Salarino, if he figured in this scene, could not witness the parting of Bassanio and Antonio which he describes in 2.8.37–50. But see 59 n. below.

1 penthouse A projecting upper storey. Gratiano may indicate either the slightly projecting gallery above the stage doors, or the whole stage roof, which could have supported the upper storey of the tiring-house.

5 lovers...clock A quasi-proverbial truism (Tilley L568). Sir Eglamour makes a similar comment in *TGV* 5.1.4–5.

6 Venus' pigeons i.e. the doves drawing Venus's chariot (rather than the lovers themselves). At the end of *Venus and Adonis* Venus is carried away by her 'silver doves'.

8 obligèd plighted.

GRATIANO That ever holds: who riseth from a feast
With that keen appetite that he sits down?
Where is the horse that doth untread again
His tedious measures with the unbated fire
That he did pace them first? All things that are
Are with more spirit chasèd than enjoyed.
How like a younger or a prodigal
The scarfèd bark puts from her native bay,
Hugged and embracèd by the strumpet wind!
How like the prodigal doth she return
With overweathered ribs and ragged sails,
Lean, rent, and beggared by the strumpet wind!

Enter LORENZO

SALARINO Here comes Lorenzo; more of this hereafter.
LORENZO Sweet friends, your patience for my long abode.
Not I but my affairs have made you wait.
When you shall please to play the thieves for wives,
I'll watch as long for you then. Approach –
Here dwells my father Jew. Ho! Who's within?

[*Enter*] JESSICA *above*[, *in boy's clothes*]

JESSICA Who are you? Tell me, for more certainty,
Albeit I'll swear that I do know your tongue.
LORENZO Lorenzo, and thy love.
JESSICA Lorenzo certain, and my love indeed,
For who love I so much? And now who knows
But you, Lorenzo, whether I am yours?
LORENZO Heaven and thy thoughts are witness that thou art.
JESSICA Here, catch this casket, it is worth the pains.
I am glad 'tis night, you do not look on me,

19 overweathered] Q1–2; over-wither'd F 26 Ho] Q2; Howe Q1; Hoa F 26 SD *Enter*] *Capell; not in* Q1–2, F
26 SD *in boy's clothes*] *Rowe; not in* Q1–2, F

9 ever holds is always true.
11 untread retrace.
12 measures paces (in a riding-school display of *manège*).
15 younger i.e. younger son, as the Prodigal was. On 15–21 see pp. 30–1 above.
16 scarfèd beflagged, dressed overall.
19 overweathered ribs i.e. timbers damaged by heavy seas.
17, 20 strumpet wind The repetition, a rhetorical figure called epistrophe, throws into relief the contrast of 'hugged and embracèd' with 'lean, rent, and beggared'.
26 father i.e. future father-in-law; but probably used sarcastically by Lorenzo. See p. 8 above, for the relationship of this scene to 2.1 of *The Jew of Malta*.

For I am much ashamed of my exchange.
But love is blind, and lovers cannot see
The pretty follies that themselves commit;
For if they could, Cupid himself would blush
To see me thus transformèd to a boy.

LORENZO Descend, for you must be my torchbearer.

JESSICA What, must I hold a candle to my shames?
They in themselves, good sooth, are too too light.
Why, 'tis an office of discovery, love,
And I should be obscured.

LORENZO So are you, sweet,
Even in the lovely garnish of a boy.
But come at once,
For the close night doth play the runaway,
And we are stayed for at Bassanio's feast.

JESSICA I will make fast the doors, and gild myself
With some moe ducats, and be with you straight.
[*Exit Jessica above*]

GRATIANO Now by my hood, a gentle and no Jew!

LORENZO Beshrew me but I love her heartily.
For she is wise, if I can judge of her,
And fair she is, if that mine eyes be true,
And true she is, as she hath proved herself:
And therefore like herself, wise, fair, and true,
Shall she be placèd in my constant soul.

46–8] *As Pope;* Even...once, / For...runaway Q1, F; Even...boy / But...night / Doth...run-away Q2 **51** SD] *Capell subst.; not in* Q1–2, F **52** gentle] Q1, F; Gentile Q2

36 ashamed...exchange embarrassed by my male disguise (with a possible hint of misgiving about the morality of her robbery and elopement).

43 light apparent (with a pun on the sense 'immodest').

44 'tis an...discovery i.e. the torchbearer's function is to show up what is happening.

46 lovely All editors accept 'lovely' as an epithet transferred from Jessica herself. But Q1's 'louely' is a possible, if old-fashioned, spelling for 'lowly'; or the compositor could have misread 'lowly' as 'louely' because of the preceding love talk.

46 garnish From the context this must mean 'costume', but *OED* gives no other instance.

48 close secretive.

48 doth...runaway is speeding by.

50 gild myself provide myself (with more gold).

51 moe Modernised to 'more' in F, but originally a distinct word, meaning 'more in number', as at 1.1.108.

52 by my hood An emphatic phrase, with no specific meaning.

52 gentle well-bred girl. As at 1.3.170, there is a pun on 'Gentile'.

53–8 Beshrew...soul These lines, which give Jessica time to come down to stage level, use a conventional figure of words which can be found also in the sestet of Sonnet 105 ('Fair, kind, and true, is all my argument') and in two poems by Nicolas Breton (*Works in Verse and Prose*, ed. A. B. Grosart, 1879, I, *Melancholic Humours*, 15).

Enter JESSICA

What, art thou come? On, gentleman, away!
Our masquing mates by this time for us stay.
Exit [*with Jessica*]

Enter ANTONIO

ANTONIO Who's there?
GRATIANO Signor Antonio?
ANTONIO Fie, fie, Gratiano, where are all the rest?
'Tis nine a clock, our friends all stay for you.
No masque tonight: the wind is come about,
Bassanio presently will go aboard.
I have sent twenty out to seek for you.
GRATIANO I am glad on't; I desire no more delight
Than to be under sail and gone tonight.
Exeunt

[2.7] *Enter* PORTIA *with* [*the Prince of*] MOROCCO *and both their trains*

PORTIA Go, draw aside the curtains and discover
The several caskets to this noble prince.
Now make your choice.
MOROCCO This first of gold, who this inscription bears,
'Who chooseth me, shall gain what many men desire.'

59 gentleman] Q1; gentlemen Q2, F 60 SD *with Jessica*] *Hanmer; not in* Q1–2, F Act 2, Scene 7 2.7] *Capell subst.; not in* Q1–2, F; *Scene III* / *Rowe* 0 SD *Enter*] Q1–2, F; *Flourish. Enter* / *Capell* 0 SD *the Prince of*] *Capell; not in* Q1–2, F 4 This] Q1, The Q2, F 5 many] Q1–2; *not in* F

59 gentleman Jessica makes a striking entry in her page's costume, causing Lorenzo laughingly to address her as 'Gentleman', as he hands her the torch and they go out together. Salarino stays with Gratiano and so witnesses the parting of Antonio and Bassanio. In changing 'gentleman' to 'gentlemen', Q2 and F cause Lorenzo to treat Jessica in a very off-hand way.

61–9 On the possibility that these lines mark a change of plan, See Textual Analysis, pp. 183–4 below. It is surprising that Antonio should act as Bassanio's messenger, but perhaps his appearance is needed here to make clear that he knows nothing whatever about the elopement.

Act 2, Scene 7

0 SD Editors have followed Capell in inserting here the 'Flo[urish of] Cornets' which is obviously misplaced at the start of 2.8. But a flourish announced an arrival, and Morocco is already in residence.

1–2 On the dramatic impact of these lines, see p. 31 above.

2 several different, various.

4 who Possibly used for 'which' to avoid a crowding of consonants.

The second silver, which this promise carries,
'Who chooseth me, shall get as much as he deserves.'
This third dull lead, with warning all as blunt,
'Who chooseth me, must give and hazard all he hath.'
How shall I know if I do choose the right?

PORTIA The one of them contains my picture, prince.
If you choose that, then I am yours withal.

MOROCCO Some god direct my judgement! Let me see:
I will survey th'inscriptions back again.
What says this leaden casket?
'Who chooseth me, must give and hazard all he hath.'
Must give – for what? For lead? Hazard for lead!
This casket threatens: men that hazard all
Do it in hope of fair advantages.
A golden mind stoops not to shows of dross;
I'll then nor give nor hazard aught for lead.
What says the silver with her virgin hue?
'Who chooseth me, shall get as much as he deserves.'
As much as he deserves – pause there, Morocco,
And weigh thy value with an even hand.
If thou be'st rated by thy estimation
Thou dost deserve enough; and yet enough
May not extend so far as to the lady;
And yet to be afeared of my deserving
Were but a weak disabling of myself.
As much as I deserve: why, that's the lady.
I do in birth deserve her, and in fortunes,
In graces, and in qualities of breeding:
But more than these, in love I do deserve.
What if I strayed no farther, but chose here?
Let's see once more this saying graved in gold:
'Who chooseth me, shall gain what many men desire.'
Why, that's the lady; all the world desires her.

18 threatens: men] *Rowe;* threatens men Q1–2, F 34 deserve] Q1–2, F; deserve her *Collier*[2], *conj. Capell*

8 all as blunt as plain and coarse as the metal it is made from (with a pun on the secondary meaning 'dull', 'unable to cut').

25 with an even hand impartially.

26 estimation 'reputation' rather than 'valuation'.

30 disabling belittling.

34 deserve There is no need to add 'her'. This intransitive form of the verb, meaning 'am worthy', accords with Morocco's liking for the language of courtly love.

From the four corners of the earth they come
To kiss this shrine, this mortal breathing saint.
The Hyrcanian deserts and the vasty wilds
Of wide Arabia are as throughfares now
For princes to come view fair Portia.
The watery kingdom, whose ambitious head
Spits in the face of heaven, is no bar
To stop the foreign spirits, but they come
As o'er a brook to see fair Portia.
One of these three contains her heavenly picture.
Is't like that lead contains her? 'Twere damnation
To think so base a thought; it were too gross
To rib her cerecloth in the òbscure grave.
Or shall I think in silver she's immured,
Being ten times undervalued to tried gold?
O sinful thought! Never so rich a gem
Was set in worse than gold. They have in England
A coin that bears the figure of an angel
Stampèd in gold; but that's insculped upon:
But here an angel in a golden bed
Lies all within. Deliver me the key:
Here do I choose, and thrive I as I may.

PORTIA There take it, prince, and if my form lie there,
Then I am yours.

[*Morocco unlocks the gold casket*]

MOROCCO O hell! What have we here?

57 Stampèd] *Rowe*[2]; Stampt Q1–2, F 62 SD] *Rowe subst.; not in* Q1–2, F 62–4] *As Capell;* O hell...death, / within...scroule, / Ile...writing Q1–2, F

40 **mortal breathing** i.e. living. Morocco elegantly if pretentiously corrects his own use of 'shrine', since shrines contained only the bones of dead saints.

41 **Hyrcanian deserts** The classical name for Ustan Duwum, south of the Caspian Sea.

43, 47 **fair Portia** This use of the rhetorical figure of epistrophe contributes to the rhapsodic tone of 39–47.

44 **watery kingdom** Neptune's realm of the sea, rhetorically contrasted with the land masses of Hyrcania and Arabia. Not a reference to Spain.

46 **spirits** i.e. men of courage (*OED* sv *sb* 13) with, as NS notes, a play on the meaning 'supernatural beings' (*OED sb* 3), as these were believed to be unable to cross water.

50 **it were** i.e. lead would be.

51 **rib** close in. In *Cym.* 3.1.19–20 England is said to be 'ribb'd and pal'd in' with rocks and water.

51 **cerecloth** The waxed cloth in which a corpse was wrapped before being enclosed in lead.

51 **òbscure** dark.

53 **ten...gold** The relative value of silver in 1600 (Clarendon).

53 **tried** assayed, purified.

56 **angel** So called because it depicted the archangel Michael.

57 **insculped upon** engraved. The word occurs nowhere else in Shakespeare so its use here has been traced to a possible source of the casket story. See p. 4 above.

A carrion death, within whose empty eye
There is a written scroll. I'll read the writing.
'All that glisters is not gold;
Often have you heard that told.
Many a man his life hath sold
But my outside to behold.
Gilded tombs do worms infold.
Had you been as wise as bold,
Young in limbs, in judgement old,
Your answer had not been inscrolled.
Fare you well, your suit is cold.'
Cold indeed, and labour lost;
Then farewell heat, and welcome frost.
Portia, adieu; I have too grieved a heart
To take a tedious leave: thus losers part.
Exit [*Morocco with his train*]

PORTIA A gentle riddance! Draw the curtains, go.
Let all of his complexion choose me so.
Exeunt. [*A flourish of cornets*]

[2.8] *Enter* SALARINO *and* SOLANIO

SALARINO Why, man, I saw Bassanio under sail,
With him is Gratiano gone along;
And in their ship I am sure Lorenzo is not.

69 tombs] *Johnson, conj. Capell;* timber Q1–2, F 74 Cold] *Capell; Mor.* Cold Q1–2, F 77 SD] *Dyce; Exit* Q1–2, F 79 SD *A flourish of cornets*] F *subst. after 2.8.0* SD*; after 2.7.77, Dyce subst.; not in* Q1–2 Act 2, Scene 8 2.8] *Capell subst.; not in* Q1–2, F*; Scene IV / Rowe* 0 SD] Q1, Q2 *subst.; Flo.Cornets / follows names,* F

63 death i.e. death's head, skull: an ironic comment on Morocco's hope to find a portrayal of his 'mortal breathing saint'.

65 All...gold This proverb is more familiar today with the synonymous 'glitters' in place of 'glisters' (Tilley A146).

69 tombs The improved metre and grammar, relevance to the context, and the possible echo of the 'whited tombs' of Matt. 23.27 (glossed 'painted' in GB), all support Johnson's emendation. But it is still possible that with 'timber' Shakespeare intended an image of woodwork covered with gold leaf or gold paint but riddled within by beetle larvae.

75 farewell...frost Morocco deliberately inverts the saying 'farewell frost'. This had the meaning 'good riddance', so we are prepared for Portia's words at 78.

79 SD *A flourish of cornets* I have moved this from the opening of the next scene, where it must be misplaced. Here it goes well with Portia's triumphant relief and is an ironic accompaniment to Morocco's departure.

Act 2, Scene 8

1–11 Why...ship Like Antonio's appearance at the end of 2.6, this makes clear to the audience that Antonio and Bassanio can in no way be held responsible for Jessica's abduction.

SOLANIO The villain Jew with outcries raised the Duke,
Who went with him to search Bassanio's ship.
SALARINO He came too late, the ship was under sail.
But there the Duke was given to understand
That in a gondola were seen together
Lorenzo and his amorous Jessica.
Besides, Antonio certified the Duke
They were not with Bassanio in his ship.
SOLANIO I never heard a passion so confused,
So strange, outrageous, and so variable,
As the dog Jew did utter in the streets:
'My daughter! O my ducats! O my daughter!
Fled with a Christian! O my Christian ducats!
Justice! The law! My ducats and my daughter!
A sealèd bag, two sealèd bags of ducats,
Of double ducats, stolen from me by my daughter!
And jewels – two stones, two rich and precious stones,
Stolen by my daughter! Justice! Find the girl!
She hath the stones upon her and the ducats!'
SALARINO Why, all the boys in Venice follow him,
Crying his stones, his daughter, and his ducats.
SOLANIO Let good Antonio look he keep his day,
Or he shall pay for this.
SALARINO Marry, well remembered:
I reasoned with a Frenchman yesterday
Who told me, in the Narrow Seas that part
The French and English, there miscarrièd
A vessel of our country richly fraught.

8 gondola] *Theobald;* Gondylo Q1–2, F; Gondalo *Rowe*

4 raised roused.

8 gondola The capital letter and the uncertain spelling of Q1–2 and F suggest that the word was unfamiliar to the compositors.

12–22 See p. 33 above for a discussion of the effect of this mockery.

12 passion passionate outburst.

15 daughter...ducats In Masuccio's story about the elopement of a miser's daughter, which Shakespeare may have read (see p. 11 above), the miser laments both his daughter and his money: 'for the last-named loss he felt no less grief than for the first' (Bullough, I, 504).

16 Christian ducats Either ducats gained from Christians or ducats now in Christian hands.

19 double ducats An accurate term, as we learn from Coryate's description of Venetian money (*Coryats Crudities* (1611), p. 285).

23–4 The jeers are bawdy: 'stones' can mean 'testicles' and coins often imply semen.

27 well remembered that reminds me. The broken line marks a change of mood.

28 reasoned spoke.

29 Narrow Seas 'i.e. the English Channel, the Straits of Dover, and the southern reaches of the North Sea' (Brown).

31 fraught laden.

I thought upon Antonio when he told me,
And wished in silence that it were not his.

SOLANIO You were best to tell Antonio what you hear.
Yet do not suddenly, for it may grieve him.

SALARINO A kinder gentleman treads not the earth.
I saw Bassanio and Antonio part:
Bassanio told him he would make some speed
Of his return: he answered, 'Do not so.
Slubber not business for my sake, Bassanio,
But stay the very riping of the time;
And for the Jew's bond which he hath of me,
Let it not enter in your mind of love.
Be merry, and employ your chiefest thoughts
To courtship, and such fair ostents of love
As shall conveniently become you there.'
And even there, his eye being big with tears,
Turning his face, he put his hand behind him,
And with affection wondrous sensible
He wrung Bassanio's hand, and so they parted.

SOLANIO I think he only loves the world for him.
I pray thee let us go and find him out
And quicken his embracèd heaviness
With some delight or other.

SALARINO Do we so.

Exeunt

40 Slubber] Q2, F; slumber Q1

40 Slubber Q2 and F substitute this word, which means 'to scamp or perform in a slovenly way', for Q1's 'Slumber', a probable misreading by the compositor of Shakespeare's manuscript.

43 mind of love love-schemes (NS).

45 ostents of love ways of showing your love. See 2.2.167 n.

46 conveniently Not the weak modern sense, but 'appropriately'. See 3.4.56 n.

49 affection...sensible amazingly strong emotion.

51 he...him i.e. Bassanio is all he lives for.

53 embracèd Rann glosses 'which he indulges too far', thus picking up the suggestion that Antonio hugs his grief. Compare Portia's use of 'rash-embraced despair', 3.2.109.

[2.9] *Enter* NERISSA *and a Servitor*

NERISSA Quick, quick, I pray thee, draw the curtain straight.
The Prince of Arragon hath tane his oath,
And comes to his election presently.

[*A flourish of cornets.*] *Enter* [*the Prince of*] ARRAGON, *his train, and* PORTIA

PORTIA Behold, there stand the caskets, noble prince.
If you choose that wherein I am contained,
Straight shall our nuptial rites be solemnised;
But if you fail, without more speech, my lord,
You must be gone from hence immediately.
ARRAGON I am enjoined by oath to observe three things:
First, never to unfold to anyone
Which casket 'twas I chose; next, if I fail
Of the right casket, never in my life
To woo a maid in way of marriage; lastly,
If I do fail in fortune of my choice,
Immediately to leave you and be gone.
PORTIA To these injunctions everyone doth swear
That comes to hazard for my worthless self.
ARRAGON And so have I addressed me. Fortune now
To my heart's hope! Gold, silver, and base lead.
'Who chooseth me, must give and hazard all he hath.'
You shall look fairer ere I give or hazard.
What says the golden chest? Ha, let me see:
'Who chooseth me, shall gain what many men desire.'
What many men desire: that 'many' may be meant
By the fool multitude that choose by show,
Not learning more than the fond eye doth teach,
Which pries not to th'interior, but like the martlet

Act 2, Scene 9 2.9] *Capell subst.; not in* Q1–2, F; *Scene V / Rowe* 3 SD *A flourish of cornets*] *As Capell subst.; not in* Q1–2; *Flor.Cornets / follows names,* F 3 SD *the Prince of*] *Capell; not in* Q1–2, F 13–14] *As Capell;* ...marriage: / Lastly,...Q1–2, F; Lastly *as separate line, Cam.*

Act 2, Scene 9

0 SD ***Servitor*** Probably identical with the Servingman of 1.2.

1 draw pull back.

1 straight immediately (as in 6).

3 to his election to make his choice.

18 addressed me prepared myself (i.e. by swearing to the three conditions).

18 Fortune Good luck.

24–5 meant By A common Elizabethan construction equivalent to our 'meant for', which replaces it in F4.

26 fond foolish.

27 martlet Another name for the swift, but probably Shakespeare meant the house martin. A martin is also the slang term for a dupe, and

Builds in the weather on the outward wall,
Even in the force and road of casualty.
I will not choose what many men desire,
Because I will not jump with common spirits,
And rank me with the barbarous multitudes.
Why then, to thee, thou silver treasure house:
Tell me once more what title thou dost bear.
'Who chooseth me, shall get as much as he deserves.'
And well said too, for who shall go about
To cozen Fortune and be honourable
Without the stamp of merit? Let none presume
To wear an undeservèd dignity.
O, that estates, degrees, and offices
Were not derived corruptly, and that clear honour
Were purchased by the merit of the wearer!
How many then should cover that stand bare!
How many be commanded that command!
How much low peasantry would then be gleaned
From the true seed of honour, and how much honour
Picked from the chaff and ruin of the times
To be new varnished! Well, but to my choice.
'Who chooseth me, shall get as much as he deserves.'
I will assume desert. Give me a key for this,
And instantly unlock my fortunes here.

[*Arragon unlocks the silver casket*]

PORTIA Too long a pause for that which you find there.

47 chaff] Q2, F; chaft Q1 51 SD] *As Delius*[3] *subst.; not in* Q1–2, F; *before 53, Rowe*

martlets are referred to again in *Mac.* 1.6.4 in a scene that makes much of deceptively fair appearances. See Caroline Spurgeon, *Shakespeare's Imagery*, 1935, pp. 187–90.

28 in the weather exposed to the weather.

29 force...casualty i.e. in the power and the path of destruction. Possibly a translation of the Latin phrase *in vi et via* (George Allen, quoted by Furness).

31 jump make one, ally myself.

36–7 go about To cozen try to cheat.

38 Without...merit Without the entitlement of his desert. A document, such as letters patent conferring a title, is authenticated when it is stamped.

40 estates, degrees, and offices These terms move from general to particular forms of distinction: estates of the realm (e.g. nobility), ranks within those estates (e.g. earls), and official posts (e.g. the Chancellorship).

43 cover keep their hats on (instead of doffing them in reverence to holders of spurious rank).

45 gleaned i.e. picked out and rejected in the process of sorting seed corn.

46 true seed the image suggests progeny and succession, as well as being an echo of the parable of the good seed (Matt. 13.25).

48 varnished This blends the meanings 'polished', as shiny grains are when cleared of chaff, and 'newly painted', as a coat-of-arms might be.

50 assume The ceremonial sense of putting on insignia (NS) reverberates later in the image of a fool 'silvered o'er' (68).

51 unlock Either imperative, because the proud prince expects a menial to open the casket for him, or optative: 'let my destiny be revealed'.

ARRAGON What's here? The portrait of a blinking idiot
Presenting me a schedule! I will read it.
How much unlike art thou to Portia!
How much unlike my hopes and my deservings.
'Who chooseth me, shall have as much as he deserves.'
Did I deserve no more than a fool's head?
Is that my prize? Are my deserts no better?

PORTIA To offend and judge are distinct offices,
And of opposèd natures.

ARRAGON What is here?

[*He reads*]

'The fire seven times tried this;
Seven times tried that judgement is
That did never choose amiss.
Some there be that shadows kiss;
Such have but a shadow's bliss.
There be fools alive iwis
Silvered o'er, and so was this.
Take what wife you will to bed,
I will ever be your head.
So be gone, you are sped.'
Still more fool I shall appear
By the time I linger here.
With one fool's head I came to woo,
But I go away with two.
Sweet, adieu; I'll keep my oath,
Patiently to bear my wroth.

[*Exit Arragon with his train*]

61 SD] Q2; *not in* Q1, F 63 judgement] Q2; judement Q1, F 72] *As* Q2; *preceded by* SH *Arrag.* Q1, F 77 wroth] Q3; wroath Q1–2, F; wrath *Theobald*; roth *Dyce*; ruth *Sisson* 77 SD] *Capell subst.*; *not in* Q1–2, F

54 schedule written scroll (the original meaning of the word, *OED* sv *sb* 1).

60–1 To...natures i.e. it is not for me to say. Portia has been the indirect cause of offence to Arragon, so it would be improper for her to judge his case, as 'no man ought to be judge in his own cause' (Tilley M341). Portia's reply is more likely to be courteous than censorious, as it would be if she meant Arragon was the offender; but she has already shown some skill in double entendres (see 2.1.20 n.).

62 this i.e. the silver of which the casket is made.

66 shadows illusions. Arragon is self-deceived.

67 iwis assuredly.

68 Silvered o'er In allusion to the silver ornamentation of court officials' dress, rather than to grey hair.

70 I...head You will always be a fool.

71 sped An ambiguous slang term, like the modern 'You've had it.' At the end of *Shr.* Petruchio says to the less fortunate husbands: 'We three are married, but you two are sped' (5.2.185).

76–8 oath...wroth...moth Kökeritz argues that the short vowel of 'moth' was a mere eye-rhyme with 'oath' and 'wroth' (*Shakespeare's Pronunciation*, 1953, p. 229). An eye-rhyme, however, would be pointless in the theatre.

77 wroth This is usually taken as a spelling for 'ruth', meaning 'grief'. It could equally well be a spelling of 'wrath'; to bear wrath would be to contain it.

PORTIA Thus hath the candle singed the moth.
O, these deliberate fools! When they do choose
They have the wisdom by their wit to lose.
NERISSA The ancient saying is no heresy:
'Hanging and wiving goes by destiny.'
PORTIA Come draw the curtain, Nerissa.

Enter a MESSENGER

MESSENGER Where is my lady?
PORTIA Here. What would my lord?
MESSENGER Madam, there is alighted at your gate
A young Venetian, one that comes before
To signify th'approaching of his lord,
From whom he bringeth sensible regreets:
To wit, besides commends and courteous breath,
Gifts of rich value. Yet I have not seen
So likely an ambassador of love.
A day in April never came so sweet
To show how costly summer was at hand
As this forespurrer comes before his lord.
PORTIA No more I pray thee, I am half afeared
Thou wilt say anon he is some kin to thee,
Thou spend'st such highday wit in praising him.
Come, come, Nerissa, for I long to see
Quick Cupid's post that comes so mannerly.
NERISSA Bassanio, Lord Love, if thy will it be!

Exeunt

78 moth] Q2; moath Q1, F 100 Bassanio, Lord Love,] *Rowe subst.*; Bassanio Lord, love Q1–2, F

78 candle...moth A very common proverb (Tilley F394).

79 deliberate deliberating, reasoning. Arragon's major premiss, 'Only the meritorious deserve honour', was sound, but his minor premiss, 'I am meritorious', was unsound, so his conclusion, 'Therefore I deserve Portia', did not follow.

82 Hanging...destiny Another proverb. 'Wedding and hanging go by destiny' (Tilley W232) crops up several times in extant sixteenth-century writings.

84 my lord This kind of riposte, used by several characters in Elizabethan drama, was a verbal trick of the time. Perhaps we are to note that Portia is still thinking of a husband ('lord'), though relieved not to have one as obsessed with rank and title as Arragon was.

86 young Venetian Presumably Gratiano is making himself of service.

88 sensible regreets tangible greetings, i.e. gifts.

89 breath words.

91 likely promising (or handsome, or both).

93 costly lavish.

97 highday wit i.e. language in its Sunday best, such as Fenton uses when he 'speaks holiday' (*Wiv.* 3.2.68).

99 post messenger.

99 mannerly in such a becoming way.

100 Bassanio...be Rowe's punctuation, which is substantively followed here, improves upon that of Q1–2 and F: 'Bassanio Lord, love if thy will it be'.

3.[1] *Enter* SOLANIO *and* SALARINO

SOLANIO Now, what news on the Rialto?

SALARINO Why, yet it lives there unchecked that Antonio hath a ship of rich lading wrecked on the Narrow Seas; the Goodwins I think they call the place – a very dangerous flat, and fatal, where the carcases of many a tall ship lie buried, as they say, if my gossip Report be an honest woman of her word.

SOLANIO I would she were as lying a gossip in that as ever knapped ginger or made her neighbours believe she wept for the death of a third husband. But it is true, without any slips of prolixity, or crossing the plain highway of talk, that the good Antonio, the honest Antonio – O that I had a title good enough to keep his name company! –

SALARINO Come, the full stop.

SOLANIO Ha, what sayest thou? Why, the end is, he hath lost a ship.

SALARINO I would it might prove the end of his losses.

SOLANIO Let me say 'amen' betimes, lest the devil cross my prayer, for here he comes in the likeness of a Jew.

Enter SHYLOCK

How now, Shylock, what news among the merchants?

Act 3, Scene 1 3.1] *Rowe subst.; not in* Q1–2; *Actus Tertius.* F 0 SD *Enter*] Q2, F; *not in* Q1 3 wrecked] *Theobald*[2]; wrackt Q1–2, F 5 gossip] Q1; gossips Q2, F 6 Report] Q3; report Q1–2, F 18 SD] *As in* Q2; *after 19,* Q1, F

Act 3, Scene 1

2 **lives** persists.

2 **unchecked** uncontradicted (from 'check' in the sense of 'stop', not in the modern sense of 'verify').

3 **Narrow Seas** See 2.8.29 n.

3–5 **the Goodwins...buried** The Goodwin Sands off the Kent coast reached six miles out into the Channel and were a byword for danger. Richard Larn, *Goodwin Sands Shipwrecks*, 1977, records the loss there of several rich cargoes in 1592–3. The name therefore has great dramatic effect, though in fact many Venetian ships did not have to brave the Sands as their ports of call were Southampton and Ghent.

5 **tall** fine, gallant.

5 **gossip Report** 'Dame Rumour' (Pooler). 'Gossip' originally meant a fellow godparent, and by extension an old friend.

7 **knapped** munched.

8 **ginger** Associated with old women in *MM* 4.3.7–8: 'ginger was not much in request, for the old women were all dead'.

9 **slips of prolixity** lapses into wordiness.

10 **crossing...talk** deviating from a straightforward account; 'beating about the bush'.

13 **Come...stop** Finish your sentence; or, since 'full stop' was a term of horsemanship, 'rein up'.

14 **what sayest thou?** what do you mean?

17 **cross** spoil, frustrate; possibly with a pun on the meaning 'to make the sign of the cross at the end of a prayer'.

18 SD **SHYLOCK** He is given his name throughout this scene, which may reflect Shakespeare's involvement in his feelings (compare 3.3). The discrepancy between Shylock's rage and distress here and the mocking account of them at 2.8.12–22

SHYLOCK You knew, none so well, none so well as you, of my daughter's flight.

SALARINO That's certain; I for my part knew the tailor that made the wings she flew withal.

SOLANIO And Shylock for his own part knew the bird was fledged, and then it is the complexion of them all to leave the dam.

SHYLOCK She is damned for it.

SALARINO That's certain – if the devil may be her judge.

SHYLOCK My own flesh and blood to rebel!

SOLANIO Out upon it, old carrion! Rebels it at these years?

SHYLOCK I say my daughter is my flesh and my blood.

SALARINO There is more difference between thy flesh and hers than between jet and ivory; more between your bloods than there is between red wine and Rhenish. But tell us, do you hear whether Antonio have had any loss at sea or no?

SHYLOCK There I have another bad match: a bankrupt, a prodigal, who dare scarce show his head on the Rialto, a beggar that was used to come so smug upon the mart. Let him look to his bond. He was wont to call me usurer; let him look to his bond. He was wont to lend money for a Christian courtesy; let him look to his bond.

SALARINO Why, I am sure if he forfeit thou wilt not take his flesh. What's that good for?

SHYLOCK To bait fish withal; if it will feed nothing else, it will feed my revenge. He hath disgraced me, and hindered me half a million,

24 fledged] Q2, F; flidge Q1 30 my blood] Q1; blood Q2, F 39 courtesy] Q2, F; cursie Q1

is theatrically overwhelming. Lichtenberg describes Macklin's entry in 1775: 'he appears hatless, with hair all flying, some of it standing up straight, a hand's breadth high, just as if it had been lifted up by a breeze from the gallows. Both hands are doubled up, and his gestures are quick and convulsive' (quoted by Furness, pp. 374–5).

23 **wings** i.e. Jessica's disguise, with a play on 'flight'.

24 **fledged** Q2 and F modernise the archaic adjective 'flidge' of Q1, which means 'fit to fly'.

25 **complexion** nature, disposition.

25 **dam** mother.

27 **if...judge** i.e. only the devil (perhaps identified with Shylock, as at 17) would damn her for such a good deed.

29 **carrion** walking corpse. Brutus speaks of 'Old feeble carrions', *JC* 2.1.130.

29 **Rebels...years?** Solanio wilfully pretends Shylock is speaking literally, of an erection.

33 **red...Rhenish** A contrast between crudeness and refinement, like that between cheap table wine and a fine hock. This fits with the mention of Rhenish as a temptation at 1.2.79, and does away with the reversal of the antithesis needed for D. A. Boughner's explanation that Jessica's rich blood is as red wine to the thin stuff in Shylock's veins ('Red wine and Rennish', *SAB* 14 (1939), 46–50). But see 49–50 n. below.

35 **prodigal** Readers who protest that Bassanio, not Antonio, is a prodigal are answered by Johnson: 'there could be, in Shylock's opinion, no prodigality more culpable than such liberality as that by which a man exposes himself to ruin for his friend'. There may also be contempt for the risks run by Antonio, in contrast to Shylock's safer trade of money-lending; compare 1.3.18 and n.

37 **mart** the Exchange.

39 **for...courtesy** i.e. out of Christian charity, rather than the meaning sometimes suggested, 'in return for a mere bow; for a song'.

42 **bait** use as a bait for, lure; so in *Err.* 2.1.94: 'Do their gay vestments his affections bait?'

43 **disgraced** 'done me disfavour' (Merchant).

43 **hindered** prevented me making.

laughed at my losses, mocked at my gains, scorned my nation, thwarted my bargains, cooled my friends, heated mine enemies – and what's his reason? I am a Jew. Hath not a Jew eyes? Hath not a Jew hands, organs, dimensions, senses, affections, passions? Fed with the same food, hurt with the same weapons, subject to the same diseases, healed by the same means, warmed and cooled by the same winter and summer as a Christian is? If you prick us, do we not bleed? If you tickle us, do we not laugh? If you poison us, do we not die? And if you wrong us, shall we not revenge? If we are like you in the rest, we will resemble you in that. If a Jew wrong a Christian, what is his humility? Revenge. If a Christian wrong a Jew, what should his sufferance be by Christian example? Why, revenge! The villainy you teach me I will execute, and it shall go hard but I will better the instruction.

Enter a [SERVING]MAN *from Antonio*

SERVINGMAN Gentlemen, my master Antonio is at his house, and desires to speak with you both.

SALARINO We have been up and down to seek him.

Enter TUBAL

SOLANIO Here comes another of the tribe; a third cannot be matched, unless the devil himself turn Jew.

Exeunt [*Salarino and Solanio with the Servingman*]

SHYLOCK How now, Tubal, what news from Genoa? Hast thou found my daughter?

TUBAL I often came where I did hear of her, but cannot find her.

57 SD SERVINGMAN] *Brown; man* Q1–2, F 58 SH] *Rowe subst.; not in* Q1–2, F 62 SD] *Capell subst.; Exeunt Gentlemen. Enter Tuball* Q1; *Exeunt Gentlemen* Q2, F

47 **dimensions** parts of the body, limbs.

47 **affections, passions** Elizabethan psychology distinguished between affections, which were the inclinations of the senses (as in the quotation in 42 n. above), and passions, which were the feelings believed to originate in the heart. See supplementary note on 4.1.47–52. Actors such as George Frederick Cooke who have 'dwelt pathetically' on 'affections' distort the effect of this speech.

49–50 **warmed...summer** Shylock's second use of the rhetorical figure chiasmus, or crossed antithesis (see 1.3.19–20); or perhaps his third (see 33 n. above).

54 **what is his humility?** i.e. in what spirit does he receive the injury? That of humility such as is enjoined on Christians?

55 **sufferance** forbearance; as at 1.3.102.

56 **revenge!** Kean made this a climax in voice and gesture, and then 'hissed out' the final sentence with 'deep concentrated malignity' (Cowden Clarke, I, 392).

56–7 **it...but** unless great difficulties prevent it; i.e. assuredly.

62 SD Tubal's entry is repeated here in Q1. Shakespeare may have failed to cross out this entry after he had inserted a passage (57 SD to 62 SD) containing an entry for Tubal. See Textual Analysis, p. 184 below.

61 **cannot be matched** cannot be found to equal the others.

SHYLOCK Why there, there, there, there! A diamond gone cost me two thousand ducats in Frankfurt! The curse never fell upon our nation till now, I never felt it till now. Two thousand ducats in that, and other precious, precious jewels! I would my daughter were dead at my foot, and the jewels in her ear: would she were hearsed at my foot, and the ducats in her coffin. No news of them, why so? And I know not what's spent in the search. Why thou loss upon loss – the thief gone with so much, and so much to find the thief, and no satisfaction, no revenge, nor no ill luck stirring but what lights o'my shoulders, no sighs but o'my breathing, no tears but o'my shedding!

TUBAL Yes, other men have ill luck too. Antonio as I heard in Genoa –

SHYLOCK What, what, what? Ill luck, ill luck?

TUBAL – hath an argosy cast away coming from Tripolis.

SHYLOCK I thank God, I thank God. Is it true, is it true?

TUBAL I spoke with some of the sailors that escaped the wreck.

SHYLOCK I thank thee, good Tubal: good news, good news! Ha, ha, heard in Genoa!

TUBAL Your daughter spent in Genoa, as I heard, one night four score ducats.

SHYLOCK Thou stick'st a dagger in me; I shall never see my gold again. Four score ducats at a sitting! Four score ducats!

TUBAL There came divers of Antonio's creditors in my company to Venice that swear he cannot choose but break.

SHYLOCK I am very glad of it. I'll plague him, I'll torture him. I am glad of it.

72 what's] Q1–2; how much is F 72 thou] Q1–2, F; then F2 75 o'my shoulders] *Rowe*[2]; a my shoulders Q1, F; on my shoulders Q2 75 o'my breathing] *Rowe*[2]; a my breathing Q1, F; of my breathing Q2 76 o'my shedding] *Rowe*[2]; a my shedding Q1, F; of my shedding Q2 79 what?] *Theobald*; what, Q1, F; what Q2 82 wreck] *Theobald*; wrack Q1–2, F 84 heard] *Neilson and Hill, conj. Kellner*; heere Q1–2, F; where? *Rowe*

67 **Frankfurt** The scene of a famous jewellery fair every September.

67 **curse** Probably Christ's prophecy of the destruction of Jerusalem is meant (Matt. 23.38). See Barbara Lewalski, 'Biblical allusion and allegory in *The Merchant of Venice*', *SQ* 13 (1962), 327–43.

71 **hearsed** coffined.

71 **coffin** Kean took advantage of the next sentence beginning with 'No' to gasp out 'No, no, no!' here, as if to efface his own curses (W. J. Fox quoted by A. C. Sprague, *Shakespeare and the Actors*, 1944, p. 24).

72 **why so?** The actor has the choice of making this an exclamation, a question (Q1, F), or a kind of deliberation (Q2).

72–3 **thou loss upon loss** Either Shylock apostrophises his loss or, Robin Hood suggests, he breaks off after 'thou' in a way that implies Tubal's enquiries have cost him further money in trying to retrieve his original loss.

80 **cast away** wrecked.

85 **heard** This emendation of Q1–2 and F 'heere' is very acceptable, as *d* and *e* were easily confused in Elizabethan handwriting, and Shylock has once already (79) eagerly echoed Tubal's words.

90 **break** go bankrupt.

TUBAL One of them showed me a ring that he had of your daughter for a monkey.

SHYLOCK Out upon her! Thou torturest me, Tubal: it was my turquoise, I had it of Leah when I was a bachelor. I would not have given it for a wilderness of monkeys.

TUBAL But Antonio is certainly undone.

SHYLOCK Nay, that's true, that very true. Go, Tubal, fee me an officer, bespeak him a fortnight before. I will have the heart of him if he forfeit, for were he out of Venice I can make what merchandise I will. Go, Tubal, and meet me at our synagogue, go, good Tubal, at our synagogue, Tubal.

Exeunt

[3.2] *Enter* BASSANIO, PORTIA, GRATIANO, [NERISSA,] *and all their trains*

PORTIA I pray you tarry, pause a day or two
Before you hazard, for in choosing wrong
I lose your company; therefore forbear a while.
There's something tells me, but it is not love,
I would not lose you; and you know yourself

95–6 turquoise] *Rowe;* Turkies Q1–2, F Act 3, Scene 2 3.2] *Rowe subst.; not in* Q1–2, F 0 SD NERISSA] *Capell; not in* Q1–2, F

95 torturest The truth or otherwise of this accusation has to be decided by actor and director. Tubal can be played as a business rival now getting his own back on Shylock, or he may simply be feeding Shylock's anger because he shares his hatred of Antonio.

95 Out...Tubal Olivier omitted this in order to concentrate the whole emotional effect upon the rest of the speech, which climaxed in the 'great, ascending first syllable' of 'wilderness' (Richard Foulkes, 'Henry Irving and Laurence Olivier as Shylock', *Theatre Notebook* 27 (1973), 26–36).

95–6 turquoise J. C. Boswell, 'Shylock's turquoise ring', *SQ* 14 (1963), 481–3, argues that the turquoise was an eastern talisman which Jessica deliberately parted with because, in the west, it was held to cause sterility.

99 fee me an officer i.e. hire a sheriff's officer at my expense to arrest Antonio.

100–1 I will...forfeit William Winter, *Shakespeare on the Stage*, 1912, pp. 191–2, describes Irving's delivery of these words as a terrifying sight: 'the jaws champing, the left hand turning the sleeve up on the right arm as far back as the elbow, and the fingers of the right hand stretched forth and quivering, as if already they were tearing out the heart of his hated enemy'.

101 make what merchandise drive what bargains.

102 synagogue A modern director and his audience may think of Shylock's visit to the synagogue as his attempt to rid himself of his vengeful thoughts, but the Elizabethans would think of it as a means of confirming them with a formal oath.

Act 3, Scene 2

0 SD *all their trains* 'All' suggests a muster of the whole company, to make the scene outshine 2.7 and 2.9. Bassanio and his followers must be as resplendent as the messenger's words at 2.9.85–94 have led us to expect.

2 in choosing if you choose.

4–6 There's...quality The tightrope act of all the willing but modest heroines in Shakespeare's middle comedies. So Beatrice: 'I confess nothing, nor I deny nothing' (*Ado* 4.1.272).

Hate counsels not in such a quality.
But lest you should not understand me well –
And yet a maiden hath no tongue but thought –
I would detain you here some month or two
Before you venture for me. I could teach you
How to choose right, but then I am forsworn.
So will I never be. So may you miss me;
But if you do, you'll make me wish a sin,
That I had been forsworn. Beshrew your eyes!
They have o'erlooked me and divided me:
One half of me is yours, the other half yours –
Mine own, I would say: but if mine then yours,
And so all yours. O these naughty times
Puts bars between the owners and their rights!
And so though yours, not yours. Prove it so,
Let Fortune go to hell for it, not I.
I speak too long, but 'tis to peize the time,
To eche it, and to draw it out in length,
To stay you from election.

20 Prove it so,] *Rowe*; (prove it so) Q1–2, F **22** peize] Q1–2, F; poize *Rowe*; peece *Rowe*[2]; piece *Johnson* **23** eche] Q1; eck Q2; ich F; eke *Johnson*

6 quality manner.

7–10 But...for me Portia is saying that she would like to keep Bassanio with her so that he might come to know her feelings, even though she cannot, in modesty, express them openly. Line 8 is not so much the folk-saying 'maidens should be seen and not heard' (Tilley M45) as the courtly convention expressed by Helena, *MND* 2.1.242: 'We should be woo'd, and were not made to woo.'

14 Beshrew A mild and affectionate imprecation, as at 2.6.53.

15 o'erlooked bewitched (as by the evil eye), *OED v* 7. In *Wiv.* 5.5.83, Pistol, acting as Hobgoblin, tells Falstaff: 'Vile worm, thou wast o'erlooked even in thy birth.'

16–18 One...yours Otto Rank's interpretation of this as a revealing verbal slip (*Zentralblat: für Psychoanalyse* I (1911), 109) has gained wide publicity through Freud's use of it in *Psychopathology of Everyday Life*. But it may be that Portia is deliberately being witty. 'Mine own I would say' then becomes a clarification rather than a correction, and means: 'I ought to say "mine" (in modesty and in deference to the hazard).'

18 naughty bad. The word, basically meaning 'worthless', is much stronger in Elizabethan than in modern English.

19 Puts The subject of this verb, 'times', is 'singular in thought' (Abbott 333).

20 Prove it so i.e. 'if it happens that I am lost to you' (Pooler).

21 Let...not I i.e. 'let fortune go to hell for robbing you of your just due, not I for violating my oath' (Benjamin Heath, *Revisal of Shakespeare's Text*, 1765, p. 117). Besides meaning 'lot, destiny', 'Fortune' is often conceived as the power that bestows that destiny. Compare 2.1.36, 2.9.37.

22 peize weigh down, retard; as in *R3* 5.3.105: 'Lest leaden slumber peize me down tomorrow'. Rowe, in his 1714 edition, and Johnson both read 'piece', in the tailoring sense of 'piece out' (= extend, by adding a piece or pieces). But the submerged image of the weights of a clock possibly leads Shakespeare's mind through 'eche' and 'draw' to the idea of the rack.

23 eche Q2 shows that the cognate 'eke' was replacing 'eche' by 1619. Shakespeare perhaps makes use of the older and more regional word to avoid the speak/eke jingle.

24 election choice; as in 2.9.3.

BASSANIO Let me choose,
For as I am, I live upon the rack.
PORTIA Upon the rack, Bassanio? Then confess
What treason there is mingled with your love.
BASSANIO None but that ugly treason of mistrust
Which makes me fear th'enjoying of my love.
There may as well be amity and life
'Tween snow and fire, as treason and my love.
PORTIA Ay, but I fear you speak upon the rack
Where men enforcèd do speak anything.
BASSANIO Promise me life and I'll confess the truth.
PORTIA Well then, confess and live.
BASSANIO 'Confess and love'
Had been the very sum of my confession.
O happy torment, when my torturer
Doth teach me answers for deliverance!
But let me to my fortune and the caskets.
PORTIA Away then! I am locked in one of them:
If you do love me, you will find me out.
Nerissa and the rest, stand all aloof.
Let music sound while he doth make his choice;
Then if he lose he makes a swan-like end,
Fading in music. That the comparison
May stand more proper, my eye shall be the stream
And watery deathbed for him. He may win,
And what is music then? Then music is

28 mistrust anxiety.

29 fear fear for. Bassanio is afraid he will not win Portia.

33 men enforcèd John Palmer in *Comic Characters in Shakespeare*, 1946, p. 54, notes that Ruy Lopez, whose trial may have been in Shakespeare's mind when he wrote the play (see p. 7 above), pleaded that he had been forced to confess to avoid being racked.

42 aloof i.e. 'at a distance' rather than 'aloft', since the two trains could scarcely be crowded into the upper stage area, especially if the musicians were placed there. See illustration 6, p. 35, for C. Walter Hodges's reconstruction of this scene.

43–7 Let music...for him Anthony Lewis (*NQ* ns 25 (1978), 126–7) thinks this passage derives from the account in Golding's Ovid of the lamentation over the dead Orpheus, whose head and hand and harp, still making music, were carried away on the river Hebrus. Between this story in *Metamorphoses* 11, 44–53 (Golding, 45–57), and that of Hesione's rescue which begins at line 194 (Golding, 217) – the source of 53–60 in this scene – Ovid recounts the legend of Midas: see 102 below.

43 music It is theatrically most effective if the music begins here as an accompaniment to Portia's evocation of a romance atmosphere in the remainder of this speech. She perhaps lingers downstage as the prize of the venture (the Golden Fleece), while the trains disperse themselves upstage.

44 swan-like end The belief that the mute swan sings before its death is as old as Plato.

48–57 The language, with its successive images of monarch, bridegroom and demi-god, acts as a spotlight upon Bassanio as he prepares for his critical choice.

Even as the flourish when true subjects bow
To a new-crownèd monarch. Such it is
As are those dulcet sounds in break of day,
That creep into the dreaming bridegroom's ear
And summon him to marriage. Now he goes
With no less presence, but with much more love,
Than young Alcides when he did redeem
The virgin tribute paid by howling Troy
To the sea-monster. I stand for sacrifice.
The rest aloof are the Dardanian wives,
With blearèd visages come forth to view
The issue of th'exploit. Go, Hercules!
Live thou, I live. With much much more dismay
I view the fight than thou that mak'st the fray.

[*Here music.*] *A song the whilst Bassanio comments on the caskets to himself*

Tell me where is fancy bred,
Or in the heart, or in the head?
How begot, how nourishèd?
Reply, reply.

61 live. With] *Johnson;* live with Q1–2, F; live, with F3; live; with *Pope* **62** I] Q1, F; To Q2 **62 SD** *Here music*] F; *not in* Q1–2; *Music within* | *Rowe; to music* | *follows* | *A song* | *Brown* **66** Reply, reply] *As line of the song, Pope; to right of* 65, Q1–2, F; *not in Rowe; as* SD, *Hanmer; preceded by* SH All *NS, conj. Lawrence*

49–50 flourish....monarch Though there had been no English coronation since 1559, Shakespeare would have been familiar with the ceremonial of stage coronations, and would have heard talk of Henri IV's crowning in Paris in 1594.

54 presence noble bearing

54 much more love Hercules rescued Hesione from the sea-monster for the sake of the reward promised him by her father, King Laomedon of Troy.

55 Alcides Hercules is called this because he was the grandson of Alcaeus.

56 howling lamenting.

57 I...sacrifice i.e. I represent the intended sacrificial victim, Hesione.

58 Dardanian wives Trojan women. These do not figure in Ovid's terse narrative, but Malone pointed out that in Caxton's *Recuyell of the Historyes of Troye* (*c.* 1474), the king and ladies and others 'went upon the downs for to see the end' (ed. H. Oskar Sommer, 1894, p. 277).

59 blearèd tear-stained.

61 Live thou i.e. if you live.

61–2 With...fray There is no stop or comma before 'with' in Q1, and the editor of Q2 seeks to make the passage intelligible by changing 'I view' to 'To view'.

62 SD *A song* No tune has survived.

62 SD *comments...himself* silently ponders and reflects on the caskets.

63 fancy Here the meaning is a superficial emotion, 'love of the eye' rather than 'love of the heart' according to Friar Lawrence's distinction: 'Young men's love then lies/Not truly in their hearts, but in their eyes' (*Rom.* 2.3.67–8).

63 bred When A. H. Fox-Strangeways pointed out (*TLS* 12 July 1923, p. 472) that this song's first three lines all rhyme with 'lead', he was seeking to clinch the argument of John Weiss (*Wit and Humour in Shakespeare*, 1876, p. 312) that by its warning against whatever is superficial the song is meant to guide Bassanio's choice. But the idea belittles Portia's integrity and Bassanio's insight. Brown sensibly comments: 'The song can prepare the audience for Bassanio's sentiments and choice without appearing to influence him at all.'

66 Reply, reply Printed to the right of the page in Q1–2 and F. For the sake of rhyme and rhythm, Pope incorporated the words into the song. Hanmer and Johnson thought they were a direction for the rest of the song to be sung as an answer to the opening questions. W. J. Lawrence suggested they were a refrain, sung like the final line by 'All' (quoted in Richmond Noble, *Shakespeare's Use of Song*, 1923, p. 49).

It is engend'red in the eye,
With gazing fed, and fancy dies
In the cradle where it lies.
Let us all ring fancy's knell.
I'll begin it – Ding, dong, bell.

ALL Ding, dong, bell.

BASSANIO So may the outward shows be least themselves:
The world is still deceived with ornament.
In law, what plea so tainted and corrupt
But, being seasoned with a gracious voice,
Obscures the show of evil? In religion,
What damnèd error but some sober brow
Will bless it and approve it with a text,
Hiding the grossness with fair ornament?
There is no vice so simple but assumes
Some mark of virtue on his outward parts.
How many cowards whose hearts are all as false
As stayers of sand, wear yet upon their chins
The beards of Hercules and frowning Mars,
Who inward searched have livers white as milk,
And these assume but valour's excrement
To render them redoubted. Look on beauty,
And you shall see 'tis purchased by the weight,

67 eye] Q1–2; eyes F 71 I'll...it] *As part of song, Johnson; distinguished from song by roman type,* Q1–2, F 71 it – Ding] *Johnson*;...it. / *Ding*...Q1–2, F 81 vice] F2; voice Q1–2, F

69 In the cradle (1) in the eye, (2) in its infancy.

72 SH ALL Presumably all the musicians sing this, as a refrain to the song, which is sung by only one of their number.

72 So Weiss (see 63 n. above) thought this showed that Bassanio had understood the relevance of the song. But it more probably refers to his unspoken thoughts as he considers the caskets.

73 shows appearances; as in 77 below.

74 still continually.

76 seasoned i.e. made acceptable. The Elizabethans used seasoning, or spices, to mask the taste of long-kept food.

77–80 Bassanio is perhaps remembering how Shylock could quote Scripture to his purpose (1.3.69–82)

78 damnèd error heresy.

78 sober brow Metonymy for 'serious-faced person'.

79 approve confirm.

81 simple uncomplicated; with a hint of 'simple-minded'.

84 stayers Usually modernised to 'stairs', which is what we hear in the theatre, but an expression similar to Herbert's 'rope of sands' in 'The Collar' could have been in Shakespeare's mind. A coward's support is unreliable, like an untrustworthy 'stay' or rope in the rigging of a ship.

86 searched probed (as by a surgeon).

86 livers...milk The liver was believed to be the seat of courage, so a white liver was, in Falstaff's words, 'the badge of pusillanimity' (*2H4* 4.3.104–5)

87 valour's excrement i.e. a brave man's beard. In Elizabethan English, 'excrement' meant 'an outgrowth or excrescence'.

88 redoubted fearsome.

89 purchased by the weight Cosmetics and false hair could be 'bought by the ounce'. 'Weight' both stresses the grossness of such artificial aids to beauty and serves to introduce the play on 'lightest' in 91.

Which therein works a miracle in nature,
Making them lightest that wear most of it.
So are those crispèd snaky golden locks
Which maketh such wanton gambols with the wind
Upon supposèd fairness, often known
To be the dowry of a second head,
The skull that bred them in the sepulchre.
Thus ornament is but the guilèd shore
To a most dangerous sea; the beauteous scarf
Veiling an Indian beauty; in a word,
The seeming truth which cunning times put on
To entrap the wisest. Therefore thou gaudy gold,
Hard food for Midas, I will none of thee,
Nor none of thee, thou pale and common drudge
'Tween man and man. But thou, thou meagre lead
Which rather threaten'st than dost promise aught,
Thy paleness moves me more than eloquence:
And here choose I. Joy be the consequence!

PORTIA [*Aside*] How all the other passions fleet to air:
As doubtful thoughts, and rash-embraced despair,

93 maketh] Q1–2; makes F; make *Pope* 101 Therefore] Q2; Therefore then Q1, F 105 threaten'st] Q1; threatnest Q2, F 106 paleness] Q1–2, F; plainness *Theobald* 108 SD] *Cam.*; *not in* Q1–2, F

91 **lightest** most wanton; with play on the meaning 'most light in weight', and therefore in value.

92 **crispèd** curled.

93 **maketh** F modernises to 'makes', keeping the singular form of the verb because 'locks' is 'singular in thought' (Abbott 333). This improves the metre, and the actor's instinctive change to 'make' will work a further improvement in the line's sound.

94 **supposèd fairness** presumed beauty.

95 **dowry** endowment. Sonnet 68 closely parallels the thought: 'Before the golden tresses of the dead,/The right of sepulchres, were shorn away,/To live a second life on second head;/Ere beauty's dead fleece made another gay' (5–8). See p. 23 above.

97 **guilèd** treacherous. We are not allowed to forget 'the peril of waters, wind, and rocks'.

99 **beauty** Many emendations have been suggested, but the line is all right as it stands. The Elizabethan dislike of a dark skin made 'Indian beauty' the rhetorical figure oxymoron: a seeming contradiction in terms.

101 **Therefore** Q1's 'Therefore then' could conceivably be right if Shakespeare meant the line to be an alexandrine. But more probably he failed to efface a word in his manuscript when he had replaced it.

102 **Hard...Midas** Midas, King of Phrygia, rashly asked Apollo that all he touched might turn to gold. Another recollection of Ovid's eleventh book (119–24). See 43–7 n. above.

103 **common drudge** menial at everyone's command.

106 **paleness** 'Pale as lead' is a common expression in Elizabethan writings. Here the contrast is between colourless lead and the *colours* of rhetoric, which are an applied embellishment, like the cosmetics that Bassanio has been talking about. Nashe, in *The Anatomy of Absurdity* (1588), declares that lovers of an ornate style 'forsake sounder arts, to follow smoother eloquence, not unlike to him that had rather have a new-painted box, though there be nothing but a halter in it, than an old barred hutch with treasure invaluable' (quoted by C. R. Baskervill, 'Bassanio as an ideal lover', *Manly Anniversary Studies*, 1923, pp. 90–103, p. 93).

109 **As** Such as.

And shudd'ring fear, and green-eyed jealousy!
O love, be moderate, allay thy ecstasy,
In measure rain thy joy, scant this excess!
I feel too much thy blessing: make it less
For fear I surfeit.

[*Bassanio opens the leaden casket*]

BASSANIO What find I here?
Fair Portia's counterfeit! What demi-god
Hath come so near creation? Move these eyes?
Or whether riding on the balls of mine
Seem they in motion? Here are severed lips
Parted with sugar breath; so sweet a bar
Should sunder such sweet friends. Here in her hairs
The painter plays the spider, and hath woven
A golden mesh t'entrap the hearts of men
Faster than gnats in cobwebs. But her eyes –
How could he see to do them? Having made one,
Methinks it should have power to steal both his
And leave itself unfurnished. Yet look how far
The substance of my praise doth wrong this shadow
In underprizing it, so far this shadow

110 shudd'ring] F; shyddring Q1–2 112 rain] Q1, F, Q3 *uncorrected*; range Q2; reine Q3 *corrected*; rein *Hanmer*[2] 114 SD] *Rowe subst.*; *not in* Q1–2, F 117 whether] F; whither Q1–2 126 unfurnished] Q1–2, F; unfinished *Rowe*

111 O love...ecstasy Portia's feelings overflow into a twelve-syllable line, or alexandrine, here and at 155 and 248.

112 rain This was understood to mean 'pour' by Beaumont and Fletcher who imitated the line in *The Laws of Candy* (acted 1619?), 3.3.57: 'pour not too fast joys on me', and also by Lansdowne, whose corresponding line in *The Jew of Venice* is 'In measure pour thy joy' (3.1.110). Q3 however spells the word 'reine', taking 'measure' not as 'moderation', but as 'a controlled pace', a term in horsemanship. 'Rain' and 'rein' may have alternated rapidly in Shakespeare's mind, but the meaning 'pour' is specially apt because of the biblical image of a blessing poured from heaven (Malachi 3.10), which is also echoed in *Temp.* 3.1.75: 'Heavens rain grace.'

115 counterfeit picture.

122 A golden mesh This conceit, which may have originated with Petrarch's 69th sonnet, is used extensively in Spenser's sonnets, and occurs also in those of Sidney, Constable, and Daniel.

123 Faster More securely.

124–6 Having...unfurnished The underlying conceit is that of the lady's eye as a sun which blinds her lover by its brilliance. Bassanio's whole speech is in 'the numbers that Petrarch flowed in' (*Rom.* 2.4.38–9).

126 unfurnished without a companion. Rowe emended to 'unfinished' and there is some support for this in a passage from *A Pair of Turtle Doves*, an anonymous English translation of J. De Flores's romance, *Bellora and Fidelio*, as quoted by Steevens: 'If Apelles...had been tasked to have drawn her counterfeit, her two bright burning lamps would so have dazzled his quick-seeing senses that...he had been enforced to have stayed his hand, and left this earthly Venus unfinished.' The work appeared in 1606, but its style is that of a generation earlier.

126 how far by the extent to which.

127 shadow semblance.

128 underprizing i.e. failing to describe it adequately.

128 so far to the same extent.

Doth limp behind the substance. Here's the scroll,
The continent and summary of my fortune.
[*He reads*]
'You that choose not by the view
Chance as fair, and choose as true.
Since this fortune falls to you,
Be content and seek no new.
If you be well pleased with this,
And hold your fortune for your bliss,
Turn you where your lady is,
And claim her with a loving kiss.'
A gentle scroll! Fair lady, by your leave,
I come by note to give, and to receive.
Like one of two contending in a prize
That thinks he hath done well in people's eyes,
Hearing applause and universal shout,
Giddy in spirit, still gazing in a doubt
Whether those peals of praise be his or no –
So, thrice-fair lady, stand I even so,
As doubtful whether what I see be true,
Until confirmed, signed, ratified by you.

PORTIA You see me, Lord Bassanio, where I stand,
Such as I am. Though for myself alone
I would not be ambitious in my wish
To wish myself much better, yet for you
I would be trebled twenty times myself,
A thousand times more fair, ten thousand times
More rich, that only to stand high in your account
I might in virtues, beauties, livings, friends,
Exceed account. But the full sum of me
Is sum of something: which to term in gross

130 SD] *Dyce; not in* Q1–2, F **139**] *As* Q1–2*; preceded by* SH *Bass.* F **145** peals] Q1, F*;* pearles Q2 **149** me, Lord] Q1–2 *subst.;* my Lord F **155** only] Q1–2, F*; not in* F2, *Rowe* **158** sum of something] *Theobald;* sume of something Q1*;* summe of something Q2*;* sum of nothing F*;* some of something *Warburton*

130 continent that which contains.

131–2 You...true A statement about Bassanio, rather than a general wish for other choosers.

140 by note 'by a bill of dues' (Merchant).

140 give...receive Asked by Cressida 'In kissing do you render or receive?', Patroclus replies 'Both take and give' (*Tro.* 4.5.37). Rowe has the SD 'Kisses her' here, but the director may choose to defer the kiss till 148, 167, or even 174.

141 prize match; for example, in fencing or wrestling.

145 peals Q2's 'pearles' is defended by Steevens by means of Elizabethan examples of the phrase 'pearls of praise'. But the image is of something heard.

156 livings material possessions.

158 sum of something F's 'nothing' obscures the gentleness of Portia's self-deprecation, which remains whether we read 'sum' or 'some'.

Is an unlessoned girl, unschooled, unpractised;
Happy in this, she is not yet so old
But she may learn; happier than this,
She is not bred so dull but she can learn;
Happiest of all, is that her gentle spirit
Commits itself to yours to be directed
As from her lord, her governor, her king.
Myself, and what is mine, to you and yours
Is now converted. But now I was the lord
Of this fair mansion, master of my servants,
Queen o'er myself; and even now, but now,
This house, these servants, and this same myself
Are yours, my lord's. I give them with this ring,
Which when you part from, lose, or give away,
Let it presage the ruin of your love,
And be my vantage to exclaim on you.

BASSANIO Madam, you have bereft me of all words.
Only my blood speaks to you in my veins,
And there is such confusion in my powers
As after some oration fairly spoke
By a belovèd prince there doth appear
Among the buzzing, pleasèd multitude,
Where every something being blent together
Turns to a wild of nothing, save of joy
Expressed, and not expressed. But when this ring
Parts from this finger, then parts life from hence:
O then be bold to say Bassanio's dead!

NERISSA My lord and lady, it is now our time,
That have stood by and seen our wishes prosper,
To cry 'good joy'. Good joy, my lord and lady!

GRATIANO My lord Bassanio, and my gentle lady,
I wish you all the joy that you can wish;

171 lord's] Q1; Lord Q2, F

165 her lord...king The same three terms are used by the reformed shrew, Kate (*Shr.* 5.2.138), in expressing the same sentiment. The Elizabethans would have approved it with a text: 'Wives, submit yourselves unto your own husbands, as unto the Lord' (Eph. 5.22, BB).

174 vantage opportunity.

174 exclaim on denounce.

177 powers faculties.

181 blent blended.

182 wild of nothing i.e. a disordered hubbub in which individual remarks ('every something') cannot be distinguished, and so are both 'expressed and not expressed'.

For I am sure you can wish none from me.
And when your honours mean to solemnise
The bargain of your faith, I do beseech you
Even at that time I may be married too.

BASSANIO With all my heart, so thou canst get a wife.

GRATIANO I thank your lordship, you have got me one.
My eyes, my lord, can look as swift as yours:
You saw the mistress, I beheld the maid.
You loved, I loved; for intermission
No more pertains to me, my lord, than you.
Your fortune stood upon the caskets there,
And so did mine too as the matter falls.
For wooing here until I sweat again,
And swearing till my very roof was dry
With oaths of love, at last – if promise last –
I got a promise of this fair one here
To have her love, provided that your fortune
Achieved her mistress.

PORTIA Is this true, Nerissa?

NERISSA Madam, it is, so you stand pleased withal.

BASSANIO And do you, Gratiano, mean good faith?

GRATIANO Yes 'faith, my lord.

BASSANIO Our feast shall be much honoured in your marriage.

GRATIANO We'll play with them the first boy for a thousand ducats.

NERISSA What, and stake down?

199 loved; for intermission] *Theobald;* lov'd for intermission, Q1–2, F; lov'd for intermission. Q3 204 roof] Q2; rough Q1, F

191 I am...me i.e. nothing you desire for yourselves can lessen my joy (because I have found a comparable happiness). Johnson's gloss of 'none from me' as 'none that I shall lose, if you gain it' grasps this idea of there being happiness to spare for all four lovers. It is preferable to the conventional politeness of 'You are so perfectly happy that you cannot want my good wishes' (Fletcher), and to the 'roguish' meaning detected by NS: 'he wishes them everything they can wish, so long (he hints) as their wishes do not clash with his own'.

195 so provided that.

198 maid For Nerissa's status, see 1.2.0 SD n.

199–200 Q1–2 and F have no stop after 'loved', and a comma after 'intermission'. Sense can be made of this if 'intermission' is taken to mean 'pastime' and 200 is taken on its own to mean 'we are in the same boat'. But Gratiano is in his fashion a serious wooer, so Theobald's punctuation has been accepted here, and 'intermission' taken in the sense 'standing idle'; Gratiano has been no less romantically active than Bassanio.

202 the matter falls it happens.

204 roof i.e. the roof of his mouth. Q1's 'rough' is a possible sixteenth-century spelling of 'roof', so there is no need to suppose a misreading of manuscript 'tong' (for 'tongue').

211 'faith An abbreviation of 'in faith', meaning 'on my honour'.

213 play wager.

215 stake down money laid on the table to cover a bet. Gratiano pounces on the bawdy meaning 'with a limp penis'. For the change of dramatic tone, see p. 35 above.

GRATIANO No, we shall ne'er win at that sport and stake down.
But who comes here? Lorenzo and his infidel!
What, and my old Venetian friend Salerio!

Enter LORENZO, JESSICA, *and* SALERIO, *a messenger from Venice*

BASSANIO Lorenzo and Salerio, welcome hither –
If that the youth of my new interest here
Have power to bid you welcome. By your leave
I bid my very friends and countrymen,
Sweet Portia, welcome.
PORTIA So do I, my lord.
They are entirely welcome.
LORENZO I thank your honour. For my part, my lord,
My purpose was not to have seen you here,
But meeting with Salerio by the way
He did entreat me past all saying nay
To come with him along.
SALERIO I did, my lord,
And I have reason for it. [*Giving letter*] Signor Antonio
Commends him to you.
BASSANIO Ere I ope his letter,
I pray you tell me how my good friend doth.
SALERIO Not sick, my lord, unless it be in mind,
Nor well, unless in mind: his letter there
Will show you his estate.
[*Bassanio*] *opens the letter*
GRATIANO Nerissa, cheer yond stranger, bid her welcome.
Your hand, Salerio; what's the news from Venice?
How doth that royal merchant, good Antonio?
I know he will be glad of our success;
We are the Jasons, we have won the fleece.

218 SD *a... Venice*] Q1–2; *not in* F 223–4 So... welcome] *As Capell; as one line* Q1–2, F 230 SD] *Theobald; not in* Q1–2, F 235 SD] Q2, F *subst.*; *open the letter* Q1

218 SD SALERIO On the identity of this character, see Textual Analysis, p. 191 below.

220–1 If... welcome If my position here, still so novel, gives me the right to welcome you.

222 very true.

224 entirely heartily.

231 Commends... you Asks to be remembered to you.

234 unless in mind i.e. unless he has fortitude to sustain him.

235 his estate the condition he is in.

236 cheer greet, welcome. Shakespeare does not necessarily imply that Portia's attendants have cold-shouldered Jessica; all attention has been fixed on Salerio.

238 royal merchant A form of superlative, like 'merchant prince'.

240–1 Gratiano's words recall 1.1.168–71, but the wordplay upon 'fleece' and 'fleets' in Salerio's reply draws a contrast between the success of the Argonauts and the failure of Antonio's present-day ventures.

SALERIO I would you had won the fleece that he hath lost.
PORTIA There are some shrewd contents in yond same paper
That steals the colour from Bassanio's cheek:
Some dear friend dead, else nothing in the world
Could turn so much the constitution
Of any constant man. What, worse and worse?
With leave, Bassanio, I am half yourself
And I must freely have the half of anything
That this same paper brings you.
BASSANIO O sweet Portia,
Here are a few of the unpleasant'st words
That ever blotted paper. Gentle lady,
When I did first impart my love to you,
I freely told you all the wealth I had
Ran in my veins: I was a gentleman.
And then I told you true; and yet, dear lady,
Rating myself at nothing, you shall see
How much I was a braggart. When I told you
My state was nothing, I should then have told you
That I was worse than nothing; for indeed
I have engaged myself to a dear friend,
Engaged my friend to his mere enemy,
To feed my means. Here is a letter, lady,
The paper as the body of my friend,
And every word in it a gaping wound
Issuing lifeblood. But is it true, Salerio?
Hath all his ventures failed? What, not one hit?
From Tripolis, from Mexico, and England,

248 freely] Q1–2, F; *not in* Q3 **266** Hath] Q1–2, F; Have *Rowe*

242 shrewd hurtful.

245 turn...constitution i.e. disturb in mind and body. The phrase approximates to the modern 'throw him off his balance'; a constant constitution was thought to consist of a stable and harmonious mixture of the humours.

251 blotted marred. Robin Hood detects a suggestion of 'tear-blotted', as if Bassanio were transferring to Antonio the emotion with which he reads the letter.

253–4 all...veins The image of blood as wealth is elaborated upon in Sonnet 67, where 'nature bankrupt is, / Beggared of blood to blush through lively veins'.

260, 261 engaged pledged, mortgaged.

261 mere absolute, deadly.

263 as like; i.e. torn open.

266 Hath The old third-person plural of the verb. See Abbott 334.

267 Tripolis See 1.3.15 n. The mention of Barbary as another place, in the next line, shows that the Levantine and not the North African Tripolis is meant (J. W. Draper, 'Shakespeare and Barbary', *Études Anglaises* 14 (1961), 306–13, p. 307).

267 Mexico See p. 13 above on the near-impossibility of a real-life merchant of Venice trading with Mexico.

From Lisbon, Barbary, and India,
And not one vessel 'scape the dreadful touch
Of merchant-marring rocks?

SALERIO Not one, my lord.
Besides, it should appear that if he had
The present money to discharge the Jew,
He would not take it. Never did I know
A creature that did bear the shape of man
So keen and greedy to confound a man.
He plies the Duke at morning and at night,
And doth impeach the freedom of the state
If they deny him justice. Twenty merchants,
The Duke himself, and the magnificoes
Of greatest port have all persuaded with him,
But none can drive him from the envious plea
Of forfeiture, of justice, and his bond.

JESSICA When I was with him, I have heard him swear
To Tubal and to Chus, his countrymen,
That he would rather have Antonio's flesh
Than twenty times the value of the sum
That he did owe him; and I know, my lord,
If law, authority, and power deny not
It will go hard with poor Antonio.

PORTIA Is it your dear friend that is thus in trouble?

BASSANIO The dearest friend to me, the kindest man,
The best conditioned and unwearied spirit
In doing courtesies; and one in whom
The ancient Roman honour more appears
Than any that draws breath in Italy.

PORTIA What sums owes he the Jew?

272 discharge pay off.

275 keen fierce.

275 confound destroy.

277 impeach discredit; perhaps with the rather stronger implication: 'accuse (the state) of treason in disobeying its own laws'.

279 magnificoes Furness quotes Minsheu's *Guide into Tongues* (1617): 'the chief men of Venice are called Magnifici, i.[e.] Magnificoes'.

280 port rank, eminence.

280 persuaded argued.

281 envious malicious.

284 Tubal...Chus Noble (pp. 104–5) points out that these names, which Shakespeare must have picked up in his reading of the Book of Genesis, are unlikely ones for Shylock's countrymen. The Jews believed themselves to be descended from Noah's eldest son, Shem, whereas Tubal and Chus were the sons of Shem's two brothers, Japhet and Ham (Gen. 10.2,6). 'Chus' is the BB form of the name; GB has 'Cush'. See Appendix, p. 197 below.

292 best conditioned most good-natured.

293 courtesies kind acts, good deeds; compare 3.1.39. The word was stronger than it is in modern English.

296–7 What...ducats Bassanio's embarrassment could, Brown thinks, account for the break in the metre. Notice the quickness of Portia's reply, which restores it.

BASSANIO For me, three thousand ducats.
PORTIA What, no more?
Pay him six thousand, and deface the bond.
Double six thousand, and then treble that,
Before a friend of this description
Shall lose a hair through Bassanio's fault.
First go with me to church, and call me wife,
And then away to Venice to your friend!
For never shall you lie by Portia's side
With an unquiet soul. You shall have gold
To pay the petty debt twenty times over.
When it is paid, bring your true friend along.
My maid Nerissa and myself meantime
Will live as maids and widows. Come away,
For you shall hence upon your wedding day.
Bid your friends welcome, show a merry cheer;
Since you are dear bought, I will love you dear.
But let me hear the letter of your friend.

BASSANIO [*Reads*] 'Sweet Bassanio, my ships have all miscarried, my creditors grow cruel, my estate is very low; my bond to the Jew is forfeit, and since in paying it, it is impossible I should live, all debts are cleared between you and I if I might but see you at my death. Notwithstanding, use your pleasure; if your love do not persuade you to come, let not my letter.'

PORTIA O love! Dispatch all business and be gone.
BASSANIO Since I have your good leave to go away,
I will make haste. But till I come again
No bed shall e'er be guilty of my stay
Nor rest be interposer 'twixt us twain.

Exeunt

297–8 What...bond] *As* F; *as one line* Q1–2 301 through] Q1–2, F; through my F2; thorough *Steevens*[2] 314 BASSANIO [*Reads*]] *Rowe*; *not in* Q1–2, F

298 deface cancel.

301 through still perhaps disyllabic in Shakespeare's time, but a monosyllable by 1632, so that F2 has 'through my'. See 4.1.169 n. 'throughly'.

311 cheer countenance.

312 dear bought The indelicacy of Portia telling Bassanio that he is costing her a lot of money has troubled critics. Some suggest that the expression means he is costly to Antonio (rather than to Portia).

312–21 These lines, after the final-sounding couplet of 313–24, could be interpolated 'second thoughts', by which Shakespeare strengthens Portia's motives for her intervention in the trial. See Textual Analysis, p. 184 below.

318 use your pleasure follow your inclination.

[3.3] *Enter* [SHYLOCK] *the Jew, and* [SOLANIO,] *and* ANTONIO, *and the Jailer*

SHYLOCK Jailer, look to him. Tell not me of mercy.
This is the fool that lent out money gratis.
Jailer, look to him.
ANTONIO Hear me yet, good Shylock –
SHYLOCK I'll have my bond, speak not against my bond;
I have sworn an oath that I will have my bond.
Thou call'dst me dog before thou hadst a cause,
But since I am a dog, beware my fangs.
The Duke shall grant me justice. I do wonder,
Thou naughty jailer, that thou art so fond
To come abroad with him at his request.
ANTONIO I pray thee hear me speak –
SHYLOCK I'll have my bond; I will not hear thee speak;
I'll have my bond, and therefore speak no more.
I'll not be made a soft and dull-eyed fool,
To shake the head, relent, and sigh, and yield
To Christian intercessors. Follow not!
I'll have no speaking, I will have my bond. *Exit*
SOLANIO It is the most impenetrable cur
That ever kept with men.
ANTONIO Let him alone.
I'll follow him no more with bootless prayers.
He seeks my life, his reason well I know:
I oft delivered from his forfeitures

Act 3, Scene 3 3.3] *Rowe subst.; not in* Q1–2, F 0 SD SHYLOCK] *Rowe; not in* Q1–2, F 0 SD SOLANIO] F; *Salerio* Q1; *Salarino* Q2 1, 4, 12 SH SHYLOCK] *Rowe; Jew* Q1–2, F 2 lent] Q1–2; lends F 17 SD] *Exit Jew* Q1–2, F 18 impenetrable] Q2, F; inpenitrable Q1

Act 3, Scene 3

0 SD SHYLOCK The use of 'Jew' in the stage direction and speech headings of this scene is significant; Shylock appears only as the moneylender, not the father.

0 SD SOLANIO Q1's *Salerio* cannot be right, as he is on the way back to Venice. See Textual Analysis, pp. 191–4 below.

4, 5 **bond** For the effect of Shylock's repetitions, see p. 36 above.

6 **dog** A deeply insulting term; compare 1.3.103 n. A speaker in Thomas Wilson's *Discourse upon Usury* (1572) says that the Hebrew word for usury, *neshech*, means 'a biting...as a dog useth to bite or gnaw upon a bone' (ed. R. H. Tawney, 1925, p. 241).

8–10 **I do...request** There may be a suggestion that Antonio is being treated by the authorities with uncommon liberality.

9 **naughty** no good, useless, See 3.2.18 n.

9 **fond** foolish.

14 **dull-eyed** easily deceived.

19 **kept** dwelt.

20 **bootless** unavailing.

22 **forfeitures** penalties (for breach of contract). Also at 25.

Many that have at times made moan to me;
Therefore he hates me.
SOLANIO I am sure the Duke
Will never grant this forfeiture to hold.
ANTONIO The Duke cannot deny the course of law;
For the commodity that strangers have
With us in Venice, if it be denied,
Will much impeach the justice of the state,
Since that the trade and profit of the city
Consisteth of all nations. Therefore go.
These griefs and losses have so bated me
That I shall hardly spare a pound of flesh
Tomorrow to my bloody creditor.
Well, jailer, on. Pray God Bassanio come
To see me pay his debt, and then I care not.

Exeunt

[3.4] *Enter* PORTIA, NERISSA, LORENZO, JESSICA, *and* [BALTHAZAR] *a man of Portia's*

LORENZO Madam, although I speak it in your presence,
You have a noble and a true conceit
Of god-like amity, which appears most strongly
In bearing thus the absence of your lord.
But if you knew to whom you show this honour,
How true a gentleman you send relief,
How dear a lover of my lord your husband,

24–5 I...hold] *As Pope; as one line,* Q1–2, F   Act 3, Scene 4   3.4] *Rowe subst.; not in* Q1–2, F   0 SD.2 BALTHAZAR] *Theobald; not in* Q1–2, F

24 Therefore Shakespeare may be emphasising (1) that Shylock is motivated by commercial jealousy rather than by racial hatred, and (2) that the feeling is of long standing and does not just date from Jessica's disappearance. Compare 1.3.34–7.

27–9 For if there is any attempt to withhold the privileges that foreigners enjoy here in Venice, the city's reputation for justice will be very much discredited. 'Commodity' means 'convenience, benefit' and hence 'commodious privileges'. As often in ordinary talk, the syntax is loose; but the sense is clear and there is no need to emend.

31 Consisteth of i.e. depends upon the equitable treatment of.

32 bated me made me lose weight. Falstaff uses the verb intransitively: 'do I not bate? do I not dwindle?' (*1H4* 3.3.2).

Act 3, Scene 4

2 conceit notion, understanding.

3 god-like amity The phrase catches the exalted tone of much Renaissance writing on male friendship. See pp. 22–4 above.

7, 17 lover This can be used of a friend in Elizabethan English. Brutus tells the Romans 'I slew my best lover' (*JC* 3.2.44–5).

I know you would be prouder of the work
Than customary bounty can enforce you.

PORTIA I never did repent for doing good,
Nor shall not now; for in companions
That do converse and waste the time together,
Whose souls do bear an egal yoke of love,
There must be needs a like proportion
Of lineaments, of manners, and of spirit;
Which makes me think that this Antonio,
Being the bosom lover of my lord,
Must needs be like my lord. If it be so,
How little is the cost I have bestowed
In purchasing the semblance of my soul
From out the state of hellish cruelty!
This comes too near the praising of myself,
Therefore no more of it: hear other things.
Lorenzo, I commit into your hands
The husbandry and manage of my house
Until my lord's return; for mine own part
I have toward heaven breathed a secret vow
To live in prayer and contemplation,
Only attended by Nerissa here,
Until her husband and my lord's return.
There is a monastery two miles off,
And there we will abide. I do desire you
Not to deny this imposition,
The which my love and some necessity
Now lays upon you.

LORENZO Madam, with all my heart
I shall obey you in all fair commands.

13 egal] Q1, F; equall Q2 21 cruelty] Q1, F; misery Q2

9 **customary bounty** i.e. your wonted generosity.

9 **enforce you** make you feel (with the implication that pride does not come easily to Portia).

12 **waste** spend (with no hint of an unfavourable meaning, but with a suggestion of making time pass quickly). Prospero says of the last night on his island, 'part of it, I'll waste / With such discourse as, I not doubt, shall make it / Go quick away' (*Temp.* 5.1.303–5).

13 **egal** Two forms of this word, 'egal' derived from Old French, and 'equal' derived from Latin, coexisted in Shakespeare's lifetime.

14 **needs** of necessity.

15 **lineaments** appearance, build.

17 **bosom lover** intimate friend and confidant.

20 **semblance of my soul** i.e. Bassanio's counterpart.

21 **state...cruelty** i.e. the state to which the diabolical cruelty of Shylock has reduced him. The phrase was too elliptical for Q2's editor, who changed 'cruelty' to 'misery'.

25 **husbandry and manage** safekeeping and management.

33 **deny this imposition** refuse the charge I am laying upon you.

PORTIA My people do already know my mind,
And will acknowledge you and Jessica
In place of Lord Bassanio and myself.
So fare you well till we shall meet again.
LORENZO Fair thoughts and happy hours attend on you.
JESSICA I wish your ladyship all heart's content.
PORTIA I thank you for your wish, and am well pleased
To wish it back on you: fare you well, Jessica.
Exeunt [*Jessica and Lorenzo*]
Now, Balthazar –
As I have ever found thee honest-true,
So let me find thee still; take this same letter,
And use thou all th'endeavour of a man
In speed to Padua. See thou render this
Into my cousin's hand, Doctor Bellario;
And look, what notes and garments he doth give thee
Bring them, I pray thee, with imagined speed
Unto the traject, to the common ferry
Which trades to Venice. Waste no time in words
But get thee gone; I shall be there before thee.
BALTHAZAR Madam, I go with all convenient speed. [*Exit*]
PORTIA Come on, Nerissa; I have work in hand
That you yet know not of. We'll see our husbands
Before they think of us.
NERISSA Shall they see us?
PORTIA They shall, Nerissa, but in such a habit
That they shall think we are accomplishèd
With that we lack. I'll hold thee any wager,

44 SD *Jessica and Lorenzo*] *Rowe subst.*; *not in* Q1–2, F 45–6] *As Pope*; *as one line* Q1–2, F 49 Padua] *Theobald*; Mantua Q1–2, F 50 cousin's hand] F; cosin hands Q1; cosins hands Q2 53 traject] *Rowe*; Tranect Q1–2, F 56 SD] Q2; *not in* Q1, F

37 **people** household.

45 **Now, Balthazar** – The broken line gives time for Lorenzo and Jessica to leave and for Balthazar to come downstage.

48 **all...man** all humanly possible effort.

49 **Padua** 'Mantua' in Q1–2 and F, but there are three later allusions to Bellario being in Padua. Shakespeare may have written 'Mantua' before he remembered that there was a renowned school of civil law at Padua. But the printer may just have misread his copy: the initial capitals could look similar in Elizabethan handwriting.

52 **with...speed** with all the speed imaginable (or, less probably, 'as fast as thought').

53 **traject** This emendation of 'tranect' is a possible anglicisation of *traghetto* which Florio's Italian dictionary translates as 'ferry'.

53 **common** public.

54 **trades to** communicates with.

56 **convenient** appropriate; but a change in the word's meaning has given rise to a stage tradition that Balthazar leaves at his own stately pace.

60 **habit** costume.

60–78 On the effect of Portia's male impersonation in this speech, see p. 36 above.

61 **accomplishèd** completed, equipped.

62 **that we lack** i.e. male genitals.

When we are both accoutred like young men
I'll prove the prettier fellow of the two,
And wear my dagger with the braver grace,
And speak between the change of man and boy
With a reed voice, and turn two mincing steps
Into a manly stride; and speak of 'frays
Like a fine bragging youth; and tell quaint lies
How honourable ladies sought my love,
Which I denying, they fell sick and died –
I could not do withal. Then I'll repent,
And wish for all that that I had not killed them;
And twenty of these puny lies I'll tell,
That men shall swear I have discontinued school
Above a twelvemonth. I have within my mind
A thousand raw tricks of these bragging jacks,
Which I will practise.

NERISSA Why, shall we turn to men?

PORTIA Fie, what a question's that,
If thou wert near a lewd interpreter!
But come, I'll tell thee all my whole device
When I am in my coach, which stays for us
At the park gate; and therefore haste away,
For we must measure twenty miles today.

Exeunt

63 accoutred] Q1, F; apparreld Q2 81 my] Q2, F; my my Q1

63 accoutred attired. The word is rare, and Q2 substitutes 'apparelled'.

66 between…boy i.e. as though my voice were breaking.

67 reed piping.

69 quaint ingenious.

72 do withal help it. *OED* Do *v* 54 cites Silvayn's *The Orator*, a possible influence on the play, p. 269: 'But what can a woman do withal, if men do love her?'

77 raw immature, naïve.

77 jacks knaves.

78 turn to be transformed into. Portia pretends Nerissa means 'sexually invite' as at 1.3.73. It means this at *Oth.* 4.1.253.

83 park gate In keeping with the tone of this scene, which is that of intrigue comedy, Belmont has become an ordinary country house of the time.

[3.5] *Enter* [LANCELOT *the*] *Clown and* JESSICA

LANCELOT Yes truly, for look you, the sins of the father are to be laid upon the children. Therefore I promise you I fear you. I was always plain with you, and so now I speak my agitation of the matter. Therefore be o'good cheer, for truly I think you are damned. There is but one hope in it that can do you any good, and that is but a kind of bastard hope neither.

JESSICA And what hope is that, I pray thee?

LANCELOT Marry, you may partly hope that your father got you not, that you are not the Jew's daughter.

JESSICA That were a kind of bastard hope indeed; so the sins of my mother should be visited upon me.

LANCELOT Truly, then, I fear you are damned both by father and mother; thus when I shun Scylla your father, I fall into Charybdis your mother. Well, you are gone both ways.

JESSICA I shall be saved by my husband; he hath made me a Christian.

LANCELOT Truly, the more to blame he; we were Christians enow before, e'en as many as could well live one by another. This making of Christians will raise the price of hogs; if we grow all to be pork eaters, we shall not shortly have a rasher on the coals for money.

Act 3, Scene 5 3.5] *Capell subst.; not in* Q1–2, F 0 SD LANCELOT *the Clown*] *Brown; Clowne* Q1–2, F; *Launcelot* / *Rowe* 1 SH LANCELOT] *Rowe, throughout; Clowne* Q1–2, F 4 o'] *Capell;* a Q1–2; of F 17 e'en] Q2, F; in Q1

Act 3, Scene 5

1–2 the sins...children Shakespeare recalls the wording of the Second Commandment as it is given in the Catechism, which has 'sins' where GB has 'iniquity' and BB has 'sin'. See Appendix, p. 196 below.

2 fear am afraid for. In *R3* 1.1.137, King Edward's physicians 'fear him mightily'.

3 plain frank.

3 agitation In error for 'cogitation' according to Eccles, but, as is the usual way with a Lancelot mistake, 'agitation' does very nicely.

4 be...cheer Merchant detects a parody of John 16.13: 'Be of good cheer, I have overcome the world' (BB). 'Damned' in place of 'saved' in the next line makes this possible, but the phrase was a common one.

6 bastard i.e. without a true cause to beget it; with a play on the usual meaning developed in 8–10.

6 neither Used to strengthen a statement, like the modern 'anyway'.

13 Scylla...Charybdis Ulysses had to sail between the monster Scylla and the whirlpool of Charybdis in the 'narrow seas' that separate Italy and Sicily (*Odyssey* 12). Malone traces this proverbial form for a choice of evils to a thirteenth-century Latin poet, Gualtier.

13 fall into With the second, bawdy, sense, 'enter sexually'.

15 saved...husband Jessica has been reading St Paul: 'the unbelieving wife is sanctified by the husband' (1 Cor. 7.14, BB).

16 enow In Elizabethan English, 'enough' is used of quantity and 'enow' of numbers, a distinction similar to that between 'more' and 'moe'.

17 one by another The double meaning 'alongside one another' and 'off each other' may be oblique social criticism.

19–20 we...money i.e. soon money won't buy even a rasher of fried bacon. 'For money' means 'in return for our money'.

Enter LORENZO

JESSICA I'll tell my husband, Lancelot, what you say: here he comes.

LORENZO I shall grow jealous of you shortly, Lancelot, if you thus get my wife into corners.

JESSICA Nay, you need not fear us, Lorenzo: Lancelot and I are out. He tells me flatly there's no mercy for me in heaven, because I am a Jew's daughter; and he says you are no good member of the commonwealth, for in converting Jews to Christians you raise the price of pork.

LORENZO I shall answer that better to the commonwealth than you can the getting up of the Negro's belly: the Moor is with child by you, Lancelot.

LANCELOT It is much that the Moor should be more than reason; but if she be less than an honest woman, she is indeed more than I took her for.

LORENZO How every fool can play upon the word! I think the best grace of wit will shortly turn into silence, and discourse grow commendable in none only but parrots. Go in, sirrah, bid them prepare for dinner.

LANCELOT That is done, sir; they have all stomachs.

LORENZO Goodly Lord, what a witsnapper are you! Then bid them prepare dinner.

LANCELOT That is done too, sir; only 'cover' is the word.

LORENZO Will you cover then, sir?

LANCELOT Not so, sir, neither; I know my duty.

LORENZO Yet more quarrelling with occasion! Wilt thou show the whole wealth of thy wit in an instant? I pray thee understand a plain man in his plain meaning: go to thy fellows, bid them cover the table, serve in the meat, and we will come in to dinner.

22 comes] Q2, F; come Q1

24 corners remote places (*OED* sv *sb*[1] 6). The jealous Leontes in *WT* accuses Hermione and Polixenes of 'skulking in corners' (1.2.289).

25 are out have quarrelled.

27–8 the commonwealth society.

31 Moor This is all we ever hear of a black attendant. A slave girl presented by Morocco would make a partner for Lancelot in the final scene, though the time scheme of their affair does not bear scrutiny.

33 more...reason i.e. 'bigger than she should be' (Ludowyk).

34–5 if she...for Ludowyk paraphrases: 'to call her "not respectable" would be to describe her flatteringly'.

40 stomachs appetites.

41 Goodly Gracious.

41 witsnapper Like 'wit-crackers' in *Ado* 5.4.101, this appears to be a Shakespearean coinage.

45 I...duty Lancelot wilfully takes 'cover' (meaning 'lay the table') to mean 'put on your hat'.

46 quarrelling with occasion i.e. taking everything that arises in conversation in a wrong sense.

LANCELOT For the table, sir, it shall be served in; for the meat, sir, it shall be covered; for your coming in to dinner, sir, why, let it be as humours and conceits shall govern. *Exit*

LORENZO O dear discretion, how his words are suited!
The fool hath planted in his memory
An army of good words; and I do know
A many fools that stand in better place,
Garnished like him, that for a tricksy word
Defy the matter. How cheer'st thou, Jessica?
And now, good sweet, say thy opinion:
How dost thou like the Lord Bassanio's wife?

JESSICA Past all expressing. It is very meet
The Lord Bassanio live an upright life,
For having such a blessing in his lady
He finds the joys of heaven here on earth,
And if on earth he do not merit it,
In reason he should never come to heaven.
Why, if two gods should play some heavenly match,
And on the wager lay two earthly women,
And Portia one, there must be something else
Pawned with the other, for the poor rude world
Hath not her fellow.

LORENZO Even such a husband
Hast thou of me, as she is for a wife.

JESSICA Nay, but ask my opinion too of that.

52 SD] *Exit Clowne,* Q1–2, F 58 cheer'st] Q1, F; far'st Q2 65–6 merit it, / In] *Pope;* meane it, it / in Q1; meane it, then / In Q2; meane it, it / Is F 71 a] F; *not in* Q1–2

52 humours and conceits Humours are of physiological origin and conceits are mental acts, but both words converge to mean 'whim': 'as the fancy takes you'.

53 O dear discretion Oh, what fine discrimination!

53 suited made suitable, adapted to the matter in hand.

54 planted drawn up ready to fire. A military term.

55 army...words i.e. useful words for a battle of wits.

55–8 and I...matter The image is of a lordly court official, decked out with insignia, who either puts off suitors by equivocations or perhaps just indulges in verbal flourishes, like Osric in *Hamlet*. Some editors think Shakespeare is praising his company's Fool at the expense of a court Fool, and take this passage as evidence that Lancelot is dressed ('garnished') as a jester.

56 A many fools many a fool.

57 tricksy ambiguous.

58 Defy the matter i.e. refuse to speak plainly.

58 How cheer'st thou 'Cheer' meant 'to assume a disposition' (*OED* sv *v* 1b), so the phrase is a vague expression of affection and concern, as Q2's change to 'far'st' shows. It could be the cue for a kiss.

65 merit it Q1's 'meane it, it' makes no sense. Q2 and F both emend unsucessfully. Pope's brilliant emendation is generally accepted; the 'it' Bassanio has to show he deserves, if he is to be admitted to heaven, is the temporal blessing of having Portia for a wife.

70 Pawned Staked.

LORENZO I will anon; first let us go to dinner.
JESSICA Nay, let me praise you while I have a stomach.
LORENZO No, pray thee, let it serve for table talk;
Then howsome'er thou speak'st, 'mong other things
I shall digest it.
JESSICA Well, I'll set you forth.
Exeunt

4.[1] *Enter the* DUKE, *the Magnificoes*, ANTONIO, BASSANIO, [SALERIO,] *and* GRATIANO [*with others*]

DUKE What, is Antonio here?
ANTONIO Ready, so please your grace.
DUKE I am sorry for thee. Thou art come to answer
A stony adversary, an inhuman wretch,
Uncapable of pity, void and empty
From any dram of mercy.

77 howsome'er] *Rowe*; how so mere Q1; howsoere Q2; how som ere F 78 SD] F; *Exit* Q1–2 Act 4, Scene 1 4.1] *Rowe subst.*; *not in* Q1–2; *Actus Quartus.* F 0 SD.2 SALERIO] *Cam.*; *not in* Q1–2, F 0 SD.2 *with others*] *Capell subst.*; *not in* Q1–2, F

75 **stomach** Now Jessica is witsnapping, with a play on the meanings 'inclination' and 'appetite'.

77 **howsome'er** Brown suggests that Q1's 'how so mere' indicates another possible pun. 'Mere' wine was wine unmixed with water.

78 **digest** With a play on the word's figurative meaning of 'making a summary' of something written or said.

78 **set you forth** Punning on the two meanings 'extol' and 'dish up'.

Act 4, Scene 1

0 SD On the Elizabethan stage (illustration 7, p. 38), Antonio and his friends would enter by one stage door which is then taken to give access to the street, and the Duke and Magnificoes would then enter by the other stage door, and seat themselves in the space no longer required for the caskets, which now had its curtain drawn back. Many different arrangements have since been attempted (see, for example, illustration 13, p. 51). The Old Vic in 1961 linked the courtroom by a loggia to a wide canal bridge across which Shylock made a jaunty arrival and downcast departure.

0 SD *Magnificoes* Shakespeare would have learnt from contemporary writers and travellers that law cases in Venice were heard by large groups of judges elected from the whole body of the nobility. In actual fact, no Doge had presided over a court for two hundred years. See p. 16 above.

0 **SD.2** ***with others*** This addition is an editorial convention, based in turn on the theatrical convention of a crowded courtroom which is given some support by 'Make room' at 16. But the scene can be adequately filled by the named characters, plus a couple of Magnificoes. Contemporary paintings of ceremonies and events in the Doges' Palace do not show any public gallery. See W. M. Merchant, 'On looking at *The Merchant of Venice*', in *Nineteenth Century British Theatre*, ed. K. Richards and P. Thomson, 1971, pp. 171–8, and Richard Foulkes, 'The staging of the trial scene in Irving's *The Merchant of Venice*', *ETJ* 28 (1976), 312–17.

2 **Ready** Present. The word also carries a nuance of 'prepared'; at 260 Antonio says he is 'well prepared' to die.

3 **answer** defend yourself against the charges of.

5 **Uncapable** Pooler's gloss 'unable to contain' is supported by the phrase 'void and empty' which follows. 'Incapable' could have the same meaning, as in Sonnet 113.13: 'Incapable of more, replete with you'.

6 **From** Perhaps used in place of 'of' for euphony. Prepositions were more variable then than now; Shakespeare uses 'empty' with 'in' in *AYLI* 2.7.93.

ANTONIO I have heard
Your grace hath tane great pains to qualify
His rigorous course; but since he stands obdùrate
And that no lawful means can carry me
Out of his envy's reach, I do oppose
My patience to his fury, and am armed
To suffer with a quietness of spirit
The very tyranny and rage of his.

DUKE Go one and call the Jew into the court.

SALERIO He is ready at the door; he comes, my lord.

Enter SHYLOCK

DUKE Make room and let him stand before our face.
Shylock, the world thinks, and I think so too,
That thou but leadest this fashion of thy malice
To the last hour of act, and then 'tis thought
Thou'lt show thy mercy and remorse more strange
Than is thy strange apparent cruelty.
And where thou now exacts the penalty,
Which is a pound of this poor merchant's flesh,
Thou wilt not only loose the forfeiture
But, touched with human gentleness and love,
Forgive a moiety of the principal,
Glancing an eye of pity on his losses
That have of late so huddled on his back,
Enow to press a royal merchant down
And pluck commiseration of his state
From brassy bosoms and rough hearts of flint,

24 loose] Q1–2F; lose *Rowe* 30 his state] Q2, F; this states Q1 31 flint] Q2; flints Q1, F

7 qualify moderate.

8 obdùrate Stressed on the second syllable, as in *R3* 1.3.346: 'Withal obdurate, do not hear him plead.'

10 envy malice. Pooler quotes a definition of Envy in Gower's *Confessio Amantis* which includes joy at another's sorrow as well as the more usual meaning of sorrow at another's joy.

13 tyranny cruel power.

16 Make...face The line indicates Shylock's effective entry through the group of Antonio's friends (who draw back with distaste) to an isolated position confronting them.

18 thou...fashion you are only keeping up the pretence.

19 the last...act i.e. the brink of performing it.

20 remorse pity (the usual sense in Shakespeare).

20–1 strange...strange The first means 'striking, remarkable', the second 'abnormal' with a hint of 'alien'.

22 exacts Used instead of 'exact'st' for euphony.

24 loose let go of. The image arises from the literal sense of 'bond'.

26 moiety portion (not necessarily a half).

29 Enow Enough (see 3.5.16 n.).

29 royal merchant i.e. even such a substantial merchant prince as Antonio. See 3.2.238 n.

From stubborn Turks, and Tartars never trained
To offices of tender courtesy.
We all expect a gentle answer, Jew.
SHYLOCK I have possessed your grace of what I purpose,
And by our holy Sabaoth have I sworn
To have the due and forfeit of my bond.
If you deny it, let the danger light
Upon your charter and your city's freedom!
You'll ask me why I rather choose to have
A weight of carrion flesh than to receive
Three thousand ducats. I'll not answer that –
But say it is my humour: is it answered?
What if my house be troubled with a rat,
And I be pleased to give ten thousand ducats
To have it baned? What, are you answered yet?
Some men there are love not a gaping pig;

35, 85, 89, 122, 127, 139, 172, 291, 297, 300, 314 SH SHYLOCK] *Rowe; Jew* Q1–2, F 36 Sabaoth] Q1; Sabbath Q2, F

32 Turks, and Tartars Classed with Jews as infidels, as in the Good Friday collect quoted by Merchant, which prays for the conversion of 'all Jews, Turks, Infidels, and Heretics'.

33 offices duties.

33 courtesy civilised customs; as when Orlando says to his brother: 'The courtesy of nations allows you my better' (*AYLI* 1.1.46).

34 gentle Again a pun on 'Gentile'.

35 SH SHYLOCK In Q1, which may reproduce the speech headings of Shakespeare's manuscript, Shylock is called *Jew* in speech headings up to the point of Portia saying 'Then must the Jew be merciful', after which he becomes *Shylock* (179). When Portia begins to give judgement (240) the speech headings are again *Jew*. From 'Is that the law?' (310) they revert, with one exception (314), to *Shylock*. The variations suggest that Shakespeare thinks of Shylock primarily as a person, rather than a stereotype, when Portia is pleading with him and when he is defeated.

36 Sabaoth By using this word Shakespeare puts his audience in mind of a phrase in the *Te Deum*, 'Holy, Holy, Holy, Lord God of Sabaoth', and so is able to give Shylock's words religious fervour without himself appearing profane. The word means 'armies' in Hebrew, but Elizabethans seem to have taken it to mean 'heavenly repose' and thought it was the same word as 'Sabbath': hence the change in Q2 and F.

37 due and forfeit 'the forfeit which is due' (G. Allen, quoted by Furness). Shylock uses for emphasis the rhetorical figure called hendiadys–two linked nouns in place of a noun and modifier.

39 charter...freedom The terms belong to an English city granted privileges by a feudal monarch, rather than to the independent republic of Venice. See p. 16 above for a discussion of the way Shakespeare interests and involves his audience by blending the familiar with the exotic.

43 But...answered? Johnson attributes this refusal to give a reasoned answer to the fact that 'Shylock gratifies his own malignity by such answers as he knows will aggravate the pain of the enquirer.'

43 humour probably the older meaning 'fixation of character' rather than 'whim', since Shylock goes on to speak of true phobias (D. H. Bishop, 'Shylock's humour', *SAB* 23 (1948), 174–80). Today, with a similar abuse of medical terms, we would use 'allergy'.

47 gaping pig Possibly a recollection of Nashe, *Piers Pennilesse, his Supplication to the Devil* (1592; *Works*, ed. R. B. McKerrow, 1904–10, I, 188): 'Some will take on like a mad man, if they see a pig come to the table.' Gustav Ungerer thinks the allusion is to satirical pictures of Jews with, or as, pigs, and points out that there was an iconographic tradition of pigs, some of them playing bagpipes, as a symbol of heresy ('Shylock's gaping pig' in *Elizabethan and Modern Studies presented to Professor Willem Schrickx*, 1985, pp. 267–76). Shylock is not however talking of his own hatred, which is reserved for Antonio.

Some that are mad if they behold a cat;
And others when the bagpipe sings i'the nose
Cannot contain their urine: for affection
Masters oft passion, sways it to the mood
Of what it likes or loathes. Now for your answer:
As there is no firm reason to be rendered
Why he cannot abide a gaping pig,
Why he a harmless necessary cat,
Why he a woollen bagpipe, but of force
Must yield to such inevitable shame
As to offend, himself being offended:
So can I give no reason, nor I will not,
More than a lodged hate and a certain loathing
I bear Antonio, that I follow thus
A losing suit against him. Are you answered?

BASSANIO This is no answer, thou unfeeling man,
To excuse the current of thy cruelty.

SHYLOCK I am not bound to please thee with my answers.

BASSANIO Do all men kill the things they do not love?

SHYLOCK Hates any man the thing he would not kill?

BASSANIO Every offence is not a hate at first.

SHYLOCK What, wouldst thou have a serpent sting thee twice?

50–1 urine: for affection / Masters oft] *conj. Bulloch;* urine for affection. / Maisters of Q1–2, F; urine for affection. / Masterless *Rowe;* urine; for affection, / Master of *Rann, conj. Thirlby;* urine; for affection / Mistress of *Capell, conj. Thirlby;* urine: for affections / Masters of *Steevens*[2], *conj. Hawkins;* urine: for affection / Masters our *conj. Malone* 51 sways] Q1–2, F; sway *Warburton* 56 woollen] Q1–2, F; swollen *Steevens*[3], *conj. Hawkins;* wawling *Hudson, conj. Capell* 65, 67, 69, 246, 252, 255, 258, SH SHYLOCK] Q2; *Jew* Q1, F 65 answers] Q1; answere Q2, F

49 sings i'the nose For the melancholy nature of bagpipe music see 1.1.53 where the subject, as here, is 'humours'.

49–50 And...urine In translating a French book about ghosts (*A Treatise of Spectres* (1605)) Zachary Jones added a story of his own to the anecdote of a man who was forced to 'go away and make water' when he heard a viol: 'Another gentleman of this quality lived of late in Devon near Exeter, who could not endure the playing on a bagpipe.' Some such anecdote was still going the rounds in 1612–16, when it cropped up in Jonson's revision of his *Every Man in His Humour* (4.2.19–22).

49–52 And . . . loathes See supplementary note, p. 179 below.

56 woollen The leather of a bagpipe is usually covered with cloth; or it could be sheepskin with the wool left on.

56 of force involuntarily.

60 lodged fixed.

60 certain steadfast.

62 losing unprofitable.

64 current Shylock's cruelty is thought of as a humour (perhaps black bile) flowing through his body.

65–9 I am...twice This line-by-line exchange is the rhetorical device of stichomythia, which the Elizabethans imitated from Seneca's tragedies. It is especially appropriate here as it catches the dramatic tension of a quasi-forensic interrogation.

68 offence offence taken, displeasure. Shylock's reply picks up the meaning of 'offence given' or 'injury'.

ANTONIO I pray you think you question with the Jew.
You may as well go stand upon the beach
And bid the main flood bate his usual height;
You may as well use question with the wolf
Why he hath made the ewe bleat for the lamb;
You may as well forbid the mountain pines
To wag their high tops and to make no noise
When they are fretten with the gusts of heaven;
You may as well do anything most hard
As seek to soften that – than which what's harder? –
His Jewish heart. Therefore I do beseech you
Make no moe offers, use no farther means,
But with all brief and plain conveniency
Let me have judgement, and the Jew his will.

BASSANIO For thy three thousand ducats here is six.

SHYLOCK If every ducat in six thousand ducats
Were in six parts, and every part a ducat,
I would not draw them; I would have my bond.

DUKE How shalt thou hope for mercy, rendering none?

SHYLOCK What judgement shall I dread, doing no wrong?
You have among you many a purchased slave,
Which, like your asses and your dogs and mules,
You use in abject and in slavish parts
Because you bought them. Shall I say to you,
'Let them be free! Marry them to your heirs!
Why sweat they under burdens? Let their beds
Be made as soft as yours, and let their palates
Be seasoned with such viands'? You will answer,
'The slaves are ours.' So do I answer you.

73 You may as] Q1 *corrected*, Q2; *not in* Q1 *uncorrected*; Or even as F 74 Why...made] Q1 *corrected*, Q2; *not in* Q1 *uncorrected*, F 74 bleat] F; bleak Q1–2 75 mountain] F; mountaine of Q1–2 79 what's] Q1–2; what F

70 question dispute, debate.

73–4 You...lamb Unlikely to be an allusion to Ruy Lopez (*lupus* = wolf); rather, as Ralph Nash has shown, this is a stock image from Virgil's *Aeneid* 9, 565–6 ('Shylock's wolvish spirit', *SQ* 10 (1959), 125–8).

74 bleat The 'bleake' of Q1–2 may be what Shakespeare wrote; 'blake' is Somerset dialect for 'bleat'.

76 wag sway. The word could be used in a serious context in Elizabethan English.

82 brief...conveniency 'suitable brevity and directness' (Myrick).

87 draw take.

88 How...none? A significant echo of the text 'For he shall have judgement without mercy that sheweth no mercy' (Jas. 2.13, BB).

90 many...slave Venice had hundreds of slaves – Slavs, Tartars, Moors, and Africans. In 1594 an English sea captain sold a cargo of '*mori neri*' in Venice. The trade died out for lack of supplies early in the next century (Robert Smith, 'In search of Carpaccio's African gondolier', *Italian Studies* 34 (1979), 45–59).

92 parts tasks, duties (*OED* sv *sb* 8).

The pound of flesh which I demand of him
Is dearly bought; 'tis mine, and I will have it.
If you deny me, fie upon your law:
There is no force in the decrees of Venice.
I stand for judgement. Answer: shall I have it?

DUKE Upon my power I may dismiss this court,
Unless Bellario, a learned doctor
Whom I have sent for to determine this,
Come here today.

SALERIO My lord, here stays without
A messenger with letters from the doctor,
New come from Padua.

DUKE Bring us the letters. Call the messenger.

BASSANIO Good cheer, Antonio! What, man, courage yet!
The Jew shall have my flesh, blood, bones, and all,
Ere thou shalt lose for me one drop of blood.

ANTONIO I am a tainted wether of the flock,
Meetest for death; the weakest kind of fruit
Drops earliest to the ground, and so let me.
You cannot better be employed, Bassanio,
Than to live still and write mine epitaph.

Enter NERISSA [*disguised as a lawyer's clerk*]

DUKE Came you from Padua, from Bellario?

NERISSA From both, my lord: [*Presenting letter*] Bellario greets your
grace.

BASSANIO Why dost thou whet thy knife so earnestly?

SHYLOCK To cut the forfeiture from that bankrupt there.

GRATIANO Not on thy sole, but on thy soul, harsh Jew,
Thou mak'st thy knife keen. But no metal can,

100 'tis] Q2, F; as Q1 118 SD *disguised...clerk*] *Rowe subst.*; *not in* Q1–2, F 120 From...grace] *As one line* Q1–2; *as two lines divided after* both F 120 both, my lord:] *Theobald*; From both? my L. Q1; From both, my L. Q2; From both. / My Lord F 123 sole...soul] *Hanmer*; soule...soule Q1–2; soale...soule F

106 determine 'resolve the matter in dispute' (*OED* sv *v* 13).

107 without outside.

114 tainted sick. The word does not necessarily imply guilt or anxiety.

114 wether castrated ram. Antonio may mean he is expendable because he has no family of his own. But the image may relate to Shylock, seen either as a shepherd culling a useless beast from the Christian flock (suggested by his talk of Jacob in 1.3), or as a dog worrying sheep.

121 whet *Gernutus* has 'The bloody Jew now ready is / With whetted blade in hand' (part 2, stanza 15). If the ballad is later than the play, this could be a recollection of stage business.

123 sole...soul Shylock is stropping his knife on the sole of his shoe. The wordplay occurs elsewhere (*Rom.* 1.4.15; *JC* 1.1.14) and 'on thy soul' is paralleled by Henry IV accusing Prince Hal of whetting murderous thoughts on his stony heart (*2H4* 4.5.106–7).

No, not the hangman's axe, bear half the keenness
Of thy sharp envy. Can no prayers pierce thee?
SHYLOCK No, none that thou hast wit enough to make.
GRATIANO O be thou damned, inexecrable dog,
And for thy life let justice be accused!
Thou almost mak'st me waver in my faith,
To hold opinion with Pythagoras
That souls of animals infuse themselves
Into the trunks of men. Thy currish spirit
Governed a wolf, who – hanged for human slaughter –
Even from the gallows did his fell soul fleet,
And whilst thou layest in thy unhallowed dam
Infused itself in thee; for thy desires
Are wolfish, bloody, starved, and ravenous.
SHYLOCK Till thou canst rail the seal from off my bond
Thou but offend'st thy lungs to speak so loud.
Repair thy wit, good youth, or it will fall
To cureless ruin. I stand here for law.
DUKE This letter from Bellario doth commend
A young and learned doctor to our court:
Where is he?
NERISSA He attendeth here hard by
To know your answer whether you'll admit him.

128 inexecrable] Q1–2, F; inexorable F3 142 cureless] Q1–2; endlesse F

125 hangman's executioner's.

127 wit intelligence, sense. So at 141 below.

128 inexecrable F4 emends to 'inexorable'. But 'inexecrable', meaning 'that cannot be execrated enough', applies better to a dog than does 'inexorable', and Shakespeare's expression appears to be imitated as 'execrable dog' by the A-version reporter of *Doctor Faustus* (Paul Merchant in *NQ* ns 14 (1967), 135).

129 And...accused i.e. it is a failure of justice that you have been allowed to live thus long.

130–3 Thou...men Like Malvolio (*TN* 4.2.55–6), and like Golding in the dedicatory epistle to his translation of the *Metamorphoses*, Gratiano knows that theologians consider the doctrine of the transmigration of souls to be a heresy.

134 wolf Usurers were often called wolves; the wolf is an emblem of Envy in sixteenth-century literature; and predatory animals were occasionally tried and executed in Europe till the late seventeenth century. In view of these facts, a specific reference to Lopez is unlikely here. See Ralph Nash, 'Shylock's wolvish spirit', *SQ* 10 (1959), 125–8, and compare 73–4 n. above.

134 who...slaughter The grammatical nominative absolute is used dramatically to convey Gratiano's passion.

135 fell deadly.

135 fleet pass out (used of the soul leaving the body: see *OED* Fleet v^1 10b).

139 rail Kean dwelt on this word with a 'prolonged, grating, guttural tone of utter contempt' (Furness, from his father).

140 Thou...offend'st You are only hurting. An oblique stage direction: Gratiano has been shouting.

141–2 Repair...ruin Shylock's house image is characteristic of him. Compare 371–2 below.

DUKE With all my heart. Some three or four of you
Go give him courteous conduct to this place.
[*Exeunt officials*]
Meantime the court shall hear Bellario's letter.

[*Reads*] 'Your grace shall understand, that at the receipt of your letter I am very sick; but in the instant that your messenger came, in loving visitation was with me a young doctor of Rome: his name is Balthazar. I acquainted him with the cause in controversy between the Jew and Antonio the merchant. We turned o'er many books together; he is furnished with my opinion which, bettered with his own learning, the greatness whereof I cannot enough commend, comes with him at my importunity, to fill up your grace's request in my stead. I beseech you let his lack of years be no impediment to let him lack a reverend estimation, for I never knew so young a body with so old a head. I leave him to your gracious acceptance, whose trial shall better publish his commendation.'

Enter PORTIA [*disguised as Doctor Balthazar, followed by officials*]

You hear the learn'd Bellario what he writes,
And here I take it is the doctor come.
Give me your hand. Come you from old Bellario?

PORTIA I did, my lord.

DUKE You are welcome; take your place.
Are you acquainted with the difference
That holds this present question in the court?

148 SD] *This edn; not in* Q1–2, F 150 SD] *NS subst.; not in* Q1–2, F; *giving it to a Clerk. Cle. reads* / *Capell;* SH *Nerissa* / *Sisson* 162 SD *disguised…officials*] *This edn; for Balthazar* Q1–2, F; *dressed like a doctor of laws* / *Rowe* 163 you] *NS; Duke.* You Q1–2, F 165 Come] Q1–2; Came F

150–62 Your…commendation The recurrence of the speech heading *Duke* at the end of this letter (163) does not imply that the letter is read out by a clerk: similar speech headings after something has been read aloud occur at 2.7.74 and 2.9.72.

151–2 in loving visitation on a friendly visit.

153 Balthazar Shakespeare uses this name for four other characters, which makes it unlikely that it was chosen here to echo 'Beltashazzar', the Babylonian name of Daniel (N. Nathan, 'Balthasar, Daniel and Portia', *NQ* ns 4 (1957), 334–5). *The Spanish Tragedy* is a more likely source, but in any case 'Baldessaro' is a common Italian name.

158–9 let his…him lack Alexander Schmidt tried to untangle this: 'equivalent either to "let his lack of years be no motive to let him lack" or "be no impediment to let him have"'. The second of these has a pun on 'let' meaning both 'allow' and 'hinder' (*Shakespeare Lexicon*, 1886, p. 1420).

161 trial Either the proceedings over which Balthazar will preside, or the test to which his reputation will be put.

161–2 better…commendation widen (more than my letter can) the regard in which he is held.

166 your place It is difficult to see what this is. Perhaps the Duke indicates a place beside him on a wide judgement seat, like a magistrates' traditional bench. But the actress of Portia is likely to want to keep her freedom of movement on the open stage.

167–8 difference…question dispute which is the subject of the present investigation.

PORTIA I am informèd throughly of the cause.
Which is the merchant here and which the Jew?
DUKE Antonio and old Shylock, both stand forth.
PORTIA Is your name Shylock?
SHYLOCK Shylock is my name.
PORTIA Of a strange nature is the suit you follow,
Yet in such rule that the Venetian law
Cannot impugn you as you do proceed.
– You stand within his danger, do you not?
ANTONIO Ay, so he says.
PORTIA Do you confess the bond?
ANTONIO I do.
PORTIA Then must the Jew be merciful.
SHYLOCK On what compulsion must I? Tell me that.
PORTIA The quality of mercy is not strained,
It droppeth as the gentle rain from heaven
Upon the place beneath. It is twice blest:
It blesseth him that gives, and him that takes.
'Tis mightiest in the mightiest, it becomes
The thronèd monarch better than his crown.
His sceptre shows the force of temporal power,
The attribute to awe and majesty,
Wherein doth sit the dread and fear of kings;
But mercy is above this sceptred sway.
It is enthronèd in the hearts of kings,
It is an attribute to God himself,
And earthly power doth then show likest God's

169 throughly] Q1–2, F; thoroughly *Steevens*[2]

169 informèd throughly 'Throughly' is modernised to 'thoroughly' by a few editors, but 'inform'd thoroughly' does not have the rhythmic assurance of 'informèd throughly'.

174 in such rule so regular, so much in order.

175 impugn oppose.

176 within his danger at his mercy. Merchant explains it as coming from the legal French phrase *en son danger*.

178–9 must...must Portia's 'must' expresses a moral imperative; Shylock's, external coercion.

180 strained constrained, forced; but the rain image seems to follow from another meaning, 'filtered, squeezed out'.

181 gentle rain A recollection of Ecclus. 35.19: 'Oh, how fair a thing is mercy in the time of anguish and trouble! It is like a cloud of rain, that cometh in the time of a drought' (GB). See Appendix, p. 199 below, for Shakespeare's use of Wisdom literature in this play.

188 Wherein...kings In which (symbolically) resides the power of kings to command dread and fear.

192–3 And...justice The source of this idea, Seneca's *De Clementia* 1.19.8–9, is followed even more closely in *Edward III*, thought to be in part by Shakespeare: 'And kings approach the nearest unto God / By giving life and safety unto men' (5.1.41).

When mercy seasons justice. Therefore, Jew,
Though justice be thy plea, consider this:
That in the course of justice, none of us
Should see salvation. We do pray for mercy,
And that same prayer doth teach us all to render
The deeds of mercy. I have spoke thus much
To mitigate the justice of thy plea,
Which if thou follow, this strict court of Venice
Must needs give sentence 'gainst the merchant there.

SHYLOCK My deeds upon my head! I crave the law,
The penalty and forfeit of my bond.

PORTIA Is he not able to discharge the money?

BASSANIO Yes, here I tender it for him in the court,
Yea, twice the sum; if that will not suffice,
I will be bound to pay it ten times o'er
On forfeit of my hands, my head, my heart.
If this will not suffice, it must appear
That malice bears down truth. And I beseech you
Wrest once the law to your authority;
To do a great right, do a little wrong,
And curb this cruel devil of his will.

PORTIA It must not be; there is no power in Venice
Can alter a decree establishèd.
'Twill be recorded for a precedent,
And many an error by the same example
Will rush into the state: it cannot be.

206 twice] Q1–2, F; thrice *Dyce*[2], *conj. Ritson*

193–8 Therefore...mercy Though Portia's arguments may remind Venetian Christians of the Lord's Prayer, they have a specifically Hebrew resonance as well. Compare Psalm 143.2: 'Enter not into judgement with thy servants, O Lord, for no flesh is righteous in thy sight', and Ecclus. 28.2: 'Forgive thy neighbour the hurt that he hath done thee, so shall thy sins be forgiven thee also, when thou prayest' (GB; BB virtually the same).

195 none of us An allusion to the doctrine of original sin and the impossibility of salvation by good works alone.

199 To...plea To moderate your plea for strict justice.

202 My...head This recalls the shout of the crowd before the Crucifixion: 'His blood be on us, and on our children' (Matt. 27.25). See 292 n. below.

206 twice See below, 223 and n. and 230.

210 malice...truth Johnson paraphrases: 'Malice oppresses honesty.' Rann glosses 'truth' as 'the strict rule of equity'.

211 once i.e. for once.

216 precedent Shakespeare is thinking in terms of English law, which is based on previous cases rather than on a code. Equity courts however were not originally bound by precedent. For the relation of the play's trial to English law, see pp. 16–18 above.

217 error 'a departure from constitutional practice' (NS).

SHYLOCK A Daniel come to judgement; yea a Daniel!
O wise young judge, how I do honour thee!
PORTIA I pray you let me look upon the bond.
SHYLOCK Here 'tis, most reverend doctor, here it is.
PORTIA Shylock, there's thrice thy money offered thee.
SHYLOCK An oath, an oath. I have an oath in heaven!
Shall I lay perjury upon my soul?
No, not for Venice.
PORTIA Why, this bond is forfeit,
And lawfully by this the Jew may claim
A pound of flesh, to be by him cut off
Nearest the merchant's heart. Be merciful:
Take thrice thy money; bid me tear the bond.
SHYLOCK When it is paid, according to the tenour.
It doth appear you are a worthy judge,
You know the law, your exposition
Hath been most sound. I charge you by the law,
Whereof you are a well-deserving pillar,
Proceed to judgement. By my soul I swear
There is no power in the tongue of man
To alter me. I stay here on my bond.
ANTONIO Most heartily I do beseech the court
To give the judgement.
PORTIA Why then, thus it is:
You must prepare your bosom for his knife.
SHYLOCK O noble judge, O excellent young man!
PORTIA For the intent and purpose of the law
Hath full relation to the penalty
Which here appeareth due upon the bond.

219, 222, 231, 242 SH SHYLOCK] Q1–2; *Jew* F **226** No] Q2, F; Not Q1 **231** tenour] Q2; tenure Q1, F

219 Daniel. In the Apocrypha's story of Susannah and the Elders, Daniel is 'a young childe' (i.e. a youth) who makes sure that the lying elders are convicted out of their own mouths. The story was familiar in sixteenth-century art and literature; it is retold by Greene and by Nashe, and Daniel is the name of the incorruptible judge in the morality play, *The Nice Wanton* (1560).

223 thrice The discrepancy between 'thrice' here and at 230, and 'twice' at 206 above, could be due to a slip on Shakespeare's part or to a compositor's misreading. But perhaps Portia, whose money it is and who has already said 'Double six thousand' (3.2.299), is deliberately raising the offer.

231 tenour In legal parlance, this refers to the actual wording of a document as distinct from its overall effect.

233 exposition A five-syllabled word; the *-ion* ending could be given its full value as two syllables on occasion, as by Morocco at 2.1.1.

238 stay take my stand.

243 intent and purpose 'meaning and intention' (Ludowyk).

244 Hath...to 'Fully authorises' (Riverside).

SHYLOCK 'Tis very true. O wise and upright judge,
How much more elder art thou than thy looks!
PORTIA Therefore lay bare your bosom.
SHYLOCK Ay, his breast.
So says the bond, doth it not, noble judge?
'Nearest his heart': those are the very words.
PORTIA It is so. Are there balance here to weigh
The flesh?
SHYLOCK I have them ready.
PORTIA Have by some surgeon, Shylock, on your charge,
To stop his wounds, lest he do bleed to death.
SHYLOCK Is it so nominated in the bond?
PORTIA It is not so expressed, but what of that?
'Twere good you do so much for charity.
SHYLOCK I cannot find it, 'tis not in the bond.
PORTIA You, merchant: have you anything to say?
ANTONIO But little; I am armed and well prepared.
Give me your hand, Bassanio. Fare you well.
Grieve not that I am fall'n to this for you.
For herein Fortune shows herself more kind
Than is her custom: it is still her use
To let the wretched man outlive his wealth,
To view with hollow eye and wrinkled brow
An age of poverty; from which ling'ring penance
Of such misery doth she cut me off.
Commend me to your honourable wife.
Tell her the process of Antonio's end,

251–2 It...flesh] *As two lines, Malone; as one line,* Q1–2, F 254 do] Q1–2; should F 255 Is it so] Q1–2; It is not F 259 You] Q1–2; Come F

251 balance Treated as plural in order to avoid an excess of sibilants and because the object itself is double: compare 'scales'. This stage property has to be used with great care. Irving thrust it forward in a way that perhaps awakened its shopkeeping associations in a Victorian audience, because Percy Fitzgerald tells us it 'did lower the tone' (*Henry Irving: A Record of Twenty Years at the Lyceum*, 1893, p. 134). But for the Renaissance spectator the balance was a powerful classical and religious emblem; and an audience familiar with the figure crowning the Old Bailey can still recognise in Shylock's knife and scales a cynical parody of the trappings of Justice.

253 on your charge at your expense.

258 I cannot...bond Macklin delivered this with a 'savage sneer', Kean with 'a chuckle of transport' which may have been even more horrible (F. W. Hawkins, *Life of Kean*, 1869, I, 152). If, as seems probable from 302, the bond remains in Portia's hand, 'find' must mean 'find it in my heart to be so charitable'.

260 armed i.e. fortified in mind.

264 still her use her regular practice.

267 age old age.

268 misery Shakespeare nowhere stresses this word on the second syllable, so F2 regularises the metre by reading 'a misery'.

270 process manner (with perhaps an ironic nuance of 'legal proceeding').

Say how I loved you, speak me fair in death,
And when the tale is told, bid her be judge
Whether Bassanio had not once a love.
Repent but you that you shall lose your friend
And he repents not that he pays your debt.
For if the Jew do cut but deep enough
I'll pay it instantly with all my heart.

BASSANIO Antonio, I am married to a wife
Which is as dear to me as life itself;
But life itself, my wife, and all the world,
Are not with me esteemed above thy life.
I would lose all, ay, sacrifice them all
Here to this devil, to deliver you.

PORTIA Your wife would give you little thanks for that
If she were by to hear you make the offer.

GRATIANO I have a wife who I protest I love;
I would she were in heaven, so she could
Entreat some power to change this currish Jew.

NERISSA 'Tis well you offer it behind her back;
The wish would make else an unquiet house.

SHYLOCK These be the Christian husbands! I have a daughter:
Would any of the stock of Barabbas
Had been her husband, rather than a Christian!
We trifle time; I pray thee pursue sentence.

PORTIA A pound of that same merchant's flesh is thine,
The court awards it, and the law doth give it.

SHYLOCK Most rightful judge!

PORTIA And you must cut this flesh from off his breast;
The law allows it, and the court awards it.

SHYLOCK Most learned judge! A sentence: come, prepare.

282 all, ay] Q3 *corrected, Pope;* all, I Q1–2, F, Q3 *uncorrected*

271 speak me fair speak well of me.

274 Repent Regret (as in next line also).

277 all my heart A jest similar to the dying Mercutio's prediction that he will soon be 'a grave man' (*Rom.* 3.1.98). Merchant points out that such witty nonchalance, or *sprezzatura*, was a virtue of the Renaissance gentleman.

279 Which Less definite than 'who': 'I am married to such a wife, that she is as dear to me...' (Abbott 266).

288 power heavenly being.

292 Barabbas Stressed on the first syllable, as in Marlowe's *Jew of Malta*. At the crowd's demand, Pilate released Barabbas, who was a thief, rather than Jesus; perhaps 202 above put Shakespeare in mind of the name. Shylock would rather his daughter had married a Jewish thief than a Christian thief such as Lorenzo.

294 pursue Stressed on the first syllable.

PORTIA Tarry a little, there is something else.
This bond doth give thee here no jot of blood.
The words expressly are 'a pound of flesh'.
Take then thy bond, take thou thy pound of flesh,
But in the cutting it, if thou dost shed
One drop of Christian blood, thy lands and goods
Are by the laws of Venice confiscate
Unto the state of Venice.
GRATIANO O upright judge!
Mark, Jew – O learned judge!
SHYLOCK Is that the law?
PORTIA Thyself shall see the Act.
For as thou urgest justice, be assured
Thou shalt have justice more than thou desirest.
GRATIANO O learned judge! Mark, Jew: a learned judge.
SHYLOCK I take this offer then. Pay the bond thrice
And let the Christian go.
BASSANIO Here is the money.
PORTIA Soft.
The Jew shall have all justice; soft, no haste;
He shall have nothing but the penalty.
GRATIANO O Jew, an upright judge, a learned judge!
PORTIA Therefore prepare thee to cut off the flesh.
Shed thou no blood, nor cut thou less nor more
But just a pound of flesh. If thou tak'st more
Or less than a just pound, be it but so much
As makes it light or heavy in the substance
Or the division of the twentieth part
Of one poor scruple – nay, if the scale do turn
But in the estimation of a hair,
Thou diest, and all thy goods are confiscate.

312 desirest] Q2, F; desirst Q1 314 this] Q1–2, F; his Q3 316–17 Soft...haste] *As Capell; as one line*, Q1–2, F
323 but] Q1–2; *not in* F

307 confiscate Words such as this, which were derived from Latin past participles, were treated as participial adjectives in Elizabethan English and so did not take the *-d* ending.

310 Is that the law? The stage business of letting knife and scales fall to the ground at this point, favoured by some nineteenth-century actors, was finally abandoned by Irving in 1884.

316 Soft i.e. not so fast.

317 all justice exactly what is allowed by law (with an ironic play on the meaning 'fully satisfying justice').

323 just exact.

324–6 in the substance...scruple I take 325 to be parenthetical, so that the meaning is 'by the gross weight of a mere scruple, or even the twentieth part of one'. The scruple was an apothecary's measure, weighing a little over one gram, and the twentieth part of this, called a grain, was 65 milligrams.

326–7 turn...hair i.e. is uneven by only a hair's breadth.

GRATIANO A second Daniel; a Daniel, Jew!
Now, infidel, I have you on the hip.
PORTIA Why doth the Jew pause? Take thy forfeiture.
SHYLOCK Give me my principal, and let me go.
BASSANIO I have it ready for thee; here it is.
PORTIA He hath refused it in the open court.
He shall have merely justice and his bond.
GRATIANO A Daniel, still say I, a second Daniel!
I thank thee, Jew, for teaching me that word.
SHYLOCK Shall I not have barely my principal?
PORTIA Thou shalt have nothing but the forfeiture,
To be so taken at thy peril, Jew.
SHYLOCK Why then, the devil give him good of it!
I'll stay no longer question.
PORTIA Tarry, Jew:
The law hath yet another hold on you.
It is enacted in the laws of Venice,
If it be proved against an alien
That by direct or indirect attempts
He seek the life of any citizen,
The party 'gainst the which he doth contrive
Shall seize one half his goods, the other half
Comes to the privy coffer of the state,
And the offender's life lies in the mercy
Of the Duke only, 'gainst all other voice.
In which predicament I say thou stand'st;
For it appears by manifest proceeding
That indirectly, and directly too,
Thou hast contrived against the very life
Of the defendant, and thou hast incurred

330 you] Q1–2; thee F 342 longer] Q1, F; longer heere in Q2 349 one] Q1, F; on Q2

330 **on the hip** Compare 1.3.38 and n.

335 **merely** There seems to be some play here between the usual modern sense of 'only' and the older sense of 'absolute' (compare 'mere enemy', 3.2.261). Both meanings were equally available to Shakespeare.

342 **I'll...question** I will not wait to hear the case debated any longer.

348 **contrive** scheme; as in *R2* 1.3.189: 'To plot, contrive, or complot any ill'.

349 **seize** take possession of. A legal term.

350 **privy coffer** A term which would be familiar to an English audience, as it was used of the sovereign's personal fortune.

352 **'gainst all other voice** without appeal. This may indicate that the limitless powers of a stage Duke were known by Shakespeare not to be enjoyed by the Doge of Venice.

The danger formerly by me rehearsed.
Down, therefore, and beg mercy of the Duke.

GRATIANO Beg that thou mayst have leave to hang thyself –
And yet, thy wealth being forfeit to the state,
Thou hast not left the value of a cord;
Therefore thou must be hanged at the state's charge.

DUKE That thou shalt see the difference of our spirit,
I pardon thee thy life before thou ask it.
For half thy wealth, it is Antonio's;
The other half comes to the general state,
Which humbleness may drive unto a fine.

PORTIA Ay, for the state, not for Antonio.

SHYLOCK Nay, take my life and all, pardon not that:
You take my house when you do take the prop
That doth sustain my house; you take my life
When you do take the means whereby I live.

PORTIA What mercy can you render him, Antonio?

GRATIANO A halter gratis – nothing else, for God's sake.

ANTONIO So please my lord the Duke and all the court
To quit the fine for one half of his goods,
I am content, so he will let me have
The other half in use, to render it
Upon his death unto the gentleman
That lately stole his daughter.
Two things provided more: that for this favour
He presently become a Christian;
The other, that he do record a gift,

364 spirit] Q1, F; spirits Q2

358 danger...rehearsed the aforesaid due penalties of the law. Legal jargon.

364 our Probably the royal first person plural; perhaps also a collective plural, implying 'of us Christians'.

365 pardon remit.

369 Ay...Antonio Portia's interpolation makes it clear that the Duke is speaking of the state's share of Shylock's property, not of Antonio's share. She thus leaves Antonio free to 'render mercy' at 374 below.

370–3 Nay...live On the echo of *The Jew of Malta*, see p. 7 above; on the emotional effect of this as a turning-point in the action, see p. 39.

371, 372 house...house A timber-framed house is here a metaphor of life; the image and the thing imaged fuse with great dramatic force, thanks to the biblical use of 'house' to mean a clan or extended family and its descendants.

377 quit remit. *OED*, however, illustrates this meaning with no other example than this passage (*OED* sv *v* 4) – though the meaning 'clear, absolve' is very close to it.

379 in use in trust. Antonio is offering, provided the state, on its part, exacts nothing from Shylock, to administer in a productive way the half of Shylock's fortune to which he is entitled, and to make it over on Shylock's death to Lorenzo and Jessica. 'Use' need not imply usury, though the choice of the word here is disturbing.

383 presently immediately.

384 record a gift sign a legal deed of gift.

Here in the court, of all he dies possessed
Unto his son Lorenzo and his daughter.

DUKE He shall do this, or else I do recant
The pardon that I late pronouncèd here.

PORTIA Art thou contented, Jew? What dost thou say?

SHYLOCK I am content.

PORTIA Clerk, draw a deed of gift.

SHYLOCK I pray you give me leave to go from hence;
I am not well. Send the deed after me
And I will sign it.

DUKE Get thee gone, but do it.

GRATIANO In christening shalt thou have two godfathers:
Had I been judge, thou shouldst have had ten more,
To bring thee to the gallows, not to the font.

Exit [*Shylock*]

DUKE Sir, I entreat you home with me to dinner.

PORTIA I humbly do desire your grace of pardon.
I must away this night toward Padua,
And it is meet I presently set forth.

DUKE I am sorry that your leisure serves you not.
Antonio, gratify this gentleman,
For in my mind you are much bound to him.

Exit Duke and his train

BASSANIO Most worthy gentleman, I and my friend
Have by your wisdom been this day acquitted
Of grievous penalties, in lieu whereof
Three thousand ducats due unto the Jew
We freely cope your courteous pains withal.

394 SH GRATIANO] Q2, F; *Shy.* Q1 396 not to] Q1, F; not Q2 396 SD *Shylock*] *Rowe; not in* Q1–2, F 398 grace of] Q1–2, F; Graces Q3

385 possessed possessed of.

395 ten more i.e. to bring the number up to the twelve required for a jury. The jest that jurymen were godfathers, because they sent the condemned man to God's judgement, was an old one; Malone notes an occurrence of it as early as the year of Shakespeare's birth.

396 SD Kean's withering stare at Gratiano was an important part of his effective exit. Inspired perhaps by the belief of Victorian critics that Shylock is about to die, Irving went out a broken man. Another actor who shall be nameless went out bleeding to death from a self-inflicted stab-wound. Olivier uttered a terrible off-stage howl.

398 of for; as in *Oth.* 3.3.212: 'I humbly do beseech you of your pardon.'

402 gratify reward.

403 bound If the Duke puns mildly here he helps relax the tension of the scene and so prepares us for a change of mood.

405–6 acquitted Of freed from.

408 cope The financial images which follow suggest that the meaning is 'give in exchange for' (*OED* sv v^3, from Old English *ceapan*, to buy and sell), rather than 'match, meet' (*OED* v^2, from Old French *couper*, strike, encounter in battle). We still speak of a horse-coper.

ANTONIO And stand indebted over and above
In love and service to you evermore.
PORTIA He is well paid that is well satisfied;
And I delivering you am satisfied
And therein do account myself well paid;
My mind was never yet more mercenary.
I pray you know me when we meet again.
I wish you well, and so I take my leave.
BASSANIO Dear sir, of force I must attempt you further.
Take some remembrance of us as a tribute,
Not as a fee. Grant me two things, I pray you:
Not to deny me, and to pardon me.
PORTIA You press me far, and therefore I will yield.
Give me your gloves, I'll wear them for your sake;
And for your love I'll take this ring from you.
Do not draw back your hand; I'll take no more,
And you in love shall not deny me this.
BASSANIO This ring, good sir? Alas, it is a trifle;
I will not shame myself to give you this.
PORTIA I will have nothing else but only this;
And now methinks I have a mind to it.
BASSANIO There's more depends on this than on the value.
The dearest ring in Venice will I give you,
And find it out by proclamation.
Only for this I pray you pardon me.
PORTIA I see, sir, you are liberal in offers.
You taught me first to beg, and now methinks
You teach me how a beggar should be answered.
BASSANIO Good sir, this ring was given me by my wife,
And when she put it on, she made me vow
That I should neither sell, nor give, nor lose it.

419 a] Q2; *not in* Q1, F

415 know...again A polite phrase meaning 'consider this as an introduction'; Portia plays on the further senses 'recognise' and 'have carnal knowledge of'.

417 Dear sir Bassanio now runs after Portia, and the ensuing dialogue gains its effect from the audience knowing they are husband and wife.

417 of force necessarily.

422 Give...sake Probably spoken to Antonio, before Portia turns back to Bassanio.

423 love affectionate gratitude; but with an ironic overtone of 'so much for your love!'

430 There's...value 'More than the cost of the ring is at stake' (Brown). An awkward phrase, as the second 'on' is superfluous.

PORTIA That scuse serves many men to save their gifts;
And if your wife be not a mad woman,
And know how well I have deserved this ring,
She would not hold out enemy for ever
For giving it to me. Well, peace be with you.
Exeunt [*Portia and Nerissa*]

ANTONIO My lord Bassanio, let him have the ring.
Let his deservings and my love withal
Be valued 'gainst your wife's commandement.

BASSANIO Go, Gratiano, run and overtake him;
Give him the ring, and bring him if thou canst
Unto Antonio's house. Away, make haste.
Exit Gratiano
Come, you and I will thither presently,
And in the morning early will we both
Fly toward Belmont. Come, Antonio.
Exeunt

[4.2] *Enter* [PORTIA *and*] NERISSA

PORTIA Enquire the Jew's house out, give him this deed,
And let him sign it. We'll away tonight
And be a day before our husbands home.
This deed will be well welcome to Lorenzo.

Enter GRATIANO

GRATIANO Fair sir, you are well o'ertane.
My lord Bassanio upon more advice
Hath sent you here this ring, and doth entreat
Your company at dinner.

444 SD *Portia and Nerissa*] *Theobald subst.; not in* Q1–2, F

Act 4, Scene 2 4.2] *Capell subst.; not in* Q1–2, F
0 SD PORTIA *and*] F; *not in* Q1–2

440 scuse This is an alternative form of 'excuse' rather than a contraction made to fit the metre.

443 hold...enemy i.e. continue to be your enemy.

447 commandement A four-syllable word. Shakespeare makes use of the same old spelling and pronunciation in *1H6*: 'From him I have express commandement' (1.3.20).

Act 4, Scene 2

4.2 Rowe has no change of scene here, but one is indicated by Gratiano's speedy exit at 4.1.450 to catch up with the lawyer, as he now does.

5 Fair...o'ertane i.e. I am glad I've caught up with you. A short line since Gratiano is out of breath.

6 more advice further reflection, second thoughts.

PORTIA That cannot be.
His ring I do accept most thankfully,
And so I pray you tell him. Furthermore,
I pray you show my youth old Shylock's house.
GRATIANO That will I do.
NERISSA [*To Portia*] Sir, I would speak with you.
[*Aside*] I'll see if I can get my husband's ring
Which I did make him swear to keep for ever.
PORTIA Thou mayst, I warrant. We shall have old swearing
That they did give the rings away to men;
But we'll outface them, and outswear them too.
– Away, make haste, thou know'st where I will tarry.
NERISSA Come, good sir, will you show me to this house?
[*Exeunt*]

5.[1] *Enter* LORENZO *and* JESSICA

LORENZO The moon shines bright. In such a night as this,
When the sweet wind did gently kiss the trees,
And they did make no noise, in such a night
Troilus methinks mounted the Troyan walls
And sighed his soul toward the Grecian tents,
Where Cressid lay that night.
JESSICA In such a night
Did Thisbe fearfully o'ertrip the dew,

9 His] Q1, F; This Q2 12 SD] *This edn; not in* Q1–2, F 13 SD] *Capell; not in* Q1–2, F 19 SD] F; *not in* Q1–2
Act 5, Scene 1 5.1] *Rowe subst.; not in* Q1–2; *Actus Quintus.* F 1 The...this] *As one line,* Q1, F; *as two lines divided after* bright Q2

15 old extraordinary; as in *Ado* 5.2.96, 'yonder's old coil at home', and in *Mac.* 2.3.2–3, 'old turning the key'. We still say 'a high old time'. The return to the familiar, jesting language of 1.2 and 3.4 helps to distance the high drama of the trial.

Act 5, Scene 1

1–14 For the dramatic force of this rhetorically patterned dialogue about famous and ill-fated lovers, see p. 4 above.

4 Troilus A memory of Chaucer's *Troilus and Criseyde*, 5: in the stanza beginning line 645, the sighing Troilus watches the moon wane, and in the stanza beginning line 666 he walks on the walls of Troy, gazing at the Greek camp to which Criseyde has been taken in an exchange of prisoners. Ann Thompson points out that this is the only reference by Shakespeare to the lovers (outside of *Troilus and Cressida*) which is not comic or satirical (*Shakespeare's Chaucer*, 1978, p. 65).

7, 10, 13 Thisbe...Dido...Medea Their stories, in this order, are told in Chaucer's *Legend of Good Women*, which he himself regarded as a sequel to *Troilus and Criseyde*, and which followed it in sixteenth-century editions (J. Hunter, *New Illustrations to Shakespeare*, 1845, I, 309–15).

7 dew This belongs to the previous morning in Chaucer (*Legend*, 775).

And saw the lion's shadow ere himself,
And ran dismayed away.

LORENZO In such a night
Stood Dido with a willow in her hand
Upon the wild sea banks, and waft her love
To come again to Carthage.

JESSICA In such a night
Medea gathered the enchanted herbs
That did renew old Aeson.

LORENZO In such a night
Did Jessica steal from the wealthy Jew
And with an unthrift love did run from Venice
As far as Belmont.

JESSICA In such a night
Did young Lorenzo swear he loved her well,
Stealing her soul with many vows of faith,
And ne'er a true one.

LORENZO In such a night
Did pretty Jessica (like a little shrew)
Slander her love, and he forgave it her.

JESSICA I would outnight you, did nobody come:
But hark, I hear the footing of a man.

8 lion's shadow The animal is a lioness both in Chaucer (*Legend*, 805) and in Ovid's *Metamorphoses* 4, 97. In both poems Pyramus finds Thisbe's blood-stained garment, concludes she has been killed by a lion, and kills himself. 'Shadow' implies moonshine, and Shakespeare again associates Pyramus with the moon in *Tit.* 2.3.231–2. Bottom and his friends actually turn the moon into a character when they enact the story in *A Midsummer Night's Dream*.

10–12 Dido...Carthage Chaucer relates how Dido was abandoned by Aeneas (*Legend*, 924 ff.), but the details here are from Chaucer's tale of Ariadne, who was abandoned by Theseus on an island in the 'wild sea' (*Legend*, 2164). She went 'high upon a rock' and tied her handkerchief to a pole, to call him back (2187 ff.). The willow is substituted as the traditional symbol of forsaken love, of which Shakespeare makes moving use in Desdemona's 'Willow Song' (*Oth.* 4.3. 40–57).

11 waft Always 'beckoned' in Shakespeare; never merely 'waved'.

13–14 Medea...Aeson After helping Jason win the Golden Fleece (compare 1.1.169 and 3.2.240), the witch Medea concocted a herbal broth with which she rejuvenated his father, Aeson (see p. 41 above). The incident is not in Chaucer's poem, but comes from Shakespeare's favourite passage of the *Metamorphoses* (7, 159–293), where much is made of the full moon.

15 steal creep away. But the occurrence of 'unthrift' in the next line hints at the presence of the word's more usual meaning. Jessica has stolen and prodigally spent her father's gold.

19 Stealing her soul This too has the shade of a more serious meaning than its teasing context implies; Lorenzo has converted Jessica to Christianity.

Enter [STEPHANO,] *a messenger*

LORENZO Who comes so fast in silence of the night?
STEPHANO A friend.
LORENZO A friend? What friend? Your name, I pray you, friend?
STEPHANO Stephano is my name, and I bring word
My mistress will before the break of day
Be here at Belmont. She doth stray about
By holy crosses where she kneels and prays
For happy wedlock hours.
LORENZO Who comes with her?
STEPHANO None but a holy hermit and her maid.
I pray you, is my master yet returned?
LORENZO He is not, nor we have not heard from him.
But go we in, I pray thee, Jessica,
And ceremoniously let us prepare
Some welcome for the mistress of the house.

Enter [LANCELOT,] *the Clown*

LANCELOT Sola, sola! Wo ha, ho! Sola, sola!
LORENZO Who calls?
LANCELOT Sola! Did you see Master Lorenzo? Master Lorenzo, sola, sola!

24 SD STEPHANO] *Theobald; not in* Q1–2, F 26, 28, 33 SH STEPHANO] *Reed² subst.; Messenger* Q1–2, F *subst.* 27 A friend] Q1–2, F; *not in Pope* 38 SD LANCELOT, *the Clown*] *Brown; Clowne* Q1–2, F; *Launcelot / Rowe* 39, 41, 44, 46 SH LANCELOT] *Rowe; Clowne* Q1–2, F 41 Master Lorenzo? Master Lorenzo] *Cam., conj. Thirlby;* M.*Lorenzo*, & M.*Lorenzo* Q1, F; M.*Lorenzo*, M.*Lorenzo* Q2; M.*Lorenzo*, and M.*Lorenza* F2; M.*Lorenzo* and Mrs *Lorenza* F3

24 SD *Enter* STEPHANO Neville Coghill thought that Stephano and later Portia and Nerissa needed to enter through the auditorium, since the tiring-house at the back of the stage represented Portia's house (*The Triple Bond*, ed. J. G. Price, 1975, p. 235). But the drawn curtain of the central space would suffice to indicate the house, leaving characters returning from Venice one or other of the two main doors on to the stage to enter by.

27 **friend** Like Portia at 2.9.84, Lorenzo is bandying words with Stephano, who is probably identical with the Messenger of that scene. Stephano had replied in a mock-military manner to Lorenzo's challenge. Compare 'My friend Stephano' at 51 below.

30–2 **She...hours** A different course of action from that Portia announced at 3.4.26–32, but this passes unnoticed in the theatre.

33 **hermit** His failure to appear troubled Johnson, but probably he was never more than a verbal touch of romance.

37 **ceremoniously** A grammatically transferred word: 'Let us prepare some ceremonious welcome.'

38 SD Lancelot enters from the house, pretending he cannot see Lorenzo despite the bright moonlight.

39 **Sola** Brown points out that this hunting cry is used as such in a hunting scene in *LLL* (4.1.149).

39 **Wo ha, ho** A falconer's call (*OED* Wo 1).

41 **Master Lorenzo? Master Lorenzo** Q1 and F read 'M.Lorenzo, & M.Lorenzo'. F2 and F3, in altering this as if they thought it denoted a couple – Master and Mistress Lorenzo – ignored the 'him' of 46, which suggests that Shakespeare did not have any such pair in mind.

LORENZO Leave holloaing, man! Here!
LANCELOT Sola! Where, where?
LORENZO Here!
LANCELOT Tell him there's a post come from my master, with his horn full of good news: my master will be here ere morning, sweet soul.

LORENZO Let's in and there expect their coming.
And yet no matter: why should we go in?
My friend Stephano, signify I pray you,
Within the house, your mistress is at hand,
And bring your music forth into the air.
[*Exit Stephano*]
How sweet the moonlight sleeps upon this bank!
Here will we sit, and let the sounds of music
Creep in our ears; soft stillness and the night
Become the touches of sweet harmony.
Sit, Jessica. Look how the floor of heaven
Is thick inlaid with patens of bright gold.

47–8 Morning, sweet soul.] Q2; morning sweete soule. Q1, F; morning, sweet love. F2; morning. *Rowe* 49 Let's] Q1–2, F; Sweet love, let's *Rowe*; Sweet soul, let's *Reed* 51 Stephano] Q2; Stephen Q1, F 53 SD] *Hanmer subst.*; *not in* Q1–2, F 56 ears; soft] F2; ears soft Q1–2, F 59 patens] Q1, F; pattents Q2; patterns F2; patines *Malone*

46 post courier.

46–7 horn...news i.e. like a cornucopia or horn of plenty.

47 morning Most editors give Lancelot an exit here; but why should he not stay and see the fun?

47–8 sweet soul Many editors place this at the beginning of 49, which is two syllables short of a regular blank verse line without it. In 1926 Greg suggested (NS, p. 106) that 'sweete soule' constituted the catchwords at the end of an inserted passage, and that the copyist or compositor then dropped the corresponding words at the start of 49 instead of the catchwords, which were left standing at the end of Lancelot's speech. Later, Greg dropped his own 'elaborate conjecture' of an interpolation, but still believed the words were the opening of 49. Robin Hood suggests that an interpolation had to be made when Shakespeare realised that Bassanio's homecoming needed to be announced, and that the passage was inserted between 38 and 49, with 'sweete soule' as the conclusion to Lancelot's speech, and 49 made a slightly short line to convey a sense of urgency. He thinks the expression reflects some clowning business on Lancelot's part. It could also simply express 'kind' Lancelot's affection for Bassanio.

49 expect await.

50 no matter 'Used to give an emphatic negative to a previous statement or implication' (Onions).

52 your mistress The fact that Lorenzo does not mention the master of the house indicates that the announcement of Bassanio's return (38 SD to 49) is indeed an interpolation.

53 music i.e. a group of musicians, as in 'The Queen's Musick'.

57 Become Befit, suit.

57 touches strains; with a hint of the meaning 'influences'.

59 patens A paten was the small dish or plate used in the Holy Communion, and this association is thought by most editors to fit the reverence of Lorenzo's tone. The conceit may be that patens inset into the floor of heaven would appear from below like the gilded bosses of an elaborate Elizabethan ceiling, reflecting points of light. F2's 'patterns' may however be the right emendation, especially as the constellations were thought of as establishing the design of earthly events. The zodiac was often represented in inlaid floors, such as the once famous one of Becket's shrine at Canterbury. Q2's 'pattents' has never been explained.

There's not the smallest orb which thou behold'st
But in his motion like an angel sings,
Still choiring to the young-eyed cherubins.
Such harmony is in immortal souls,
But whilst this muddy vesture of decay
Doth grossly close it in, we cannot hear it.

[*Enter* STEPHANO *with musicians*]

Come, ho! and wake Diana with a hymn.
With sweetest touches pierce your mistress' ear,
And draw her home with music.

Music plays

JESSICA I am never merry when I hear sweet music.
LORENZO The reason is your spirits are attentive.
For do but note a wild and wanton herd
Or race of youthful and unhandled colts

65 it in] Q1; in it Q2, F; us in it *Rowe*; us in *Rowe*[2] **65** SD] *Capell subst.*; *not in* Q1–2, F **68** SD] Q2; *play Musique* Q1, F

60–1 smallest...sings The idea that the concentric spheres of the Ptolemaic universe produced music by their friction was familiar in the sixteenth century, mainly through Cicero's *Somnium Scipionis*, which inspired Montaigne to write of 'the revolutions, motions, cadences, and carols of the asters [i.e. stars] and planets' (*The Essays of Montaigne done into English by John Florio*, Tudor Translations, 1902, I, 104). Because the stars, being in a fixed sphere, could not strictly be said to sing individually, some have taken Shakespeare's orbs to be an echo of Job 38.7: 'the morning stars sang together'. But 'sang' is not used in sixteenth-century translations.

62 Still choiring continually singing together. An echo of the *Te Deum* as translated in the Book of Common Prayer: 'To thee Cherubin and Seraphin continually do cry.'

62 young-eyed Two traditions about the nature of the cherubim are linked by this compound adjective. In Renaissance art they are commonly represented as beautiful winged children, often without bodies. In the Bible, however, they appear in the vision of Ezekiel as mysterious 'living beings' with eyes all over their bodies (Ezek. 10.12).

62 cherubins This irregular plural, along with its alternative form 'cherubims', occurs frequently until the middle of the seventeenth century.

63 Such...souls i.e. as the 'great world' of the heavenly bodies makes music, so too does the world of men.

64 muddy vesture of decay i.e. the body, thought of as made from the dust of the earth, as in Gen. 2.7.

65 it...it It is probable that both pronouns stand for the music of creation, but the first 'it' could be a kind of collective singular for the 'immortal souls' – 'each and every soul'.

66 wake Diana call forth the moon (which appears, from 92, to have gone behind a cloud). NS however takes 'wake' to mean 'keep vigil for' and identifies the virgin Portia with Diana.

67 touches strains; as at 57. For John Stevens the word implies that Stephano's musicians are a consort of strings ('Shakespeare and the music of the Elizabethan stage', *Shakespeare in Music*, ed. P. Hartnoll, 1964, pp. 3–48, p. 29).

68 draw...music The legendary drawing power of music, an anticipation of the allusion to Orpheus at 79–80, follows naturally on talk of its supernatural origins. Shakespeare will make full dramatic use of the idea in Ariel's music in *Temp.*

69 merry light-hearted.

70 spirits faculties (*OED* sv *sb* 18, but with a nuance of 17d, 'liveliness': hence the image of young colts).

72 race 'herd or stud' (Onions).

72 unhandled colts i.e. young stallions which are not yet broken in. Ariel's music in *Temp.* 4.1.175–8 tames an unruly group of characters who are 'like unbacked colts'.

Fetching mad bounds, bellowing and neighing loud –
Which is the hot condition of their blood –
If they but hear perchance a trumpet sound,
Or any air of music touch their ears,
You shall perceive them make a mutual stand,
Their savage eyes turned to a modest gaze
By the sweet power of music. Therefore the poet
Did feign that Orpheus drew trees, stones, and floods;
Since naught so stockish, hard, and full of rage,
But music for the time doth change his nature.
The man that hath no music in himself,
Nor is not moved with concord of sweet sounds,
Is fit for treasons, stratagems, and spoils;
The motions of his spirit are dull as night
And his affections dark as Erebus.
Let no such man be trusted. Mark the music.

Enter PORTIA *and* NERISSA

PORTIA That light we see is burning in my hall.
How far that little candle throws his beams!
So shines a good deed in a naughty world.
NERISSA When the moon shone we did not see the candle.
PORTIA So doth the greater glory dim the less:
A substitute shines brightly as a king
Until a king be by, and then his state

87 Erebus] F2; *Terebus* Q1–2; *Erobus* F; *Tenebris* Q3

74 hot Blood was thought of literally as a hot fluid, or humour, abundant in young animals.

77 mutual Here, 'simultaneous'.

79 the poet Ovid in *Metamorphoses* 10, 86 ff. The song that opens Act 3 of *H8*, 'Orpheus with his lute', is based on the same legend.

81 stockish...rage These terms appropriately qualify the nouns 'trees, stones, and floods' in the preceding line. A favourite rhetorical device, strikingly illustrated by a song in Sidney's *Arcadia*: 'Virtue, beauty and speech, did strike, wound, charm / My heart, eyes, ears, with wonder, love, delight' (ed. J. Robertson, 1973, p. 229).

82 for the time Primarily 'for the moment', but with a touch of the musical meaning of 'time': 'by effect of its tempo'.

83–8 The man...trusted Shylock calls fife music 'vile squealing' (2.5.29), and in *JC* the conspirator Cassius 'hears no music' (1.2.204).

85 spoils plunder.

86 The motions...night The impulses of his mind are as sinisterly impenetrable as is darkness.

87 Erebus In classical legend the place of darkness between Earth and Hades.

91 So...world A reminiscence of Matt. 5.14–16: 'Let your light so shine before men, that they may see your good works' (GB and BB), made very familiar by the Communion service.

91 naughty worthless, wicked.

92–3 When...less The proverbial saying 'to be like stars to the moon' (Tilley / Dent s826.2) may have originated in Horace's *Odes* 1, 12, 47, where the 'Julian star', Augustus, is said to be *velut inter ignis luna minores* – 'as the moon among lesser lights'. The king image which follows suggests Shakespeare had the Ode in mind, perhaps because it refers to Orpheus drawing trees, streams, and winds by his music (compare 80).

Empties itself, as doth an inland brook
Into the main of waters. Music, hark!

NERISSA It is your music, madam, of the house.

PORTIA Nothing is good, I see, without respect;
Methinks it sounds much sweeter than by day.

NERISSA Silence bestows that virtue on it, madam.

PORTIA The crow doth sing as sweetly as the lark
When neither is attended; and I think
The nightingale, if she should sing by day
When every goose is cackling, would be thought
No better a musician than the wren.
How many things by season seasoned are
To their right praise and true perfection.
Peace, ho! The moon sleeps with Endymion
And would not be awaked!

[*Music ceases*]

LORENZO That is the voice,
Or I am much deceived, of Portia!

PORTIA He knows me as the blind man knows the cuckoo
By the bad voice.

LORENZO Dear lady, welcome home!

PORTIA We have been praying for our husbands' welfare,
Which speed we hope the better for our words.
Are they returned?

LORENZO Madam, they are not yet.

97 hark] Q1–2; harke. *Musicke* F 109 Peace, ho!] *Malone;* Peace, how Q1–2, F; Peace! How *Pope* 110 SD] F; *not in* Q1–2 114 husbands' welfare] Q1, F; husband health Q2

96–7 inland...waters 'All rivers run into the sea' is another semi-proverb (Tilley R140) associated with various possible ideas, such as the passage of time, ineluctable mortality, or, as here, the natural principle of subordination.

98 music a group of musicians; as at 53 above.

99 Nothing...respect A commonplace. Used again in *Ham.* 2.2.249. The meaning is made clear by Donne's last lines to 'The Progess of the Soul': 'There's nothing simply good, nor ill alone, / Of every quality comparison / The only measure is, and judge, opinion' (*Complete English Poems*, ed. A. J. Smith, 1974, p. 193).

101 virtue special quality.

103 attended expected. Compare *OED* Attend *v* 15. This makes better sense here than 'listened to' or 'accompanied'.

107 season With a play on the meanings 'time' and 'spice', which is extended to 'seasoned'.

109 Peace, ho! Malone's modernisation of Q1–2 seems more likely than a whispered 'Peace! how...' because it enables Portia to raise her voice and so be recognised by Lorenzo in spite of the darkness. 'Howe' means 'Ho!' at 2.6.26.

109 the moon...Endymion Endymion was the shepherd on Mount Latmos who, in Greek legend, was loved by the moon. Capell suggested that Portia is speaking of Jessica and Lorenzo asleep in one another's arms. The director has to weigh up the effectiveness of this tableau against its weakening of the scene's steady expectancy. If the remark is an elaborate way of saying the moon has gone behind a cloud (see 92), its mythological wit helps restore the mood – and the Portia – of 3.2.53–62, before Bassanio claims her anew.

115 speed prosper.

But there is come a messenger before
To signify their coming.

PORTIA Go in, Nerissa:
Give order to my servants that they take
No note at all of our being absent hence –
Nor you Lorenzo, Jessica nor you.
[*A tucket sounds*]

LORENZO Your husband is at hand, I hear his trumpet.
We are no telltales, madam; fear you not.

PORTIA This night methinks is but the daylight sick,
It looks a little paler; 'tis a day
Such as the day is when the sun is hid.

Enter BASSANIO, ANTONIO, GRATIANO, *and their followers*

BASSANIO We should hold day with the Antipodes,
If you would walk in absence of the sun.

PORTIA Let me give light, but let me not be light,
For a light wife doth make a heavy husband,
And never be Bassanio so for me –
But God sort all! You are welcome home, my lord.

BASSANIO I thank you, madam. Give welcome to my friend.
This is the man, this is Antonio,
To whom I am so infinitely bound.

PORTIA You should in all sense be much bound to him,
For as I hear he was much bound for you.

121 SD] F; *not in* Q1–2

118 Go in No exit is given for Nerissa, who perhaps stays where she is because the tucket sounds. If, mindful of the need to keep up the pretence that she and Portia have stayed at home, she does go in, Gratiano can go into the house in search of her, so that both of them make a noisy, quarrelsome re-entry at 142.

119–20 take...all of make no remark at all on.

121 SD *tucket* A distinctive 'signature tune' on a trumpet. Bassanio is the only private citizen in Shakespeare to have his own tucket; perhaps he is now to be considered the ruler of Belmont. See J. S. Mansfield, *Music in the English Drama from Shakespeare to Purcell*, 1956, p. 28.

127–8 We...sun Malone glosses: 'If you would always walk in the night it would be day with us, as it now is on the other side of the globe.' Bassanio responds to Portia's remark as if they are in the middle of a quiet conversation. In this way Shakespeare, by a kind of under-playing or theatrical litotes, solves his problem of how to satisfy our expectations of this meeting; he also imparts to Antonio (and to us) the feeling that Belmont is home.

129 be light be wanton.

130 heavy unhappy, heavy-hearted.

132 God sort all All is as God disposes. Said with slight foreboding: Bassanio will shortly be a 'heavy husband'.

136 in all sense in the fullest meaning of the word.

136 bound Portia in fact plays on three meanings: 'indebted', 'pledged', and 'imprisoned'.

ANTONIO No more than I am well acquitted of.
PORTIA Sir, you are very welcome to our house.
It must appear in other ways than words:
Therefore I scant this breathing courtesy.
GRATIANO [*To Nerissa*] By yonder moon I swear you do me wrong!
In faith, I gave it to the judge's clerk,
Would he were gelt that had it, for my part,
Since you do take it, love, so much at heart.
PORTIA A quarrel ho, already! What's the matter?
GRATIANO About a hoop of gold, a paltry ring
That she did give me, whose poesy was
For all the world like cutler's poetry
Upon a knife: 'Love me, and leave me not.'
NERISSA What talk you of the poesy or the value?
You swore to me when I did give it you.
That you would wear it till your hour of death,
And that it should lie with you in your grave.
Though not for me, yet for your vehement oaths
You should have been respective and have kept it.
Gave it a judge's clerk! No, God's my judge
The clerk will ne'er wear hair on's face that had it.
GRATIANO He will, and if he live to be a man.
NERISSA Ay, if a woman live to be a man.
GRATIANO Now by this hand, I gave it to a youth,
A kind of boy, a little scrubbèd boy
No higher than thyself, the judge's clerk,

142 SD] *Rowe; not in* Q1–2, F **148** give] Q1–2, F; give to *Collier*[2], *conj. Steevens* **148, 151** poesy] Q2 *subst.*; posie Q1, F **152** it] Q2, F; *not in* Q1 **157** No...judge] Q1–2; but well I know F

138 acquitted of freed from.

141 this breathing courtesy i.e. these verbal compliments.

142 By yonder moon An unpropitious oath, as Juliet tells Romeo: 'O swear not by the moon, th'inconstant moon' (*Rom.* 2.2.109).

144 gelt gelded.

148 poesy The motto inscribed on the inside of a ring was called its posy. The less common Q2 spelling is used here as it may be a trisyllable, which the metre requires.

149 cutler's poetry i.e. phrase or verse inscribed on a knife handle. The expression is a scornful one, like our 'cracker-mottoes'.

150 leave part with; as at 172 and 196 below. At *TGV* 4.4.74, where a ring is also in question, Julia says 'It seems you lov'd not her, to leave her token.'

156 respective 'regardful of the circumstances under which you received it' (Pooler).

157 No...judge F1 substitutes 'But well I know', in deference to the 1606 decree against stage profanity.

161 hand Nerissa may be clutching it to display its ringless state.

162 scrubbèd stunted; like the low-growing bushes we call 'scrub'.

A prating boy that begged it as a fee;
I could not for my heart deny it him.

PORTIA You were to blame, I must be plain with you,
To part so slightly with your wife's first gift,
A thing stuck on with oaths upon your finger
And so riveted with faith unto your flesh.
I gave my love a ring, and made him swear
Never to part with it, and here he stands.
I dare be sworn for him he would not leave it
Nor pluck it from his finger for the wealth
That the world masters. Now in faith, Gratiano,
You give your wife too unkind a cause of grief;
And 'twere to me, I should be mad at it.

BASSANIO [*Aside*] Why, I were best to cut my left hand off
And swear I lost the ring defending it.

GRATIANO My lord Bassanio gave his ring away
Unto the judge that begged it, and indeed
Deserved it too; and then the boy his clerk
That took some pains in writing, he begged mine,
And neither man nor master would take aught
But the two rings.

PORTIA What ring gave you, my lord?
Not that, I hope, which you received of me?

BASSANIO If I could add a lie unto a fault,
I would deny it; but you see my finger
Hath not the ring upon it, it is gone.

PORTIA Even so void is your false heart of truth.
By heaven, I will ne'er come in your bed
Until I see the ring.

NERISSA Nor I in yours
Till I again see mine.

BASSANIO Sweet Portia,
If you did know to whom I gave the ring,
If you did know for whom I gave the ring,
And would conceive for what I gave the ring,
And how unwillingly I left the ring,

177 SD] *Theobald; not in* Q1–2, F 191–2 Nor...mine] *As two lines,* Q1–2; *as one line,* F

174 masters possesses.

176 And If.

193–7, 199–202 Bassanio makes a frenetic use of the rhetorical figure epistrophe as a persuasive device, which Portia coolly parodies.

196 left parted with.

When naught would be accepted but the ring,
You would abate the strength of your displeasure.

PORTIA If you had known the virtue of the ring,
Or half her worthiness that gave the ring,
Or your own honour to contain the ring,
You would not then have parted with the ring.
What man is there so much unreasonable,
If you had pleased to have defended it
With any terms of zeal, wanted the modesty
To urge the thing held as a ceremony?
Nerissa teaches me what to believe:
I'll die for't, but some woman had the ring!

BASSANIO No by my honour, madam, by my soul
No woman had it, but a civil doctor,
Which did refuse three thousand ducats of me,
And begged the ring, the which I did deny him,
And suffered him to go displeased away,
Even he that had held up the very life
Of my dear friend. What should I say, sweet lady?
I was enforced to send it after him;
I was beset with shame and courtesy;
My honour would not let ingratitude
So much besmear it. Pardon me, good lady,
For by these blessèd candles of the night,
Had you been there I think you would have begged
The ring of me to give the worthy doctor.

PORTIA Let not that doctor e'er come near my house.
Since he hath got the jewel that I loved
And that which you did swear to keep for me,
I will become as liberal as you;
I'll not deny him anything I have,
No, not my body, nor my husband's bed:
Know him I shall, I am well sure of it.

214 had...up] Q1, F; did uphold Q2

199 virtue inherent value (or possibly the magical power of the stones set in the ring).

201 contain retain (*OED* sv *v* 13c).

205 wanted the modesty as to have been so lacking in delicacy.

206 urge press for.

206 ceremony i.e. something held sacred, a symbol.

210 civil doctor doctor of civil law.

214 held up preserved.

217 beset with assailed by feelings of.

220 candles, stars. A favourite Shakespearean metaphor, as in Romeo's 'Night's candles are burnt out' (*Rom.* 3.5.9).

226 liberal generous; with a play on the meaning 'licentious'.

229 Know him A deliberate echo of the quibble in 4.1.415.

Lie not a night from home. Watch me like Argus.
If you do not, if I be left alone,
Now by mine honour which is yet mine own,
I'll have that doctor for my bedfellow.
NERISSA And I his clerk; therefore be well advised
How you do leave me to mine own protection.
GRATIANO Well, do you so. Let not me take him then,
For if I do, I'll mar the young clerk's pen.
ANTONIO I am th'unhappy subject of these quarrels.
PORTIA Sir, grieve not you; you are welcome notwithstanding.
BASSANIO Portia, forgive me this enforcèd wrong;
And in the hearing of these many friends
I swear to thee, even by thine own fair eyes
Wherein I see myself –
PORTIA Mark you but that?
In both my eyes he doubly sees himself:
In each eye one. Swear by your double self,
And there's an oath of credit!
BASSANIO Nay, but hear me.
Pardon this fault, and by my soul I swear
I nevermore will break an oath with thee.
ANTONIO I once did lend my body for his wealth,
Which but for him that had your husband's ring
Had quite miscarried. I dare be bound again,
My soul upon the forfeit, that your lord
Will nevermore break faith advisedly.
PORTIA Then you shall be his surety. Give him this,
And bid him keep it better than the other.
ANTONIO Here, Lord Bassanio, swear to keep this ring.
BASSANIO By heaven, it is the same I gave the doctor!

233 my] Q2, F; mine Q1 239] *As one line*, Q1–2; *as two lines divided after* you F

230 Lie...home not sleep a single night away from home.

230 Argus The watchful guardian in classical fables; only two of his hundred eyes closed in sleep at any one time.

232 mine own intact.

234 be well advised take care.

237 pen A bawdy quibble: penis.

242 A deliberate glance back at the high-complimentary style of 3.2.116–18, 123–6 – not now so well received.

245 double With a play on the meanings 'two-fold' and 'two-faced, meretricious'.

246 of credit worthy of belief (said ironically).

249 wealth material well-being; as in the Book of Common Prayer Litany: 'In all time of our tribulation, in all time of our wealth', and the Prayer for the Sovereign: 'Grant her in health and wealth long to live.'

251 Had...miscarried Would have been entirely lost.

253 advisedly knowingly.

PORTIA I had it of him; pardon me, Bassanio,
For by this ring the doctor lay with me.
NERISSA And pardon me, my gentle Gratiano,
For that same scrubbèd boy the doctor's clerk,
In lieu of this, last night did lie with me.
GRATIANO Why, this is like the mending of highways
In summer where the ways are fair enough!
What, are we cuckolds ere we have deserved it?
PORTIA Speak not so grossly; you are all amazed.
Here is a letter, read it at your leisure;
It comes from Padua, from Bellario.
There you shall find that Portia was the doctor,
Nerissa there her clerk. Lorenzo here
Shall witness I set forth as soon as you,
And even but now returned; I have not yet
Entered my house. Antonio, you are welcome;
And I have better news in store for you
Than you expect. Unseal this letter soon;
There you shall find three of your argosies
Are richly come to harbour suddenly.
You shall not know by what strange accident
I chancèd on this letter.
ANTONIO I am dumb.
BASSANIO Were you the doctor and I knew you not?
GRATIANO Were you the clerk that is to make me cuckold?
NERISSA Ay, but the clerk that never means to do it,
Unless he live until he be a man.
BASSANIO Sweet doctor, you shall be my bedfellow;
When I am absent, then lie with my wife.
ANTONIO Sweet lady, you have given me life and living;
For here I read for certain that my ships
Are safely come to road.

262 In lieu of In return for.

263–4 mending...enough i.e. cynical and preposterous. Each parish had the obligation to maintain its roads in good repair – a duty notoriously neglected in winter when most necessary but accepted as a pleasant pastime in summer when not necessary at all. Gratiano seems to be saying that the women have embarked on affairs before their marriages have been put to the test.

266 amazed bewildered.

275 soon quickly.

278–9 You...letter 'A beautiful example of Shakespeare's dramatic impudence' (NS). Its airiness is theatrically emphasised as Portia triumphantly watches the men poring over their letters.

286 life and living Perhaps spoken with a slight stress on 'and'; Portia has already saved Antonio's life and now she has restored his livelihood.

288 road anchorage.

PORTIA How now, Lorenzo?
My clerk hath some good comforts too for you.
NERISSA Ay, and I'll give them him without a fee.
There do I give to you and Jessica
From the rich Jew, a special deed of gift
After his death of all he dies possessed of.
LORENZO Fair ladies, you drop manna in the way
Of starvèd people.
PORTIA It is almost morning;
And yet I am sure you are not satisfied
Of these events at full. Let us go in,
And charge us there upon inter'gatories,
And we will answer all things faithfully.
GRATIANO Let it be so. The first inter'gatory
That my Nerissa shall be sworn on is:
Whether till the next night she had rather stay,
Or go to bed now, being two hours to day.
But were the day come, I should wish it dark,
Till I were couching with the doctor's clerk.
Well, while I live I'll fear no other thing
So sore as keeping safe Nerissa's ring.

Exeunt

FINIS

298 inter'gatories] F; intergotories Q1–2; interrogatories F3 Q1 *corrected*, Q2; interrogatory F3 300 inter'gatory] F; intergory Q1 *uncorrected*; intergotory

294 manna i.e. the food from heaven which sustained the Israelites in the desert (Exod. 16.15). BB has 'manna', GB 'man'.

296–7 And...full I am sure you do not yet know all you want to about these events.

298 charge...inter'gatories An expression used of any searching examination under oath. This is Portia's last bit of legal jargon, perhaps spoken with a momentary return to her courtroom manner.

302 rather stay Nerissa's expression can convey what she thinks of this suggestion.

307 keeping 'the not keeping' (Rann).

307 ring Gratiano's last bit of bawdy, since 'ring' could mean 'vulva'. Marilyn L. Williamson points out that an anecdote in Rabelais's *Gargantua and Pantagruel* is based on this meaning (*South Atlantic Quarterly* 71 (1972), 587–94).

SUPPLEMENTARY NOTE

4.1.47–52:

Some men there are loue not a gaping pigge?
Some that are mad if they behold a Cat?
And others when the bagpipe sings ith nose,
cannot containe their vrine for affection.
Maisters of passion swayes it to the moode
of what it likes or loathes... (Q1)

Basic to any interpretation of this passage is the distinction made in Elizabethan psychology between 'affection' and 'passion'. Affection is a strong sensuous response, either of attraction or revulsion, which is thought of as arousing passion – that is, disturbing the mind. The two words are brought together at the end of *The Comedy of Errors*, when the Abbess, on being told that Antipholus's 'passion' has broken into 'extremity of rage' asks if the cause is that 'his eye / Strayed his affection in unlawful love?' (5.1.51–2).

Given this distinction, it is just possible to make sense of lines 51–2 as they stand, by taking 'Masters of passion' to refer to the various affections, or antipathies, that Shylock has listed. A singular verb with a plural subject is not uncommon in Elizabethan English. But if 'Masters' is a plural noun, its juxtaposition with the singular 'affection', together with the ambiguity of the twice-used 'it', produces a very clumsy sentence. Another suspicious feature of the passage is the full stop after 'affection'. The compositor at this stage was so short of full stops, which he had to conserve for abbreviated speech headings, that he was driven to make do with marks of interrogation in lines 47 and 48. In fact the full stop in line 50 is the last for 110 lines; only towards the end of the forme, in the bottom half of G4v, did the compositor allow himself to make use of a couple. The deliberate use of a full stop in line 50 therefore suggests an attempt to clarify a passage which may have been unpunctuated thus in the manuscript:

cannot containe their vrine for affection
maisters of passion swayes it to the moode
of what it likes or loathes...

Most editors prefer to remove the full stop, which they assume is misplaced, putting instead some intermediate mark of punctuation after 'urine', and changing 'Masters' to 'Master'. This makes 'Master of passion' a nominal clause, expanding 'affection' which is the subject of 'sways'. Although this makes very satisfactory sense, Bulloch's 1878 emendation seems to me marginally better:

for affection
Masters oft passion, sways it to the mood
Of what it likes or loathes.

Both rhythmically and syntactically the parallel verbs 'Masters' and 'sways', balanced by 'likes or loathes' in the next line, are a very Shakespearean construction. They are also typical of Shylock's speech, which is rich in active verbs. The confusion of 'of' and 'oft' is a probable one; 'oft' in the Hand D additions to *Sir Thomas More* is distinguished from 'of' only by a horizontal stroke which Shakespeare could easily have failed to make. The sole objection I can see to 'Masters oft passion' is that it is slightly awkward to say. But Shylock is seldom euphonious.

TEXTUAL ANALYSIS

The Heyes–Roberts quarto (Q1)

The textual history of *The Merchant of Venice* begins with two entries in the Stationers' Register. The first is under the date of 22 July 1598, and reads:

Iames Robertes. Entred for his copie vnder the handes of bothe the wardens, a booke of the Marchaunt of Venyce or otherwise called the Iewe of Venyce. Prouided that yt bee not prynted by the said Iames Robertes; or anye other whatsoeuer wthout lycence first had from the Right honorable the lord Chamberlen vj^{d}

For his sixpenny fee the printer James Roberts thus established his copyright in the play in the eyes of the officials ('wardens') of the Stationers' Company. The proviso however shows that he had not yet received permission to print from Shakespeare's company, the Lord Chamberlain's Men. Publication was in fact deferred until 1600, when a second entry records Roberts's transfer of his right in the work to a publisher called Heyes:

28 octobr 1600
Tho. haies. Entred for his copie vnder the handes of the Wardens & by Consent of m^{r} Robertes. A booke called the booke of the merchant of Venyce vj^{d}

These two entries for one play have given rise to various speculations. Earlier scholars believed Roberts, the official printer of playbills, to have been a book pirate whose access to the theatres enabled him to snap up such unconsidered trifles as the manuscript of *The Merchant of Venice*.[1] The condition that publication be deferred until the Lord Chamberlain (or his Men) gave permission was taken as a sign of the suspicion with which Roberts was received at Stationers' Hall. In reaction against this romantic scenario, the leaders of the 'new bibliography', early in this century, argued that Roberts made this and a few similar entries at the actors' instigation, in order to prevent the publication of corrupt or inadequate texts.[2]

The sale of the play to Roberts may, however, have been a straightforward business transaction. In the summer recess after what may have been the play's first season[3] the actors could have sold the manuscript on the understanding that printing would be delayed until any immediate theatrical currency the play might have was exhausted. When permission to print was given two years later, Roberts perhaps found himself without enough money for the venture, and as on other occasions[4] sought financial

[1] This nineteenth-century view of Roberts has been revived by A. S. Cairncross, 'Shakespeare and the "staying entries"', in *Shakespeare in the South-West: Some New Directions*, ed. T. J. Pafford, 1969, pp. 80–93.

[2] A. W. Pollard, *Shakespeare's Folios and Quartos*, 1909, pp. 66–7; W. W. Greg, *Some Aspects and Problems of London Publishing Between 1550 and 1650*, 1956, pp. 112–22.

[3] See pp. 1–2 above. [4] Brown, p. xii.

backing from another man in the book trade. The phrase 'by Consent of m^r^ Robertes' suggests that Heyes was accompanied by Roberts, or produced written authority for the transfer, when the 1600 entry was made in his favour.

Typesetting and printing must have followed within the next few weeks, as the Heyes–Roberts quarto appeared by the end of the year.[1] Its descriptive title page reads like one of the playbills Roberts was accustomed to print; a neat ambiguity keeps readers in suspense about the outcome of Shylock's malice.

The most excellent / Historie of the *Merchant / of Venice.* / With the extreame crueltie of *Shylocke* the Iewe / towards the sayd Merchant, in cutting a iust pound / of his flesh: and the obtayning of *Portia* / by the choyse of three / chests. / *As it hath beene diuers times acted by the Lord / Chamberlaine his Seruants.* / Written by William Shakespeare // [small fleuron ornament] // AT LONDON, / Printed by *I.R.* for Thomas Heyes, / and are to be sold in Paules Church-yard, at the / signe of the Greene Dragon. / 1600.

The copy for Q1

The Heyes–Roberts quarto is our only authoritative text of *The Merchant of Venice*; the second (1619) and third (1637) quartos and the First Folio text of 1623 were all printed from it. So it is especially important to try to establish the nature of the manuscript that served Roberts as copy. Since 'the book of' a play was theatrical jargon for a prompt-book, the curious phrase 'a booke called the booke of' suggests that Heyes proved his authorisation by producing the prompt-book, which would have been prepared from the playwright's manuscript or from a transcript of it. A few stage directions in Q1 are of the kind associated with prompt-books. The curt or imperative directions, '*Iessica* aboue' (2.6.26 SD), '*open the letter*' (3.2.235 SD), and '*play Musique*' (5.1.68 SD) could be by the book keeper. In 3.1 two entries are given for Tubal, at 60 and 62: the book keeper, in a preliminary inspection of the play, might have added the first of these to Shakespeare's manuscript before it was finally copied, in order to make sure that Tubal was visible to the audience when Solanio says 'Heere comes another of the Tribe' (61). He may also have clarified '*his man that was*' (that is, Shylock's former servant) by adding '*the Clowne*' to 2.5.0 SD.

There is, however, no good reason why Shakespeare should not have written all these directions himself. As an actor, he was accustomed to imperative stage directions; in making changes in his manuscript he may have left in two directions for Tubal's entry;[2] and he could himself have added the explanatory '*the Clowne*'. Moreover descriptive phrases such as '*his man that was*' are more characteristic of an authorial than of a theatrical manuscript. Other examples are 'her wayting woman *Nerrissa*' (1.2.0 SD), 'the maskers, *Gratiano* and *Salerino*' (2.6.0 SD), '*a man from* Anthonio' (3.1.57 SD), and '*Salerio* a messenger from Venice' (3.2.218 SD). Yet other directions suggest Shakespeare visualising a scene as he wrote: 'Enter *Morochus* a tawnie Moore all in white' (2.1.0 SD); '*Bassanio comments on the caskets to himselfe*' (3.2.62 SD). These directions *might* survive into a prompt-book, but there are others which would

[1] Probably in November, as plays printed in December usually carried the next year's date.
[2] Brown, p. xv.

certainly not be tolerated by the book keeper, who could not work from such vague descriptions as '*three or four followers*' (2.1.0 SD) and '*a follower or two*' (2.2.92 SD). Fluctuations between the speech headings *Launce*[*let*] and *Clowne* and between *Shy*[*lock*] and *Iew*[*e*] are uncharacteristic of a prompt-book and no book keeper would have let *Salerio* stand in the stage direction heading 3.3, since Salerio is at this point on the road to Venice; nor would he have left 4.2 without an entrance for Portia.[1] Lastly, the stage directions of the Folio indicate that the prompt-book provided for several musical effects which do not appear in Q1.[2]

All this suggests that the copy before Roberts's compositors in 1600 was a manuscript closer to the author than to the theatre. As Greg has shown,[3] there is no incompatibility here with the theory that Heyes produced the prompt-book for the Stationers' Company; he could have borrowed it as proof that the actors had at last agreed to publication, then returned it to the theatre and given Roberts the go-ahead to print the play from the manuscript which had been in his printing shop since 1598. Greg thought, however, that the directions with a prompt-book feel about them were indeed notes by the book keeper, possibly inserted 'when going through the manuscript preparatory to making the prompt copy'.[4] I venture to think that we can dispense with the book keeper. Shakespeare was a man of the theatre who, however rapidly he wrote, would keep reminding himself of the actors' and book keeper's needs, and so have gone back from time to time to enter such brief directions as *open the letter* or *play Musique*; we may add to these two the entrances at 2.4.9 and 2.6.58 which, like them, are not centred but crowded in at the right margin of the text. Overall, there is a strong probability that every word in the copy for Q1 was Shakespeare's.

We cannot, however, immediately assume that the manuscript set by Roberts's compositors was in Shakespeare's hand. Two arguments have been advanced for it having been a scribal copy. One is that although playwrights were expected to hand in a 'fair copy' to the theatre,[5] there are, as we shall see, enough anomalies in Q1 to make it unlikely that Shakespeare made his own fair copy; consequently it has to be supposed that as the company's chief dramatist he was privileged to have his plays copied by the playhouse scrivener who had no brief to tidy up or 'perfect' the manuscript which lay before him. The other argument is that another Shakespearean quarto which was set by the same compositors,[6] *Hamlet* Q2 (1603/4), displays all kinds of textual confusion, whereas Q1 of *The Merchant of Venice* is by comparison a very clean text. For some textual scholars, this makes it 'inconceivable...anyone could fancy both manuscripts were holograph'.[7] So *Hamlet* Q2 is assumed to have been set from Shakespeare's holograph and *The Merchant of Venice* Q1 from a scribal copy.

Every practising writer knows, however, that clear, fluent manuscript and illegible,

[1] These last two errors could, however, have been compositorial.

[2] W. W. Greg, *The Editorial Problem in Shakespeare*, 2nd edn, 1951, pp. 123–4; Brown, pp. xiv–xv and xix–xx.

[3] Greg, *Editorial Problem*, p. 107.

[4] *Ibid.*, p. 124.

[5] Fredson Bowers, *On Editing Shakespeare and the Elizabethan Dramatists*, 1955, pp. 13–16.

[6] John Russell Brown, 'Compositors of *Hamlet* Q2 and *The Merchant of Venice*', *SB* 7 (1955), 25–40.

[7] Fredson Bowers, 'Seven or more years?', in *Shakespeare 1971*, ed. Clifford Leech and J. M. R. Margeson (1972), p. 58.

much-emended manuscript can proceed at different times from the same hand. Both went under the name of 'foul papers' in the sixteenth century, since even the neatest authorial manuscript, if the playwright himself had not recopied it, was likely to contain small inconsistencies, some of them resulting from alterations, erasures, and insertions. QI has a number of the loose ends that characterise such authorial foul papers. Portia describes six suitors, but towards the end of the scene a servant speaks of them as 'the foure strangers' (1.2.101). Lancelot's family name begins as *Iobbe*, but by the time his father appears it has become *Gobbo*; at 3.4.49 Portia sends a servant to Mantua[1] with a letter for her cousin, but in the trial scene (4.1.109) we learn that he lives at Padua. In addition to these inconsistencies, metrical irregularities sometimes reveal that the text has not been tidied up. On the whole the play is metrically very accomplished; what appear in QI to be occasional very long lines all prove, when spoken aloud, to be the effective rhetorical device of a short line and a normal one side by side. Such subtleties make it probable that the rare unmetrical line such as 'To find the other forth, and by aduenturing both' (1.1.142) is something of a loose end.

Awkwardnesses at several points in the play suggest that Shakespeare's manuscript bore sign of his own alterations. The opening scene suffers from some repetitiousness in that first Salarino and Solanio, and then Gratiano, comment on Antonio's sadness and seek to dispel it. Gratiano (with Lorenzo) may have been inserted at line 56 in order to brighten up the comedy's rather sombre start. This could explain both the repetition of the speech heading *Sola.* at 57 for Solanio who is already speaking, and the prose passage (114–18) which links Gratiano's departure to the rest of this verse scene. Alternatively, the scene may originally have started at line 73 or thereabouts, in which case the Salarino–Solanio–Antonio conversation of the opening, separated in QI from the rest of the scene by a clear space, may have been added when Shakespeare realised he was going to need an extra pair of characters. If Salarino and Solanio were such *ad hoc* inventions it is not surprising that at first Shakespeare was uncertain about their names. They start as *Salanio* and *Salarino*, but as their names are progressively shortened in the speech headings Shakespeare appears to have realised that abbreviation was going to be confusing unless he changed one of the names. So there are speeches by *Sola.* at lines 46, 47, and 57, and at line 68 the stage direction *Exeunt Salarino, and Solanio* confirms the small alteration of one name. *Salanio* makes one more appearance, in a stage direction at the head of 2.3, but this is as likely to be a compositorial misreading as a lapse on the dramatist's part; thereafter the distinction is maintained throughout the speech headings of 2.4 and the stage directions and speech headings of 2.8 and 3.1 as the detailed table of speech headings on pp. 180–1 shows.

Another possible alteration is hinted at by the conclusion of 2.6. After Lorenzo has spoken the kind of ringing couplet that Shakespeare likes to end a scene with, Antonio enters and prevents Gratiano and Salarino[2] following Lorenzo and Jessica: 'No maske to night, the wind is come about' (65). The concluding couplet is now spoken

1 This may simply be a compositor's misreading.
2 See Commentary on 2.6.59.

by Gratiano. It may well be that Shakespeare wrote one of the masquing scenes that he excelled at before he realised that the Jessica episode was thereby made too lengthy, and that he then substituted for it the nine lines that conclude 2.6. Towards the end of 3.2 there is again what sounds like a concluding couplet (311–12). Perhaps Shakespeare only decided at a later stage to let Portia and the audience hear Antonio's letter, but in making the insertion failed to give Bassanio, as reader, a speech heading. The double entry for Tubal in 3.1 could also have resulted from a change of plan. Tubal may have been intended to make his entry at the end of Shylock's big speech (57). Shakespeare would then have seen he needed a device to get Salarino and Solanio off; he therefore inserted a summons from Antonio, an entry for Tubal, and a brief characterisation of him by the departing Solanio. Finally, Shakespeare may have got as far as line 116 of the last scene when he realised that Lorenzo needed to be able to tell Portia of Bassanio's imminent arrival, and so went back to make Lancelot give warning of it at line 38; here too there are signs of joins in the text, which are discussed in the Commentary.

A marked oddity of Q1 which could be attributed to its having been set from Shakespeare's foul papers is the way that the use of capital letters to begin verse lines decreases (though not consistently) over the course of the play. A reason could be that Shakespeare, when he started to write, followed the convention of starting each line with a capital letter, but gradually reverted to using such capitals only after an end-stopped line. That this last was his normal practice can be surmised from the Hand D additions to *Sir Thomas More*, which are very generally believed to be in Shakespeare's handwriting.[1]

The absence of capitals at the beginning of many verse lines gives the pages of Q1 a rather unprofessional appearance. This is made worse by the frequent use of capital italic *I*'s and *J*'s and even capital roman Y's to do duty for capital roman I's, and of marks of interrogation where we expect a full stop or colon. Shortage of type must be to blame for these printing defects. They do not, however, hide the fact that the punctuation of the play is remarkably sensitive. When the occasion demands, as in the verbal set-piece that opens 5.1, it is precise and grammatical; elsewhere it registers the natural pauses of the speaking voice, as when a cascade of commas marks the broken delivery of the 'Hath not a Jew eyes?' speech (3.1.42–57). Overall, the pointing is light, as it also is in the Hand D additions. But this could add weight to the argument that the manuscript used for Q1 was in Shakespeare's hand only if we knew that Roberts's compositors were accustomed, contrary to normal Elizabethan practice, to follow the punctuation of their copy. There is some evidence that they were. Brown has been able, by an examination of other works set by the same compositors,[2] to show that the light punctuation of *The Merchant of Venice* was not their invariable practice. In addition, a comparison of *Titus Andronicus* Q2 (1600), which they also set, with the 1594 first quarto which served them as copy suggests that they were 'careful and conservative' in reproducing the pointing of their copy, though inclined to increase

[1] Alexander, pp. 1345–51.

[2] Brown, 'Compositors', pp. 39–40.

the total number of stops. It is therefore possible that the light punctuation of Q1 directly reflects a very light use of stops in Shakespeare's manuscript.

Spelling, like punctuation, was an aspect of copy in which the Elizabethan printer felt no obligation to follow his author's practice. But here again Brown has shown that Roberts's compositors sometimes retained, from their copy, spellings which were at variance with prevailing practice or with their own preferences or with both.[1] This means that when we find in *The Merchant of Venice* Q1 and *Hamlet* Q2 a spelling which appears from the Hand D additions to be characteristic of Shakespeare the probability increases that both plays were printed from Shakespeare's holograph. This is the case with *-ewe* and *-owe* spellings of words whose final syllable was at the time coming to be spelt *-ew* or *-ow*, and with the spellings 'farwell', 'deare', 'sayd', and 'howre' in preference to 'farewell', 'deere', 'said', and 'houre'. In the Hand D additions, 'elevenpence' (as we would now write it) is spelt 'a leuenpence'; 'a leuen' occurs at 2.2.135 of our play and 'a leauen' at *Hamlet* 1.2.251. It can be demonstrated that the same compositor set the passages from both plays containing this word, and that in following the manuscript of another writer he set 'eleuen'. The same compositor is responsible for the unusual 'how so mere' at 3.5.77 of *The Merchant of Venice* and 'howsomeuer' at *Hamlet* 1.5.84; by contrast, in setting from a non-Shakespearean manuscript, he uses the commoner 'howsoeuer'.[2] These are small pointers to his having at least been inclined to follow the spelling of his copy.

Such idiosyncrasies of spelling could just conceivably survive the double transition from holograph to scribal copy and scribal copy to print; they are a little more likely to have survived a single process of holograph to print. Thus this spelling evidence, small though it is, may be sufficiently 'heauy in the substance' to turn the scales in favour of *The Merchant of Venice* having been printed from a legible manuscript, some of which the playwright may have copied out fair but which was largely or even wholly foul papers. Too much has been made of the discrepancy with *Hamlet*; the legibility of the Hand D additions should shift the problem from 'Why is *The Merchant of Venice* Q1 such a good text?' to 'Why is the text of *Hamlet* Q2 so bad?' In Q1 we almost certainly have *The Merchant of Venice*, a few venial printing errors apart, as it came from Shakespeare's hand.

The Pavier quarto of 1619 (Q2)

The title page of another quarto of *The Merchant of Venice* claims that it too was printed by Roberts in 1600. Since it does not include Heyes's name, many editors up to the early years of this century believed this quarto to have been printed from the manuscript acquired by Roberts in 1598, and the Heyes–Roberts quarto to have been printed from a different manuscript.[3] This means care has to be taken in making use

[1] *Ibid.*, pp. 32–9. [2] *Ibid.*, p. 38.

[3] F. J. Furnivall, *Shakspere's Merchant of Venice...A Facsimile in Photo-lithography*, n.d., describes Q2 on the title page as 'the first (tho worse) quarto'.

of such editions as the Cambridge one of 1863 and Furness's Variorum of 1888, in which this other quarto is wrongly designated Q1 or 'the Roberts quarto'. It has in fact nothing to do with Roberts. As Pollard, Greg, and Neidig demonstrated in 1909, it was printed in 1619, three years after Shakespeare's death, from a copy of the real Q1, and is one of ten plays assembled by the publisher Thomas Pavier as the first step towards a collected edition of Shakespeare's works.[1]

There can be no doubt that Q2, or the Pavier quarto, derives from Q1. Not only does it reproduce a number of Q1's errors, but at 2.2.59 it follows it in printing G O D thus, in spaced capitals, a convention that Roberts's men were accustomed to observe in devotional works. Another small but telling piece of evidence that Q1 was the copy for Q2 occurs at 4.1.350, when Shylock is told that if anyone is found guilty of an attempt on a Venetian's life, the offender's property

comes to the priuie coffer of the State,

It will be seen that the second 'f' in 'coffer' is broken, so that the two letters together look like the ligature 'ſt', with 's' in its long form. Q2's compositor read it this way and so produced the nonce-word 'coster'.

Because of this dependence on Q1, Q2 is a derivative text which lacks any real authority. Modern editions are all based on Q1. In recent decades, attempts have been made to discredit Q2 still further by the use of the new bibliographical technique of compositor determination. This, it is claimed, enables the workmanship of one compositor to be distinguished from that of another. Among the workers who set the First Folio it is thus possible to distinguish one man whose habit of 'following the matter with the mind rather than with the eye'[2] led him to omit, interpolate, or substitute words and even phrases. The Folio, like the Pavier quartos, was produced in Isaac Jaggard's printing shop. There is thus a possibility that the maverick Compositor B was employed on both enterprises. D. F. McKenzie has gone so far as to argue that the whole of Q2 was set by Compositor B and that it exhibits his 'misdirected ingenuity, deliberate tampering, and plain carelessness'.[3]

Variants which suggest that the compositor tried to carry too many words in his head are certainly a feature of Q2. They range from the substitution of a single letter ('know' for 'knew' at 3.1.20), through changes in word order (at 1.1.24 'might do at sea' becomes 'at sea might do'), the dropping or addition of single words ('you' dropped at 2.4.22, 'that' added at 3.1.90) and the changing of single words ('husband health' for 'husbands welfare' – a typical memorial vulgarisation – at 5.1.114), to the addition or alteration of whole phrases, such as 'twinkling of an eye' in place of 'twinkling' (2.2.140) and 'did uphold' for 'had held up' (5.1.214). There are also

[1] The full story of the discovery of the Pavier enterprise is told in chapter 3 of Pollard's *Shakespeare's Folios and Quartos*.

[2] Alice Walker, 'The Folio text of *1 Henry IV*', *SB* 6 (1954), 45–59, p. 53. Walker's *Textual Problems of the First Folio*, 1953, is the pioneer study of compositor determination.

[3] D. F. McKenzie, 'Compositor B's role in *The Merchant of Venice* Q2 (1619)', *SB* 12 (1959), 75–90, p. 76. See also McKenzie, 'Shakespeare's punctuation – a new beginning', *RES* 10 (1959), 361–70, and W. S. Keble, 'Compositor B, the Pavier quartos, and copy spellings', *SB* 21 (1968), 131–61.

places where we catch the compositor changing the wording of his copy in order to save himself the trouble of justifying a line of type: thus Shylock's exclamation 'would shee were hearst at my foote' is deliberately prefixed by 'O' in order to fill up the previous line (3.1.69–70). A further liberty taken in the setting of Q2 is the introduction of many more elisions than the few and strictly metrical ones of Q1. But as these are not likely to represent any difference in pronunciation, 'pray thee' and 'prethee' for example probably sounding exactly alike, these interventions scarcely deserve the indignation they have aroused.

It is not, however, possible to lay all the Q2 variants at the door of Compositor B. Even if he was already in Jaggard's employ by 1619, he would, according to printing practice of the time, have set only half the text. Peter Blayney has argued the case for Q2 having been cast off into sheets which were set, turn and turn about, by two compositors, G and H; G's work he finds to bear some resemblance to B's work on the Folio.[1] Even so, a count of each man's substantive variants, based on the division of labour suggested by Blayney, shows that 43 % occur in the sheets thought to have been set by H. Furthermore, many of these changes are beyond the reach of even a meddlesome compositor; they imply the presence, as Greg saw, of a printing-house reader. But whereas this reader struck Greg as 'displaying a lack of intelligence',[2] to me he appears intelligent and careful.

To get a fair view of Q2 we need to set aside our prejudice against its deceptive title page and the possible vagaries of Compositor B and instead to consider its positive achievements. We owe to Q2 the correction of a number of Q1's misreadings and misprints, such as its substitution of 'e'en' for 'in' at 3.5.17, and ''tis' for 'as' at 4.1.100: small changes that suggest the activity of a sensitive and alert printer's reader. Such a reader could have produced Q2's attempts to make sense of a rare syntactical tangle ('Liue thou, I liue...', 3.2.61–2) or even rarer textual crux ('he doe not meane it it...', 3.5.65–6). Needed stage directions are supplied, and those that in Q1 were printed in any available space by the right margin (probably because they had been so inserted in the manuscript) are now correctly placed and centred. Other changes show an alert recognition that Shakespeare often preferred the less common word: 'Slubber' replaces Q1 'slumber' at 2.8.40 and (unless this is a mere spelling variant) the precise legal term 'tenour' replaces the more familiar Q1 'tenure' at 4.1.231. Proper names are knowledgeably corrected: 'Neopolitane' rightly becomes 'Neapolitane' and 'Palentine' becomes 'Palatine' (1.2.33, 38), though the pedantic but inaccurate change from 'Cressed' to 'Cressada' spoils the metre at 5.1.6. The metre is however rescued at 5.1.51, where Q1 'Stephen' is given back the name 'Stephano'. A similar watchfulness accounts for the change of *Iobbe* to *Gobbo* in Lancelot's opening monologue (2.2.3–6) and the replacement of *Salerio* in 3.3 by *Salarino*.

Care has also been taken with the speech headings of Q2. Although the villain is both *Shy*[*lock*] and *Iew*[*e*] and *Launce*[*let*] is sometimes *Clowne*, attempts have been made to keep the names consistent throughout each scene, even if this plan breaks

[1] Peter Blayney, 'Compositor B and the Pavier quartos: problems of identification and their implications', *The Library*, 5th series, 27 (1972), 179–206.
[2] W. W. Greg, *The Shakespeare First Folio*, 1955, p. 159.

down in the trial scene. The form 'Salanio', which I have suggested above Shakespeare soon abandoned for 'Solanio', is kept throughout, but he and his companion are carefully differentiated in the speech headings as *Salan.* and *Salar.* This points up the significance of Q2's reallocation of speeches in the first scene. (See the detailed table of speech headings on pp. 180–1.) In Q1, Salanio is the one to suggest that Antonio is in love and then to fend off the merchant's rebuff with a number of witty images at the expense of melancholy men. In Q2 these speeches are given to Salarino. From the intrusive speech heading *Sola.* just after the entry of more friends (line 57), the press reader has perhaps assumed that one friend is interrupting the other and so reallocated both the earlier part of the speech and the previous speech to Salarino, thus making him much the more voluble of the two. In this the reader seems to have been acting very much as a literary editor. He has perhaps decided, from the sympathetic tone of Solanio's first speech (15–22), that he is the 'quiet' one. He may even have given the play a prior reading and decided, like some later critics, that Solanio is more sober and prudent than his friend: he is the one who wants the masque to be well prepared, who sees trouble coming to Antonio as the result of Jessica's elopement, and who advises Salarino to use discretion in breaking bad news to Antonio.

This is an intelligent change, but it is almost certainly a wrong one. At this stage of the play, Shakespeare is not concerned to distinguish one friend from the other; they both function as part of the exposition, laying dramatic emphasis upon Antonio's wealth and his melancholy. Besides, it would be poor theatre to anticipate the comic routine of the talker who does not let his companion get a word in edgeways, since this properly belongs to Gratiano and Lorenzo. The reader, or editor, of Q2 was, one suspects, no playgoer. He failed to see that Antonio's question, 'is hee yet possest / How much ye would?' at the end of his first speech to Shylock (1.3.53–7), constitutes a contemptuous turning aside from the moneylender to Bassanio. He spoiled Lancelot's jokes, such as they are, by laboriously correcting his 'confusions' at 2.2.16, 2.2.21 and 2.2.29. He may have missed another small joke in emending Lorenzo's 'on gentleman' at 2.6.59 to 'on gentlemen' (but so did the Folio's press reader) and I think he failed to hear the telling hesitancy in Portia's '*Bassanio*, as I think so was he calld' (1.2.95). He certainly did not have enough sense of the theatre to respond to Shylock's highly individual way of speaking, and such forms as 'moneys' (1.3.108), 'my flesh and my blood' (3.1.30), and 'a my shedding' (3.1.76) are dully normalised in Q2.

Misguided changes such as these highlight an editorial problem: how far should collation proceed along the wide spectrum of Q2's variants as they range from careful and accurate editorial corrections to compositorial blunders? Many of Q2's readings, though not acceptable as emendations, are historically interesting as showing how a Shakespeare play was read in 1619. Beyond such interventions lies a band of variants which may represent meddlesomeness or even carelessness on the part of a compositor, but could also be honest attempts to put right things which the press reader felt to be amiss with Q1. Emendations which I have given the benefit of the doubt, to the extent of admitting them to the collation, include 'pearles' in place of 'peales' (3.2.145), 'misery' for 'cruelty' (3.4.21), 'apparreld' for 'accoutered' (3.4.63), and 'presently' for 'instantly' (4.1.277). In so doing I have accorded Q2's variants more respect than they customarily receive in a modern edition. Far from wishing to lob stones into Jaggard's printing shop from the insecurity of my own glasshouse, I am grateful for the evidence that Q2 affords of the way Q1 looked to a Jacobean.

The Folio of 1623 (F)

The Folio text of *The Merchant of Venice* was set from Q1, but not from the copy already used by Jaggard for Q2. The reason we know this is that some copies of Q1 have at 4.1.73–4 the defective lines

> well vse question with the Woolfe,
> the Ewe bleake for the Lambe.

This error must have been noticed while Q1 was actually being printed; the run was stopped and the lines corrected

> You may as well vse question with the Woolfe,
> Why he hath made the Ewe bleake for the Lambe.

Q2 has the lines complete, so it must have been set from a corrected copy. But the reader or compositor of F was faced with the incomplete lines of an uncorrected copy of Q1, and made a half-hearted attempt at emendation:

> Or euen as well vse question with the Wolfe,
> The Ewe bleate for the Lambe:

The chief interest of F is that certain of its features must have originated in the theatre and others almost certainly did so. The phrase 'pray God grant' at 1.2.90 becomes simply 'wish' and 'no Gods my Iudge' at 5.1.157 is toned down to 'but well I know'. These expurgations were probably in deference to the 1606 Act against stage profanity; it has been suggested[1] that they were carried out in the printing-house, but they had not after all been found necessary when Q2 was printed by Jaggard in 1619. The change of Portia's slighting reference to the Scots at 1.2.63, where 'the Scottish Lorde' becomes 'the other Lord', could well have been made by the actors for the Court performances of 1605, and the addition of act divisions to F may be in line with the introduction of inter-act music to the indoors playhouses in James's reign. Lancelot's entry at 2.4.9 '*with a letter*' reflects the book keeper's concern with props; the book keeper too must have been the source of the seven musical directions, most of them ceremonial flourishes, which have been added in F.[2]

At first sight, it looks as if the printers of F were working from a copy of Q1 that had served as a prompt-book. But we have no proof that Shakespeare's company ever used a printed quarto in this way.[3] Had they done so they would assuredly have felt the need to rewrite the incomplete or vague stage directions of Q1, and to put right

[1] *Ibid.*, p. 155.
[2] 2.1.0 SD; 2.1.46 SD; 2.7.79 SD; 2.9.3 SD; 5.1.97 SD (not in this text); 5.1.110 SD; 5.1.121 SD.
[3] F. P. Wilson, *Shakespeare and the New Bibliography*, 1970, pp. 78–9.

a number of its errors; but these stand uncorrected in the Folio. What is likely to have happened is that the actors, rather than be parted for some weeks from the prompt-book, either used it to make alterations and additions to a copy of Q1 which they then gave to Jaggard, or they allowed Jaggard (or his deputy) to make them for himself. The latter probability is just a little stronger, because one of the musical directions is misplaced, and the error is one that the book keeper would have avoided. At the end of 2.7, *Flo. Cornets* had to be written into the scant space to the side of the opening direction of 2.8, 'Enter *Salarino* and *Solanio*', with the result that in F the two gentlemen of Venice get the flourish that was meant as an ironic accompaniment to Morocco's departure in 2.7.

Over and above these augmentations, the copy of Q1 used for F seems to have received some editing; the 'if on earth he doe not meane it' crux (3.5.65–6) is dealt with competently, and there are other sensible emendations, a few of which coincide, quite fortuitously, with those made in Q2. But the editing of F appears to have been a good deal more casual than that of Q2, as is evidenced by confusions in the speech headings at the very outset of the play. Whereas the abbreviations used in Q2 carefully kept Salarino and 'Salanio' distinct, F's compositor, apparently without a press reader's editorial guidance, plunges straight into using the abbreviation *Sal.*, then sees the problem and (perhaps with a faint sense of having been here before, because this is Compositor B again) prefixes *Salar.* to the next speech; unfortunately it is 'Salanio' who is speaking.

For the rest, F tends to normalise the grammar of Q1, and modernises its language which had already become that of a generation ago. It has one or two meddlesome verbal changes in the sections supposedly set by Compositor B: 'endlesse ruine' for the 'curelesse ruin' of Gratiano's wits (4.1.142), and a change of 'meane' to 'smal' at 1.2.6, which avoids a repetition but spoils the wordplay. Overall, F introduces more errors than it eliminates. Apart from its valuable stage directions, its readings appear rarely in the collation of this edition.

The quarto of 1637 (Q3)

One other seventeenth-century edition of *The Merchant of Venice* has been shown to have independent interest.[1] This is the third quarto, published in 1637 by Thomas Heyes's son, Laurence. It is based on a copy of Q1 which had 4.1.73–4 in the corrected form, and it shows a filial piety in being more faithful to Q1 than is either Q2 or F. Though it has some bad errors, someone proof-read it during the printing run, and so introduced, in some copies, two emendations which have generally been attributed to later editors: 'Ay' for the second 'I' in 'I wou'd lose all, I sacrifize them all' (4.1.282), and 'reine' for 'raine' in Portia's 'In measure raine thy ioy' (3.2.112). Another interesting feature of Q3 is its list of 'The Actors Names', which is the basis for the List of Characters on p. 56 above. This list does not include Salerio, and the stage direction in the text for this character's first appearance reads 'Enter... *Salerio*?

[1] Christopher Spencer, 'Shakespeare's *Merchant of Venice* in 63 editions', *SB* 25 (1972), 89–106, pp. 103–4.

a messenger from Venice.' If this question mark was written into the printed copy-text, it may indicate the first awareness of a problem that has troubled most editors: are there two, or three, Venetians with very similar names? This brings us to the most notable change introduced into the text of *The Merchant of Venice* during the present century.

Salarino, Solanio, Salerio

Earlier editors of the play were reluctant to believe that Shakespeare, after naming two characters 'Salarino' and 'Salanio' – as the names appeared in the first SD of F, and throughout Q2 which was then generally (see pp. 173–4 above) believed to be the earliest text – would have made confusion worse confounded by bringing on a third character called 'Salerio'. To have created so superfluous a character would have violated 'dramatic propriety',[1] put the actors to unnecessary expense, and shown a singular lack of inventiveness in the choice of names. Several of them therefore gave the entry at 3.2.218 to 'Salanio'. Capell, however, preferred to give it to Salarino, on the grounds that this character's name had already been spelt twice with an 'e' in the second syllable (2.6.0 SD; 3.1.60 SH – see the table on pp. 180–1), bringing it very close to 'Salerio'. In the New Shakespeare edition of 1926, Wilson concurred with Capell in making Salarino and Salerio one and the same person but decided that Shakespeare's name for him must be 'Salerio' since this occurs five times in the dialogue. He therefore substituted 'Salerio' for 'Salarino' or its variants in all previous stage directions and speech headings. All subsequent editors have followed Wilson in this, and Salarino has not put in an appearance for the past sixty years. On a number of grounds, I have restored him to the text of this edition.

The arguments against Shakespeare having envisaged three personages when writing the play are not very strong. Dramatic propriety, a tenet of the neo-classical theatre, is a concept alien to Shakespeare, who throws very minor characters into his plays at any stage of the action without pausing to ask himself if the new character's function could not be performed by an existing personage.[2] This was in no way extravagant, thanks to the Elizabethan practice of doubling parts. Even if Morocco is still blacking-off during 3.2, the actors of Old Gobbo and Arragon are available to play Salerio. To have given him this name was certainly uninventive; but the same could be said about the two Jaques in *As You Like It*, Gremio and Grumio in *The Taming of the Shrew*, and, in this very play, the use of 'Balthazar' both for Portia's steward and for the lawyer she pretends to be.

There is thus no *prima facie* case against Shakespeare having had three different personages in mind. On the other hand, the positive evidence in favour of three characters is admittedly slight. In 3.3 there may be an indication that before the trial the original pair are still in Venice awaiting Salerio's return. Although only one friend is given an entrance (*Salerio* in Q1, but both Q2 and F recognise this is impossible), there is a speech heading *Sol.* as well as one for *Sal.* The variation could, however,

[1] The phrase is Knight's (p. 427).
[2] Arthur Colby Sprague, 'Shakespeare's unnecessary characters', *S.Sur.* 20 (1967), 75–82.

Table of occurrences of the names Salarino, Solanio, and Salerio (asterisks indicate irregularities)

Act, scene, and line	Q1	Q2	F
1.1.0 SD	*Salaryno, and Salanio	*Salaryno, and Salanio	Salarino, and Salanio
8 SH	Salarino	Salarino	Sal.
15 SH	Salanio	Salanio	*Salar.
22 SH	Salar.	Salar.	Sal.
46 SH	Sola.	*Salar.	Sola.
47 SH	Sola.	*Salar.	Sola.
57 SH	Sola.	Salan.	Sola.
60 SH	Sala.	Salar.	Sala.
65 SH	Sal.	Salar.	Sal.
68 SH	Sal.	Salar.	Sal.
68 SD	Salarino, and Solanio	Salarino and Salanio	Salarino, and Solanio
2.4.0 SD	*Salaryno, and Salanio	Salarino, and Salanio	*Slarino, and Salanio
40 SH	Salari.	Salar.	Sal.
60 SH	*Saleri.	Salar.	Sal.
61 SH	Solanio	Salan.	Sol.
24 SH	Sal.	Salar.	Sal.
25 SH	Sol.	Salan.	Sol.
27 SH	Sal.	Salar.	Sal.
2.6.0 SD	*Salerino	Salarino	*Salino
3 SH	Sal.	Sal.	Sal.
6 SH	Sal.	Sal.	Sal.
21 SH	Sal.	Sal.	*Salino
2.8.0 SD	Salarino and Solanio	Salarino and Salanio	Salarino and Solanio
1 SH	Sal.	Salar.	Sal.
4 SH	Sola.	Salan.	Sol.
6 SH	Sal.	Salar.	Sal.
12 SH	Sol.	Salan.	Sol.
23 SH	Sal.	Salar.	Sal.
25 SH	Sola.	Salan.	Sol.
27 SH	Sal.	Salar.	Sal.
34 SH	Sol.	Salan.	Sol.
36 SH	Sal.	Salar.	Sal.
51 SH	Sol.	Salan.	Sol.
54 SH	Sal.	Salar.	Sal.

Table (cont.)

Act, scene, and line	Q1	Q2	F
3.1.0 SD	*Solanio and Salarino*	*Salanio and Salarino*	*Solanio and Salarino*
1 SH	*Solanio*	*Salan.*	*Sol.*
2 SH	*Salari.*	*Salar.*	*Sal.*
7 SH	*Solanio*	*Salan.*	*Sol.*
13 SH	*Salari.*	*Salar.*	*Sal.*
14 SH	*Solanio*	*Sal.*	*Sol.*
16 SH	*Salari.*	*Salar.*	*Sal.*
17 SH	*Solanio*	*Salan.*	*Sol.*
22 SH	*Salari.*	*Salar.*	*Sal.*
24 SH	*Solan.*	*Salan.*	*Sol.*
27 SH	*Salari.*	*Salar.*	*Sal.*
29 SH	*Sola.*	*Salan.*	*Sol.*
31 SH	*Salari.*	*Salar.*	*Sal.*
40 SH	*Salari.*	*Salar.*	*Sal.*
60 SH	**Saleri.*	*Salar.*	*Sal.*
61 SH	*Solanio*	*Salan.*	*Sol.*
3.2.218	*Salerio*	*Salerio*	*Salerio*
218 SD	*Salerio*	*Salerio*	*Salerio*
219	*Salerio*	*Salerio*	*Salerio*
227	*Salerio*	*Salerio*	*Salerio*
229 SH	*Sal.*	*Sal.*	*Sal.*
233 SH	*Sal.*	*Sal.*	*Sal.*
237	*Salerio*	*Salerio*	*Salerio*
241 SH	*Sal.*	*Sal.*	*Sal.*
265	*Salerio*	*Salerio*	*Salerio*
270 SH	*Sal.*	*Sal.*	*Sal.*
3.3.0 SD	**Salerio*	**Salarino*	**Solanio*
18 SH	**Sol.*	**Sol.*	*Sol.*
24 SH	*Sal.*	*Sal.*	*Sol.*
4.1.15 SH	*Salerio*	*Sal.*	*Sal.*
107 SH	*Salerio*	*Saler.*	*Sal.*

be a compositorial error. In the previous scene *a messenger from Venice* (3.2.218 SD) could imply that not only is Salerio not to be confused with the two men-about-town, but that his social status is rather different. Gratiano's 'My old Venetian friend *Salerio*' (218) need not imply equality; it can be a condescending form of address and also an explanatory phrase such as the audience would not need if it had met Salerio four times already. Salerio, with his overall view of the situation at home, can be seen as a kind of state functionary who makes as chilling an entrance into Belmont as does the black-clad Marcade into an earlier comedy of deferred nuptials, *Love's Labour's Lost*. This would accord with his role in the trial, where he is a kind of gentleman usher. The social nuances of four hundred years ago are not, however, something on which we can speak with confidence today, and it would be quite easy to make out a case, in the play's first scene, for a social difference between Solanio and Salarino on the one hand and Bassanio's more immediate group of friends on the other.

Because the positive evidence in favour of a third 'Sally' is so scanty, Wilson's elimination of Salarino who, like Solanio, is nowhere named in the dialogue seems eminently sensible. Yet it has to be recognised that it rests in large part on his belief, later retracted, that the copy for Q1 was an assembled text in which the stage directions were based on the curtailed speech headings of actors' parts: a state of things which might well give rise to a ghostly Salarino. Now that scholars agree that Q1 was printed from a very clear and possibly holograph manuscript, the onus is on any editor who wishes to follow Wilson to show why, in these circumstances, 'Salerio' could repeatedly be read as 'Salarino'. Brown suggests that the compositor or playhouse scribe mistook the dot on the i of 'Salerio' for a mark of abbreviation and consequently expanded the name to 'Salarino'. If, as many believe, the play was set from Shakespeare's own manuscript, there are two objections to this. First, Salarino's name in the entries heading 1.1 and 2.4 is spelt *Salaryno*, and we have seen that the compositors of Q1 tended to preserve the spelling of their copy. Secondly, 'Salerio' would have had to be misread 'Salarino' by the *two* compositors; according to the division of the copy suggested by Brown himself, both men set 'Salarino'.

Brown has another suggestion: 'Shakespeare modified the name when he had occasion to use it in verse.'[1] Though it is tempting to reply 'In that case, why not "My old Venetian friend Solanio"?' this is a plausible theory. Shakespeare likes his four-syllabled Italian names to end in 'io', since he can then make them trisyllabic when the metre so requires without the kind of distortion heard at 2.2.141: 'I pray thee, good *Leonardo* thinke on this'. A further point in favour of Shakespeare having decided rather late in the day on the form 'Salerio' is that the speech heading *Saleri.* (3.1.60) occurs in a passage which, as we have seen, may have been an insertion. There is, however, a world of difference between (with Wilson) employing 'Salerio' for speech headings and stage directions throughout the play, in the belief that Shakespeare always used this name for Solanio's companion and (with Brown) finding it 'simplest to regularize to Salerio'[2] in the belief that in 3.2 Shakespeare stopped writing 'Salarino' and began to write 'Salerio'. Some regularisation there has to be: the Solanio who goes out at 1.1.68 SD must be shown to be the Salanio who came in at 1.1.0 SD. But to change the Salarino who goes out for the fifth time at 3.1.62 into the Salerio who comes in for the first time at 3.2.218 demands a good deal more confidence. Before taking such a step one would like to feel sure that Salarino and Salerio were one and the same on the Jacobean stage. F gives some hint that they were,

[1] Brown, p. 2 n. [2] *Ibid.*, p. 2 n.

in changing the impossible *Salerio* of 3.3.0 SD into *Solanio* rather than into the *Salarino* of Q2. But we cannot be sure this was a theatrical change. Nor is Q3's list of characters any help. Its omission of 'Salerio' may imply there was no third gentleman, but more probably the description in the stage direction of Salerio as 'a messenger' causes him to be subsumed under the term 'Attendants' in this list.

It is always open to the director to identify Salarino with Salerio, thereby economising on minor parts and very probably fulfilling Shakespeare's final intention into the bargain. But the printed text must, I believe, retain three Venetian gentlemen with similar names because, whatever his intentions, Salarino, Solanio, and Salerio all figured in the manuscript that Shakespeare actually gave to his actors as *The Merchant of Venice*.

Appendix: Shakespeare's use of the Bible in *The Merchant of Venice*

Shakespeare is held to have displayed 'exceptional biblical knowledge'[1] in *The Merchant of Venice*. The purpose of this appendix is first to try to define in what ways Shakespeare's familiarity with Scripture, as it is revealed in this play, is exceptional; and secondly to suggest both the extent and the limits of the critical conclusions which can be drawn from this familiarity.

Elizabethans of Shakespeare's generation were accustomed to hear read aloud in church every Sunday at least four substantial passages from the Bible: lessons from the Old and the New Testament at Morning Prayer, and as a sequel the Epistle and Gospel from the Ante-communion (or 'dry communion' – the sacrament itself was celebrated only at the major festivals). Further passages from the two Testaments were read in the afternoon, at Evening Prayer. Since everyone had to attend his or her parish church or risk having to pay a sizeable fine, Shakespeare as the years passed must inevitably have become familiar with the passages 'proper' to specific Sundays. Early each year, on Sexagesima Sunday (for example), he would have listened to St Paul's description of his arduous voyages as it was rendered in the English of the Bishops' Bible, the version appointed to be read in churches for as long as he could remember. So when Shylock is made to speak of the dangers of trading ventures, not only would the phrase 'perils of the waters' have come naturally to Shakespeare, but it would have brought with it the cumulative rhythms of the passage in question from the second Epistle to the Corinthians.[2] Moreover the liturgy in which such extracts were set, and which itself was in large part derived from Scripture, imprinted itself week after week on a sensitive ear. Lorenzo's angel-like star, 'still' – that is, constantly – 'choiring to the young-eyed cherubins', recalls the *Te Deum*'s 'To thee all Angels cry aloud: the heavens and all the powers therein. To thee Cherubin and Seraphin: continually do cry'; while the next verse of the same canticle, 'Holy, holy, holy: Lord God of Sabaoth' is echoed in Shylock's 'our holy Sabaoth'.[3] And although the Psalms for the day may have been sung in Shakespeare's parish church in London in their dreary metrical versions, he would have been familiar since childhood with the Prayer Book versions in Coverdale's beautiful prose. Not only were these recited antiphonally by the Stratford congregation, but Shakespeare would have had to learn many of them by heart at his 'petty school', and at grammar school he would have construed them – that is, turned them into Latin – as he would have done passages from other Old Testament books, such as Proverbs and Ecclesiasticus.[4] At a very

[1] Noble, p. 96. I am very indebted to Noble's book throughout this appendix.

[2] Compare 2 Cor. 11 with *The Merchant of Venice* 1.3.18–21. Volume 1 of W. Horton Davies, *Worship and Theology in England*, 1970, is helpful on Elizabethan churchgoing.

[3] See Commentary on 5.1.62 and 4.1.36.

[4] T. W. Baldwin, *William Shakspere's Small Latine and Less Greeke*, 1944, 1, 682–7. The Apocrypha was included in Tudor Bibles.

tender age he would have committed to memory the Ten Commandments as they stand in the Church Catechism of the Prayer Book, so that for him and for Lancelot Gobbo (as indeed for us today) the 'sins' of the fathers are visited upon the children, and not the 'sin' as in the Bishops' Bible or the 'iniquity' as in the Geneva version.[1]

This Geneva Bible, compiled by Marian exiles and first published in 1560, was the favourite form of the Scriptures for private reading because it was relatively cheap, compact in size, and printed in roman type. There is evidence that Shakespeare read an edition of it which appeared, with a revised New Testament, in 1595; but already by that time he had made ample use in his plays of portions of the Bishops' Bible which were not among those appointed to be read aloud in church, so at one time or another he must have had access to both these versions. At the time he wrote *The Merchant of Venice* the Bishops' Bible, probably in the 1584 quarto edition, would seem to have been the more familiar to him. Verbal echoes from it outnumber those from the Geneva version by four to one. They include the proper name 'Chus' (rather than the Genevan 'Cush') and the phrases 'Staff of my age' and 'a neighbourly charity' which cannot be matched in the Geneva Bible.[2] Yet the marginal glosses which are an important feature of the Geneva Bible sometimes suggest that Shakespeare was reading that version when *The Merchant of Venice* was in the making. If that reading included the Wisdom literature of the Old Testament, a gloss on Proverbs 28.8 – 'For God will take away the wicked usurer and give his goods unto him that shall bestow them well' – may have linked itself in the dramatist's memory with a striking phrase from Proverbs 26.19 – 'So dealeth the deceitful man with his friends and sayeth, Am not I in sport?' – to inspire both Shylock's phrase 'merry sport' (rather than the 'merry jest' of *Gernutus*)[3] and the ultimate outcome of the sport in Antonio's control of Shylock's fortune, a detail not in the play's main sources.

To have read parts of the Bible in one or more of its current English versions was in no way unusual for an educated Elizabethan. The Scriptures were after all the keystone of the Reformation. What is exceptional about Shakespeare's biblical knowledge is that one segment of it appears to have been deliberately acquired or renewed with a dramatic purpose in mind: the creation of Shylock. Shakespeare is unlikely ever to have known an orthodox Jew, and any Marranos he may have met in London would have been at pains to conceal their religious origins. To get at these origins and so to endow Shylock with his pride of race, Shakespeare naturally went to the stories of the patriarchs told in the Book of Genesis. The Church Lectionary had already made him familiar with one of these stories, the account in Genesis 27 of the manner in which Jacob's 'wise mother wrought in his behalf' so that he wrested his father's blessing and inheritance from his brother Esau. But he pursued the narrative through succeeding chapters on his own initiative,[4] and in doing so conceived Shylock's imaginative involvement with Jacob: an aspect of the Jew which brings him

[1] Noble, p. 166. [2] See Commentary on 3.2.284; 2.2.54; 1.2.64.

[3] These two echoes are pointed out by Frank McCombie, 'Wisdom as touchstone in *The Merchant of Venice*', *New Blackfriars* 64 (1982), 117–18.

[4] See Commentary on 1.3.38.

to life just at the moment we are in danger of stereotyping him as the conventional stage usurer. Jacob's dealings with his brother and his long service with Laban offer Shylock the model for his own defiant enterprise in a hostile society, while the mysterious episodes of Jacob's ladder and of the wrestling angel underlie Shylock's deep sense of apartness, his Old Testament 'righteousness'. Some commentators on the play have viewed the story of Laban's sheep as a self-indictment on Shylock's part, in that it is a defence of something manifestly wrong;[1] but, as actors have always realised, the dramatic effect of Shylock's identification with Jacob in this anecdote is to give him the vitality of the born survivor.

Shakespeare's immersion in these chapters of Genesis continues to make itself felt in the rest of the play. Jacob's exaction of a blessing from the blind Isaac is parodied, perhaps unconsciously, in Lancelot's scene with Old Gobbo. In swearing by Jacob's staff Shylock is made to recall Jacob's boast in Genesis 32 that this was all he had in the world to begin with. Shylock's wife bears the name of one of the two wives of Jacob who figure in Genesis 29–33. 'Hagar's offspring', first heard of in Genesis 16, reappear in Genesis 28 when the granddaughter of Abraham's bondmaid Hagar marries Esau, whose descendants are destined to serve those of Jacob.[2] In such ways Shakespeare makes use of what was essentially a humanistic knowledge of the life of Jacob as related in Genesis, a knowledge no different in kind from his study of Plutarch's Lives.

Another aspect of Shakespeare's recourse to the Bible in his realisation of the Jew shows itself in Shylock's allusions to the Gospels. These differ from the Genesis allusions in that their effect depends on their being immediately recognised by the audience. On Shylock's first meeting with Bassanio, his detestation of the Christians breaks out in the dactylic rhythm and harsh consonants of 'to eat of the habitation which your prophet the Nazarite conjured the devil into': a phrase of virulent contempt which must have startled early audiences and indeed so shocked Johnson that he omitted it from his edition. Nowadays it falls short of this effect, since only a portion of the audience realise that Shylock's words travesty the Gospel narrative about Jesus miraculously healing two demented men. Shakespeare could, however, count on his audience knowing the sayings of Jesus thoroughly, and elsewhere he manipulates their knowledge to achieve sharp dramatic irony at Shylock's expense. When Shylock calls Antonio 'a fawning publican', Shakespeare may intend him to be suggesting that Antonio is a lackey of the people in power; but he certainly intends the audience to recall and to attribute to Shylock the self-righteousness of the Pharisee when, in the Gospel parable, he dissociates himself from the publican. 'The curse never fell upon our nation till now' had specific meaning for an audience that remembered Jesus's prophecy over Jerusalem – 'Behold your habitation shall be left to you desolate' – and thought of the Diaspora as retribution upon the Jews who had elected to save Barabbas and let Jesus be crucified: another part of the Gospel story

[1] See Brown's valuable note on this passage.
[2] See Commentary on 2.2.69–70; 2.5.35; 2.5.42.

recalled in Shylock's wish that 'any of the stock of Barabbas' had been Jessica's husband, rather than a Christian.[1]

These are only a few specimens of the play's biblical echoes. Many more have been detected, making a conceivable total well in excess of the fifty or so noted in the Commentary to this edition. In the eyes of several recent critics, this profusion points to the play being intended as a religious allegory. Thus for Barbara Lewalski, the biblical language of *The Merchant of Venice* 'clearly reveals an important theological meaning', the supremacy of the New Law over the Old.[2] Frank McCombie traces in the play's echoes of Wisdom literature the biblical quest for the Divine Sophia, who, once she is found, comes down from her beautiful mountain to rescue the righteous and then returns there to dwell with all who love her.[3] To view the play in this light it is necessary to believe that Shakespeare's use of a phrase or reference always reflects his reading of Scripture and that its biblical source was immediately evident to the audience; that an Elizabethan audience would have considered theological matters a proper concern of comedy; and that it was ready, at the end of the day, to attribute a distinct moral meaning to the play it had witnessed. None of these assumptions can be made with confidence. Though Shakespeare, as we have seen, exploited his audience's familiarity with certain parts of the Bible, many of the phrases he used did not carry their biblical context with them because, though of biblical origin, they had passed into current speech long before the Tudor translations gained wide currency. Shakespeare himself is no more likely to have been consciously quoting 2 Sam. 17.8 when he wrote 'Pluck the young sucking cubs from the she-bear' than we have in mind Matt. 23.27 when we speak of 'whited sepulchres' (though this last *is* from the Tudor translations). Lancelot's 'old proverb', 'God's grace is gear enough', was the wisdom of the tribe rather than a quotation from Corinthians 12.19.[4] Nor did allusions to Daniel's judgement against the Elders or even to the Prodigal Son have an immediate biblical ring to Elizabethan ears. Such stories, through their retelling in works such as *The Golden Legend*, or their use as subjects for embroidery, painted cloths, and tapestries (successive monarchs cherished the Whitehall tapestries of the Prodigal Son), had become an integral part of English folklore, much in the way that incidents in *The Pilgrim's Progress* have for over a century been part of the folklore of African societies.

Good folk tales apart, the Bible as a source of edification would not have been in the forefront of people's minds when they went to the theatre. It is true that there had been a strong tradition of biblical parody in medieval drama, but in *The Merchant of Venice* such parody, if and when it occurs, is limited to Lancelot's part. 'The devil can cite Scripture for his purpose', and in much medieval drama the Devil had degenerated into the Vice who in his turn begat such Elizabethan stage clowns as Lancelot. But even in his lines there are indications that Shakespeare tried to avoid the direct recall of biblical phrases. When Lancelot promises to return 'in the

[1] See Commentary on 1.3.28; 1.3.33; 3.1.67; 4.1.292.

[2] Barbara Lewalski, 'Biblical allusion and allegory in *The Merchant of Venice*', *SQ* 13 (1962), 328.

[3] See n. 3, p. 197 above.

[4] See Commentary on 2.1.29; 2.2.124.

twinkling', it is officious of Q2's editor to add 'of an eye' and so put us in mind of the expression's Pauline origin. For by the end of the sixteenth century the medieval comprehensiveness in drama was giving way to the Renaissance principle of decorum, which can be biblically summed up as 'to everything there is a season... A time to mourn and a time to dance'. There was a time for preaching, and a time for play-acting. A play about Jews and Christians inevitably reflected the Christian beliefs of its writer, but its original audience might have been considerably surprised to be told that it *expounded* them. They were simply there and taken for granted like the air people breathed: the shared cultural environment of writer, watcher, and reader.

Finally, as I have tried to show in my Introduction, the concept of a play's overall meaning, the bird's-eye view, is basically alien to the theatrical experience, in which our responses change from minute to minute as they do in the flux of daily living. Though the mind of the individual auditor preserves some total effect of a play, he or she does not go home nursing some nugget of 'meaning', but animatedly recalling this or that moment of the action. Certain of these moments fix themselves in our memory because they are reinforced with conscious or subliminal recollections of verses from Scripture. For this reason, while we need to make our way circumspectly among the theological readings of the play, recent explanations of its biblical echoes[1] even beyond the many recorded by Noble, are valuable in a time which has lost the habit of reading the Bible.

[1] For example, John S. Coolidge, 'Law and love in *The Merchant of Venice*', *SQ* 27 (1976), 243–63.

READING LIST

This list comprises the books and articles on *The Merchant of Venice* which the editor has found the most informative or the most critically stimulating. It is offered as a guide to those who may wish to undertake further study of the play.

Auden, W. H. 'Brothers and others', in *The Dyer's Hand*, 1963, pp. 232–5.

Berek, Peter. 'The Jew as Renaissance Man', *Renaissance Quarterly* 51 (1998), 128–62

Berkowitz, Joel. 'A true Jewish Jew: three Yiddish Shylocks', *Theatre Survey* 37 (1996), 75–88 (also in Berkowitz's *Shakespeare on the American Yiddish Stage*, 2002)

Bloom, Harold (ed.). *Major Literary Characters: Shylock*, 1991

Brown, John Russell. *Shakespeare and His Comedies*, 1957, pp. 45–81

'The realization of Shylock', in *Early Shakespeare* (*Stratford-upon-Avon Studies 3*), 1961, pp. 186–209

'Creating a role: Shylock', in *Shakespeare's Plays in Performance*, 1966, pp. 83–103

Bullough, Geoffrey. *Narrative and Dramatic Sources of Shakespeare*, II, 1958, pp. 443–514

Bulman, James C. *Shakespeare in Performance: The Merchant of Venice*, 1991, second edn. forthcoming

Cohen, Walter. '*The Merchant of Venice* and the possibilities of historical criticism', *ELH* 49 (1982), 765–89

Coyle, Martin (ed.). *New Casebooks: The Merchant of Venice*, 1998

Cusack, Sinead. 'Portia in *The Merchant of Venice*', in *Players of Shakespeare 1*, ed. Philip Brockbank, 1985, 29–40

Danson, Lawrence. *The Harmonies of 'The Merchant of Venice'*, 1978

Dessen, Alan C. 'The Elizabethan stage Jew and Christian example: Gerontus, Barabas, and Shylock', *MLQ* 35 (1974), 231–45

Doran, Gregory. 'Solanio in *The Merchant of Venice*', in *Players of Shakespeare 3*, ed. Russell Jackson and Robert Smallwood, 1993, 68–76

Edelman, Charles (ed.). *Shakespeare in Production: The Merchant of Venice*, 2002

Fan Shen, 'Shakespeare in China: *The Merchant of Venice*', *Asian Theatre Journal* 5 (1988), 23–37

Findlay, Deborah. 'Portia in *The Merchant of Venice*', in *Players of Shakespeare 3*, ed. Russell Jackson and Robert Smallwood, 1993, 52–67

Golder, John, and Richard Madelaine (ed.). *O Brave New World: Two Centuries of Shakespeare on the Australian Stage*, 2001

Granville-Barker, Harley. *Prefaces to Shakespeare*, II, 1930, pp. 67–110

Gross, John. *Shylock: Four Hundred Years in the Life of a Legend*, 1992

Halio, Jay L. (ed.). *The Merchant of Venice*, 1993

Hankey, Julie. 'Victorian Portias: Shakespeare's borderline heroine', *SQ* 45 (1994), 426–48
Holmer, Joan Ozark. *The Merchant of Venice: Choice, Hazard, and Consequence*, 1995
Hortmann, Wilhelm. *Shakespeare on the German Stage: The Twentieth Century*, 1998
Horwich, Richard. 'Riddle and dilemma in *The Merchant of Venice*', *SEL* 17 (1977), 191–200
Jones, Norman. *God and the Moneylenders*. London, 1989
Lerner, Laurence. 'Wilhelm S and Shylock', *S.Sur 48* (1995), 61–8
Luscombe, Christopher. 'Launcelot Gobbo in *The Merchant of Venice* and Moth in *Love's Labour's Lost*', in *Players of Shakespeare 4*, ed. Robert Smallwood, 1998, 18–29
McDiarmid, Ian. 'Shylock in *The Merchant of Venice*', in *Players of Shakespeare 2*, ed. Russell Jackson and Robert Smallwood, 1988, 45–54
Nevo, Ruth. *Comic Transformations in Shakespeare*, 1980, pp. 115–41
Odell, G. C. *Shakespeare from Betterton to Irving*, 1920
Orgel, Stephen. 'Shylock's tribe', in *Shakespeare and the Mediterranean: the Selected Proceedings of the International Shakespeare Association World Congress, Valencia, 2001*, ed. Tom Clayton, Susan Brock and Vicente Fores, forthcoming
Oz, Avraham. *The Yoke of Love: Prophetic Riddles in The Merchant of Venice*, 1995
Rabkin, Norman. *Shakespeare and the Problem of Meaning*, 1981, pp. 1–32
Rozmovits, Linda. *Shakespeare and the Politics of Culture in Late Victorian England*, 1998
Salingar, Leo. *Shakespeare and the Traditions of Comedy*, 1974
Shaheen, Naseeb. *Biblical References in Shakespeare's Plays*, 1999
Shapiro, James. *Shakespeare and the Jews*, 1996
Shattuck, Charles. *Shakespeare on the American Stage: From Booth and Barrett to Sothern and Marlowe*, 1987
Smith, Bruce R. *Homosexual Desire in Shakespeare's England: A Cultural Poetics*, 1991
Sokol, B. J. 'Prejudice and law in *The Merchant of Venice*', *S.Sur 51* (1998), 159–73
Sprague, A. C. *Shakespeare and the Actors*, 1944
Stewart, Patrick. 'Shylock', in *Players of Shakespeare*, ed. Philip Brockbank, 1985, pp. 11–28.
Wilders, John (ed.). *Shakespeare: 'The Merchant of Venice': A Casebook*, 1969
Williams, Simon. *Shakespeare on the German Stage, Volume I: 1586–1914*, 1990
Yaffe, Martin. *Shylock and the Jewish Question*, 1997